DOUBLE EXPOSURE

Take Three

Compiled and Photographed
by
Roddy McDowall

WILLIAM MORROW AND COMPANY, INC.
New York

It is the policy of William Morrow and Company, Inc., and its imprints and affiliates, recognizing the importance of preserving what has been written, to print the books we publish on acid-free paper, and we exert our best efforts to that end.

Library of Congress Cataloging-in-Publication Data

McDowall, Roddy.
Double exposure, take III / Roddy McDowall.
p. cm.
ISBN 0-688-10063-5
1. Entertainers—Portraits. 2. Entertainers—Biography.
I. Title. II. Title: Double exposure, take 3. III. Title: Double exposure, take three.
PN1583.M36 1992
791'.092'2—dc20 91-48056
CIP

Printed in Japan

First Edition

1 2 3 4 5 6 7 8 9 10

BOOK DESIGN BY DAVID CHARLSEN

Contents

for Steven Jongeward

Geneviève Bujold
BY
Jeremy Irons

Geneviève Bujold.

Pronounce it right, and that mouth comes to mind—
crushed-velvet sensitive on the verge of flicking
wide to a dazzling smile.
A true actress.
By which I mean a disliker of bullshit.

When we worked together she was to play a
faltering actress of forty.
She rejected the dazzling wardrobe carefully chosen.
She rejected the glamorous makeup.
I *am* an actress of forty she said. These *are* my clothes—the
clothes I wear. This *is* my face that I live in.
Why should I lie and dress them up?

So she played in *her* clothes, with *her* face.
No dressing up, no covering.
Naked, as it were.
And her truth and strength shone through.

Ballsy Lady.

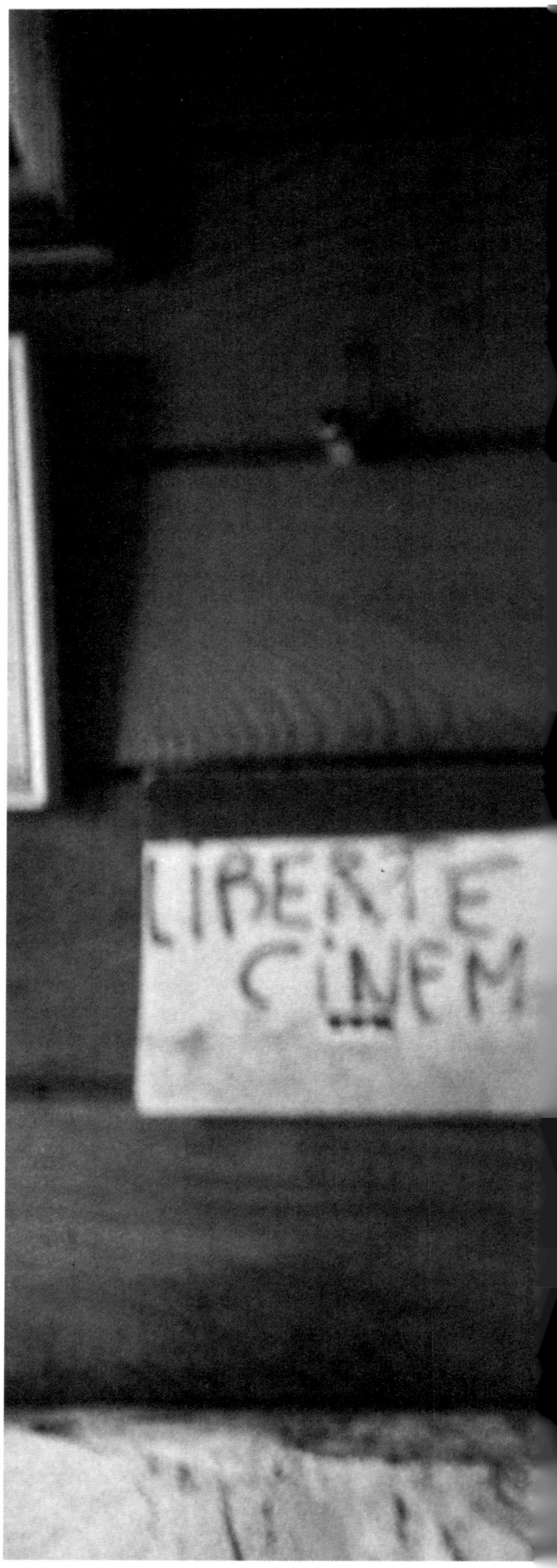

Malibu, California *1990*

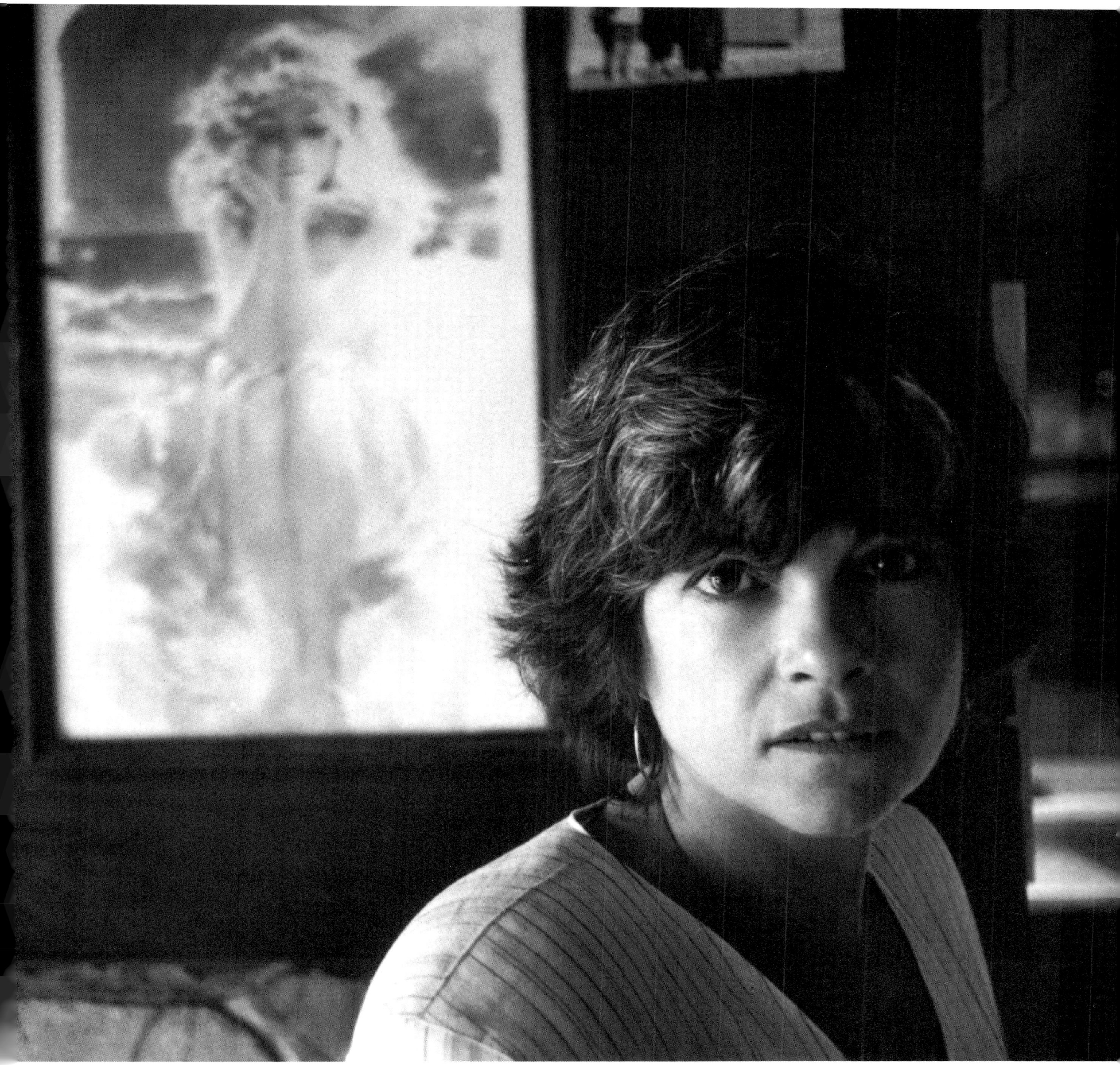

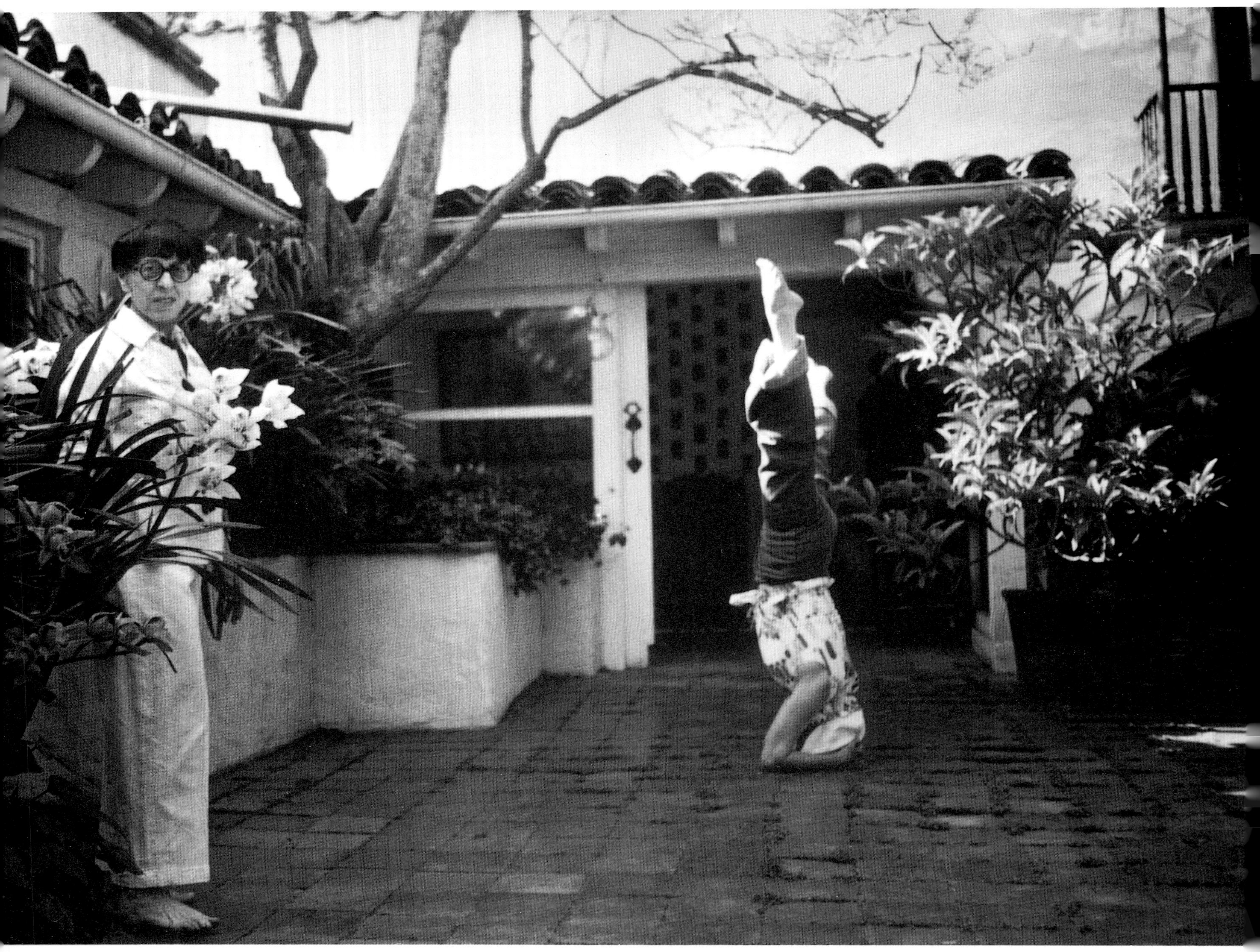

Edith Head
BY
Elizabeth Taylor

Edith Head was one of the people I loved most in the world. She was friend, confidante, and was always there for me, like "another mother." I won't try to describe her magical talent; it is there for all of us to see.

But it was her method of working that was so phenomenal. She got "inside" the characters and helped create their persona as much as the actors and directors did. She would find little personality quirks for each different individual, like a funny cup, a favorite scarf, or pockets in odd places, sort of built-in props for each new role.

As the lady I loved, she was wildly funny and totally giving—and she was *so* wise. She looked at all the craziness of Hollywood behind those dark glasses of hers with a most lovely sense of ironic sanity. She had a very practical way of putting panic into its proper perspective, and always made you end up laughing. Nothing amazed her or fazed her, including her friend Ava Gardner standing on her head for no apparent reason.

I miss her very much.

Beverly Hills *1974*

Johnny Depp
BY
Tim Burton

there was a young man
everyone thought was quite handsome.
so he tied up his face
and he held it for ransom.

he made everybody
back up 20 feet,
then he ran off
with his head
down a darkly
lit street.

the whole town
wondered why he'd
threatened his face,
they couldn't understand,
... it was that kind of place.

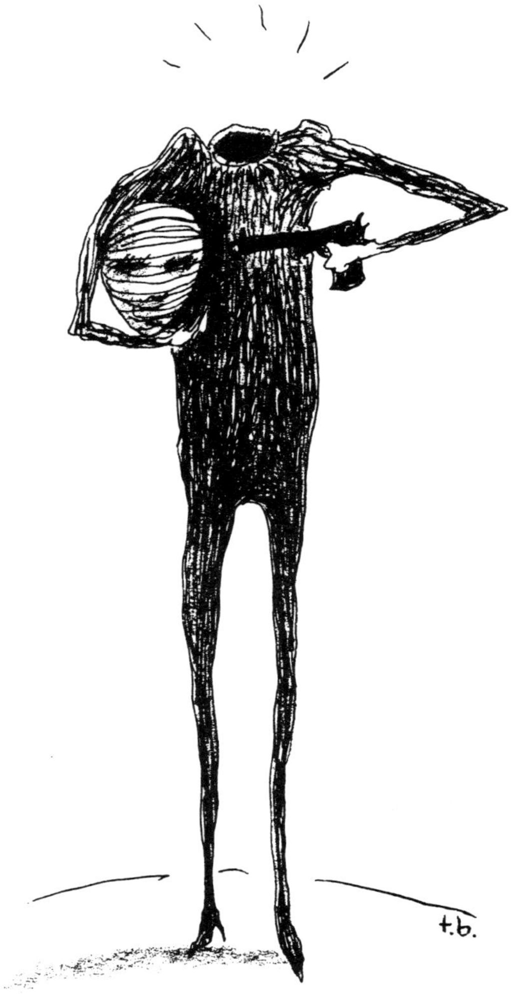

Studio City, California 1991

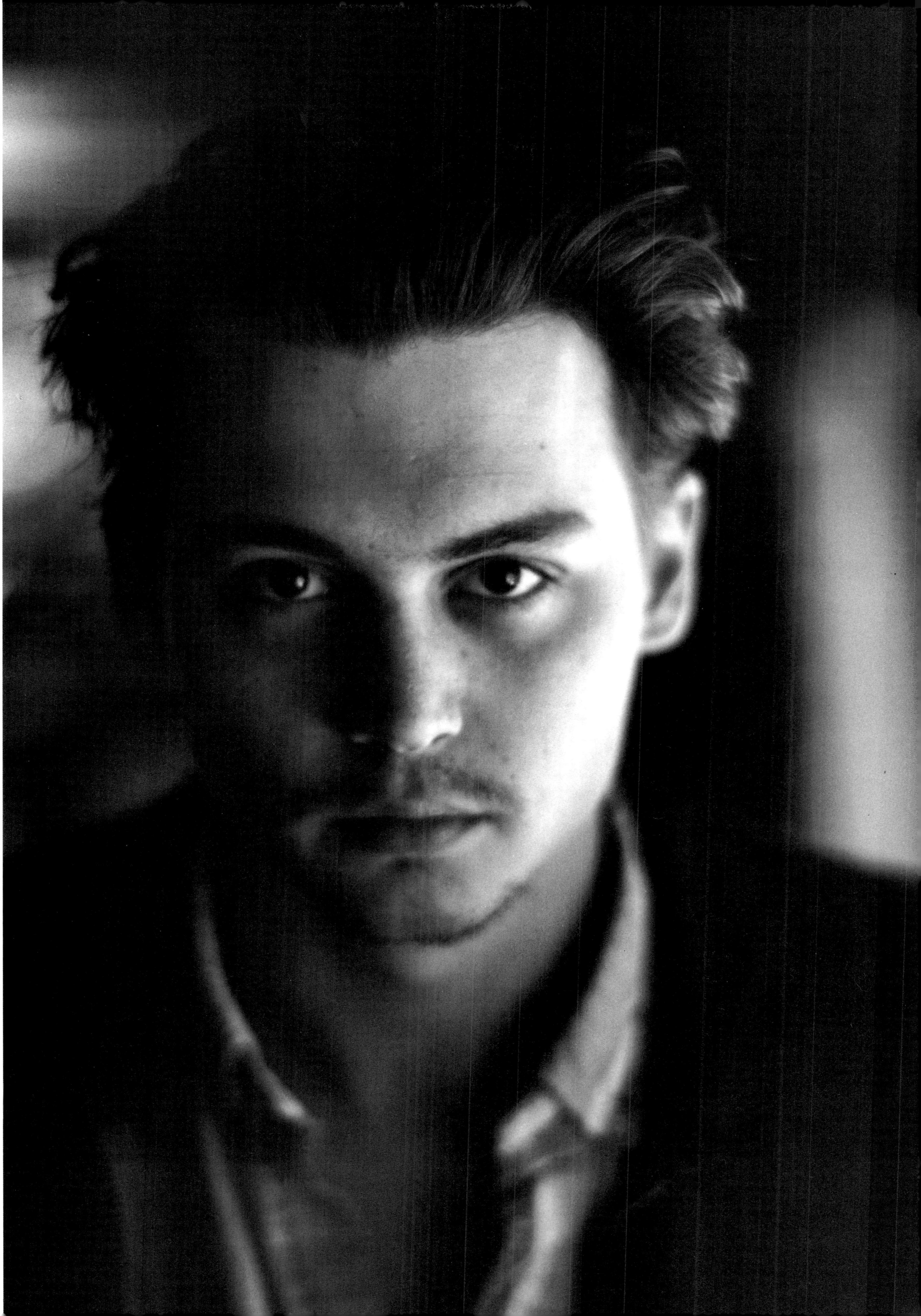

Joan Plowright
BY
Tracey Ullman

I have always been told I look like a young Joan Plowright. I didn't fully appreciate this compliment until she became my mother for three months in the film *I Love You to Death.*

I had been living in America for a few years and felt free of our inhibiting class structure, and on the first day of rehearsal I thought, "If some Grand Dame of the British Theatre walks in here enunciating and making me feel like the girl from suburbia with the plastic platform boots, who used to pay 80 pence to sit in the Upper Circle and watch her in *Saturday, Sunday, Monday,* I'll go bloody mad!!" But no, Joan said, "Hello, love," and put her arm around me, and from that moment on I had a mother, a friend, and an eating partner—Joan is a gourmand!!

Within days I was able to rib her about being "Lady Olivier"—"Do you put your tiara on in the lunch break in the privacy of your motor home, Joan?" "Oh shut up, Tracey!" she'd say with a hint of Scunthorpe, her hometown, in her voice.

What a joy that whole movie experience was, and when it was released, I couldn't get over how alike Joan and I are—our rounded cheeks, twinkling brown eyes, and noses that aren't large enough for surgery, but give us *character.* (I hope your self-esteem is greater than mine, Joan.) I wish I could also have Joan's dignity, common sense, grace, and aroma (yes, Joan even smells nice). I'm very proud to be asked to attempt to describe Ms. Plowright when so many others could do so more eloquently, or from longer acquaintance, but she's so truly great that it only took me a short time to see it.

Hollywood 1989

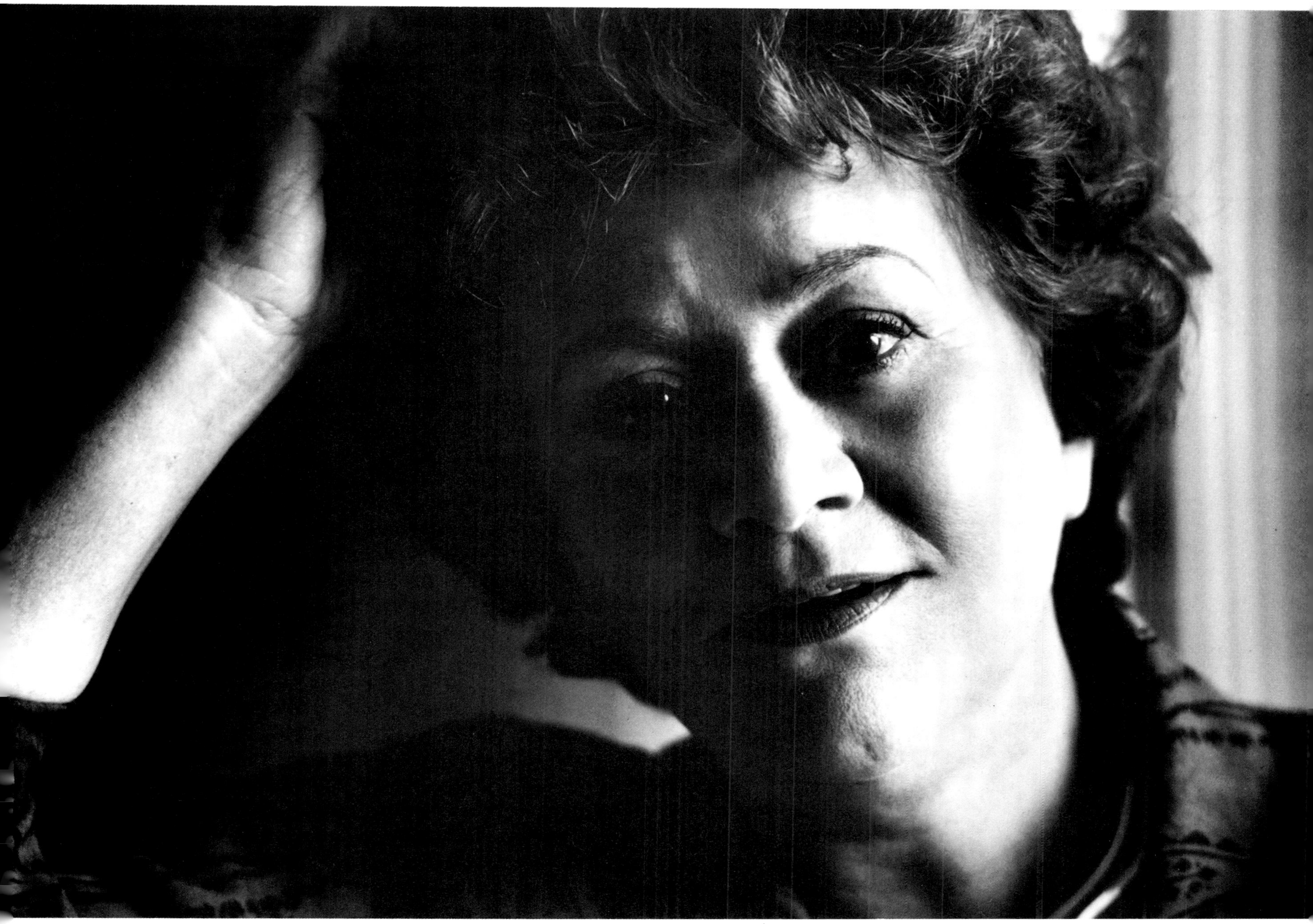

Richard Avedon
BY
Audrey Hepburn

The first thing I saw when I came to America thirty-eight years ago was the Statue of Liberty. The second . . . Richard Avedon.

Producer Gilbert Miller had brought over a total unknown to appear on Broadway. To deal with this unknown quantity he decided to make her arrival known with the utmost quality. Before I knew it, I was in front of Richard Avedon's cameras, lights flashing, music going, Richard snapping away a mile a minute, darting from one angle to another like a hummingbird, everywhere at once, weaving his spell which I am still under today.

For Richard I have happily
swung from swings,
stood in clouds of steam,
been drenched with rain,
and descended endless flights of stairs
without looking
and without breaking my neck

I treasure every picture Richard has ever taken of me over the years, as I do his unchanging friendship. Only with Richard have I been able to shed my innate self-consciousness in front of a camera. Is it his sweetness? His sense of fun? The assurance that you know you are going to end up looking the way you *wished* you looked? Or is it the knowledge that you are in the presence of someone who will not rest until he has captured the best of his subject as seen through his gifted eyes?

In fact, Richard has never rested, never relaxed on his laurels. He could so easily have continued to be the unsurpassed fashion photographer of our day, or the most sought after portraitist of the most beautiful women in the world.

But Richard's sensitivity and intelligence drove him on to deeper portraits of *life.* Life etched on faces often aged and ravaged by time. Portraits, beautiful and deeply touching in their honesty. A most moving example of these are the photographs Richard took of his father during his last years.

We owe so much to Richard's genius. How many young models found fame and fortune thanks to Richard Avedon? How many women became an international "beauty" because they

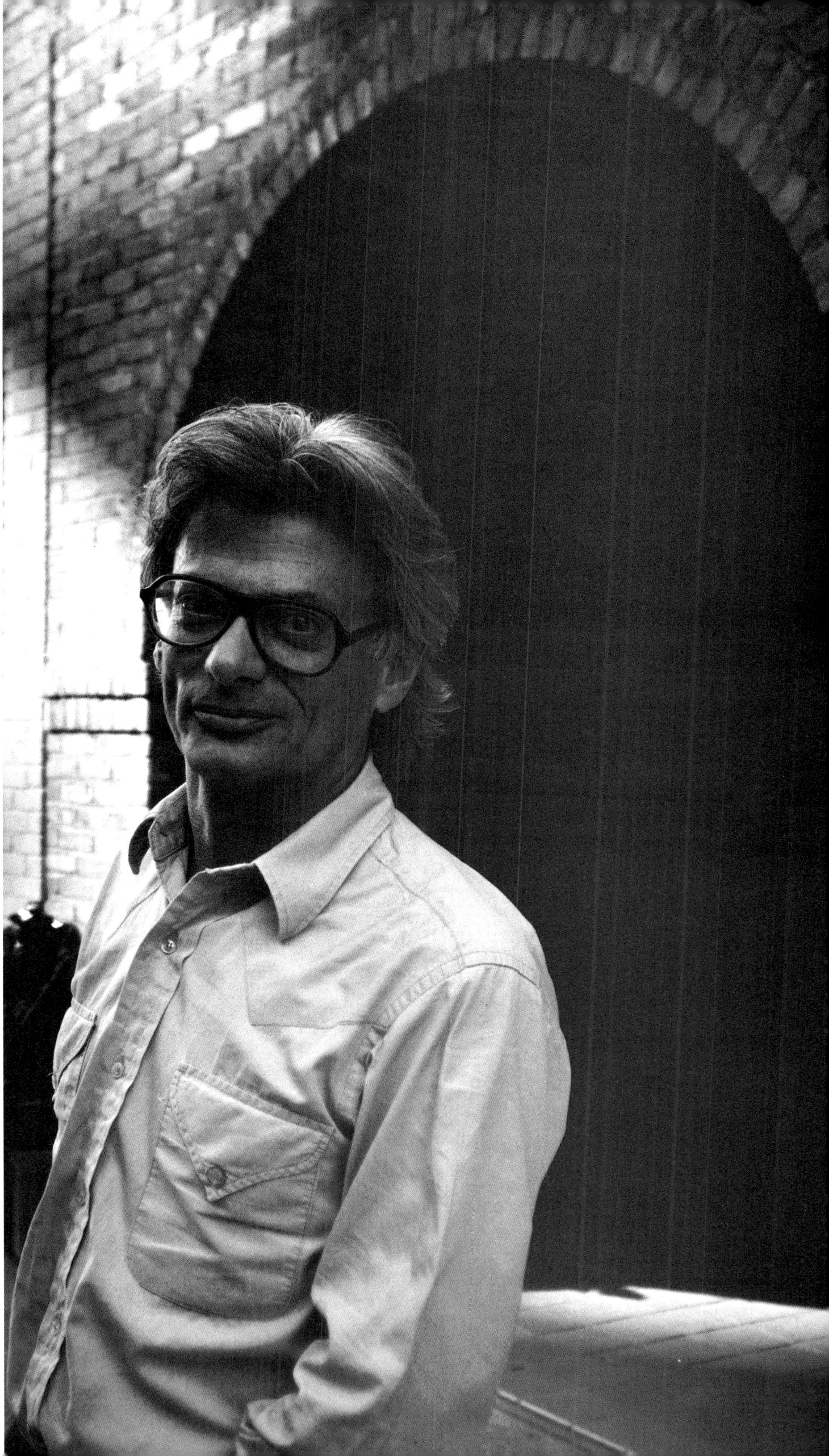

merited his camera? How many unknowns (like myself) were put on the map by Richard? And how many already famous faces gained a new and contemporary aura given the mark of Richard Avedon?

Not only has he helped others achieve a new dimension to their lives, their dreams, but his talent has given *us* a lifetime of seeing, through his lens, his eyes,

always searching,
always changing,
always renewing.
never satisfied,
but creating and recreating unforgettable images
of style
of wit
of depth
of truth
and always of
beauty.

❑

Mary Astor
BY
Gavin Lambert

In the twilight of the major studio era, Mary Astor made her 107th film, *Return to Peyton Place.* I was also working at 20th Century-Fox at the time, and watched her rehearse a scene. She was cast in the supporting role of a puritanical small-town mother, determined to remove a "shocking" novel from the shelves of the local library. The director, José Ferrer, liked what she did in the run-through and was ready to shoot. But not Astor. "Something's missing," she said quietly. "I have to make it more *real.*"

And on the screen, instead of a conventional prude, you saw an almost tragically wrong-headed woman. Once again she had found the vital slant—the "who" of a part, as she called it. Because she was so beautiful, Mary Astor played nothing but sweetly romantic heroines in more than 30 silent movies, and had to wait until her third talkie, *Holiday,* to find a role with a "who." Typically, she made the rich girl wholly charming at first so that her hard, materialistic side came as a surprise; and she revealed it almost apologetically, implying that she had been brought up to believe in money and status as the most important things in life. In the same way, the first impression she created in *Red Dust* was of a primly controlled woman, which made her sexual obsession with Clark Gable completely unexpected; her "other woman" in *Dodsworth* was so appealingly vulnerable that Walter Huston's return to his wife seemed like an unhappy ending for both of them; and in *The Prisoner of Zenda* she made an ordinary *femme fatale* role extraordinary, underscoring the bitterness of a discarded mistress in her scenes with Douglas Fairbanks, Jr.

1941, of course, was Mary Astor's *annus mirabilis,* the epic bitch of *The Great Lie* and the conniving Brigid O'Shaughnessy of *The Maltese Falcon.* By then she had acquired an unmistakable star aura, but instead of projecting a star image, she concentrated on the vital slant. In the case of *The Great Lie,* the physical and imaginative stress of being a concert pianist. Her Sandra is equally believable as bitch and artist. In the case of *The Maltese Falcon,* she assumes the most innocent, breathless, persuasive mask of truth for the screen's most epic liar.

It was her last leading role. At thirty-five she had no interest in trying to look younger, and no hang-ups about switching to "character" parts because she had always played them. The 40s in fact became her richest period. Two wonderfully contrasted mothers, salt of the Midwest earth in *Meet Me in St. Louis,* and tough, explosive casino owner in *Desert Fury.* The giddiest high-society man-chaser of them all in *The Palm Beach Story* (which, surprisingly, she didn't enjoy making), and a trip to the other side of the tracks as the indelibly lonely, aging whore of *Act of Violence.* In the 50s and 60s, opportunities dwindled and her enthusiasm, understandably, started to fade. After *Return to Peyton Place,* only two (silly) movies allowed her to create a momentarily electrifying "who," as the predatory patron of a young writer in *Youngblood Hawke* and, in her farewell performance, as the deceptively frail little old murderess of *Hush, Hush, Sweet Charlotte.*

But writing had always fascinated her, which is not surprising in view of the way she approached her roles, and after her retirement Mary Astor wrote several novels and a remarkable autobiography, *A Life on Film.* This search for her own "who" is as alert and original as her best performances. On screen, she gave the impression that a kind of cool assurance was second nature; in fact, it was painfully acquired. Her life was extraordinarily turbulent. A grasping stage mother, a possessive and domineering father, a chaotic affair with John Barrymore when she was only 18, the later "scandal" of her diaries (partly forged) recounting her affair with George Kaufman, her first husband killed in a plane crash, three more marriages that ended in divorce, alcoholism, rehabilitation, going off alone to a small Mexican town "to park my typewriter and put down one word after another and see what happened . . ." It sounds like soap opera to the nth degree, but comes out like life because she tells it with such intelligence, humor, and grace. On the page, no less than on the screen, you can't take your eyes off Mary Astor. She will always be mysteriously clear.

Woodland Hills, California *1979*

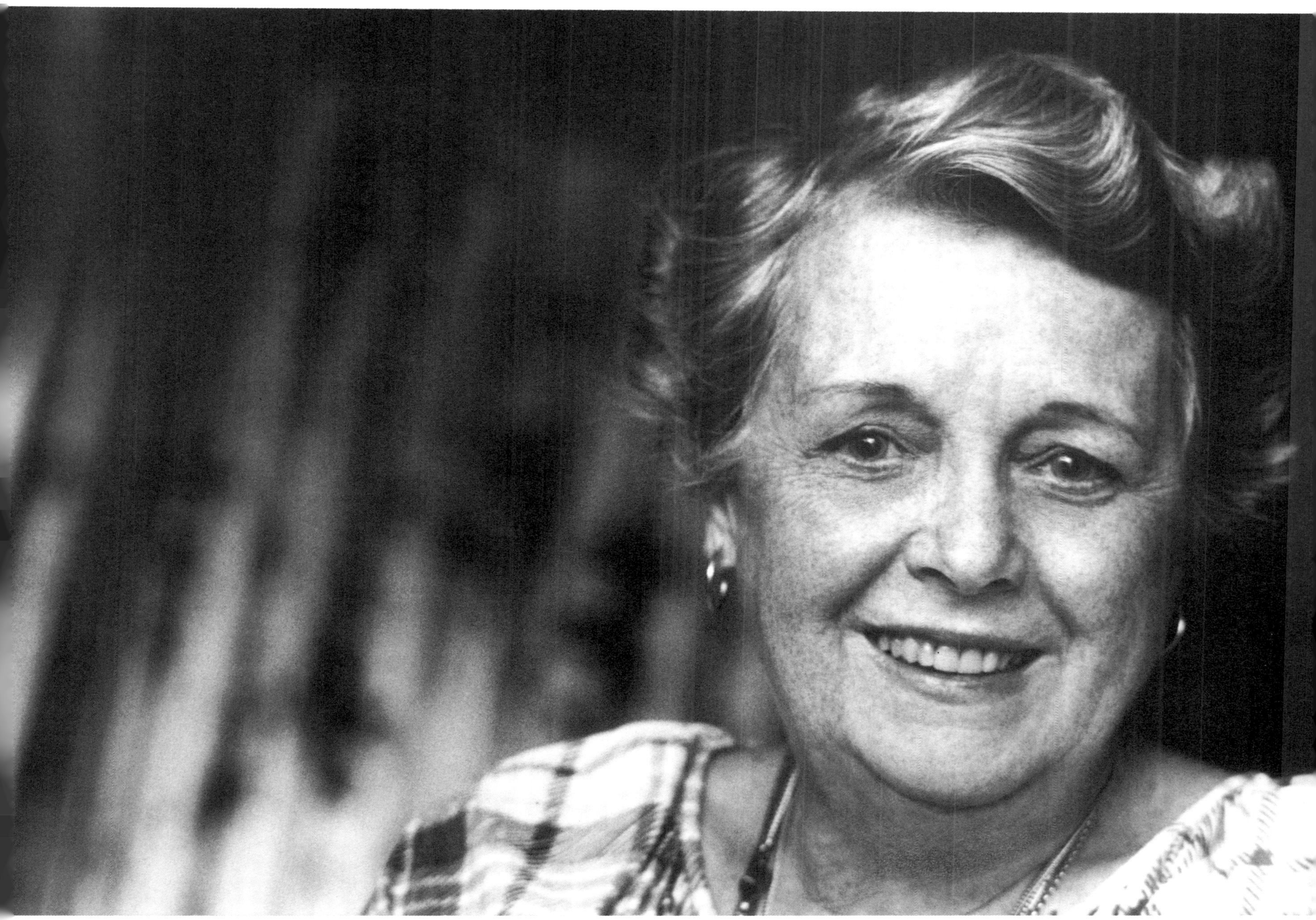

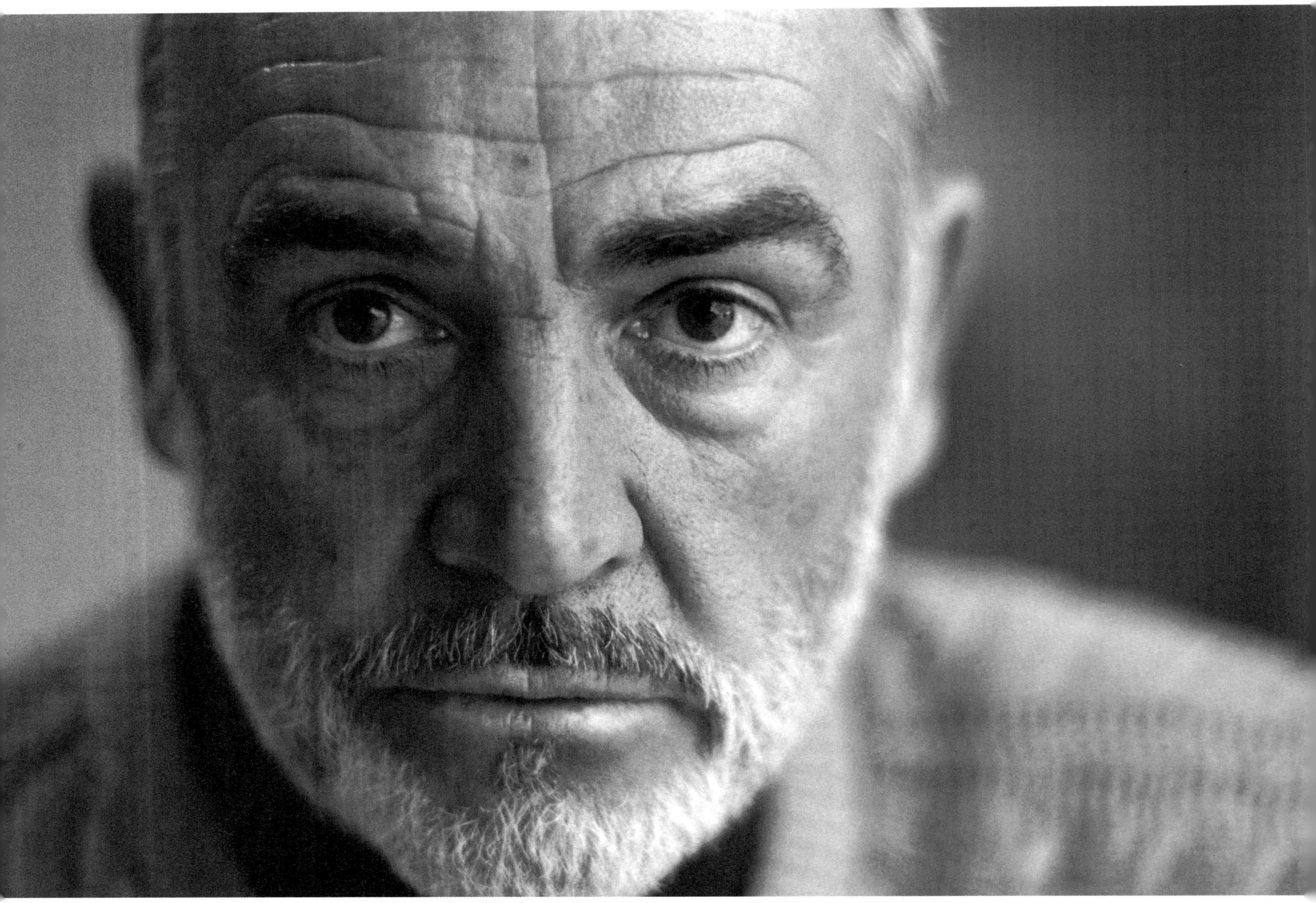

Sean Connery
BY
Harrison Ford

I haven't known Sean very long. But we did a movie together and that's like being in a foxhole with a guy. You get to know pretty quick if you can trust him, if you can depend on him.

Sean is trustworthy, and dependable, and smart, and quick. For years I admired what he brought to the screen. And now I admire the man. What we saw was what I got.

Beverly Hills *1990*

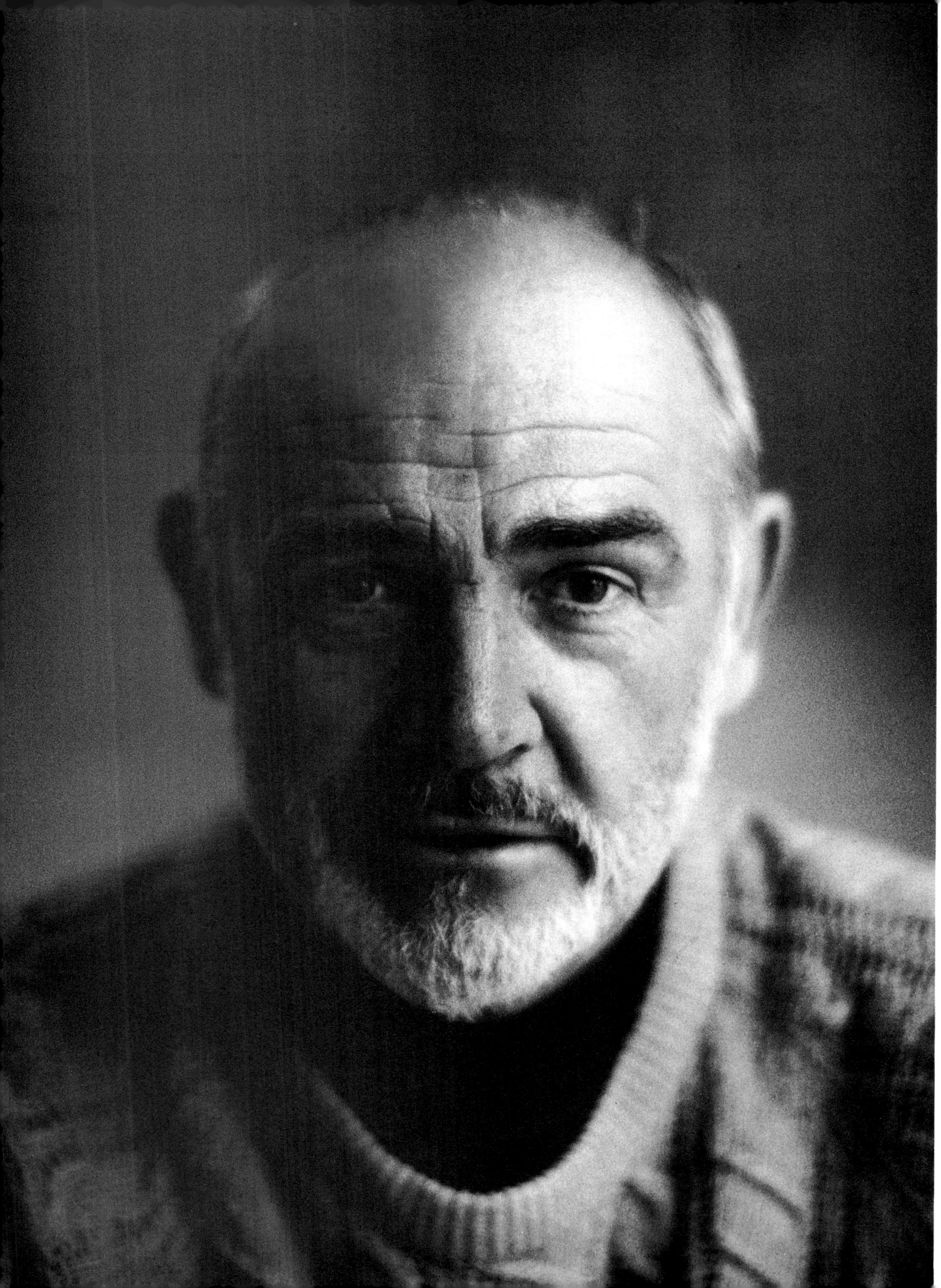

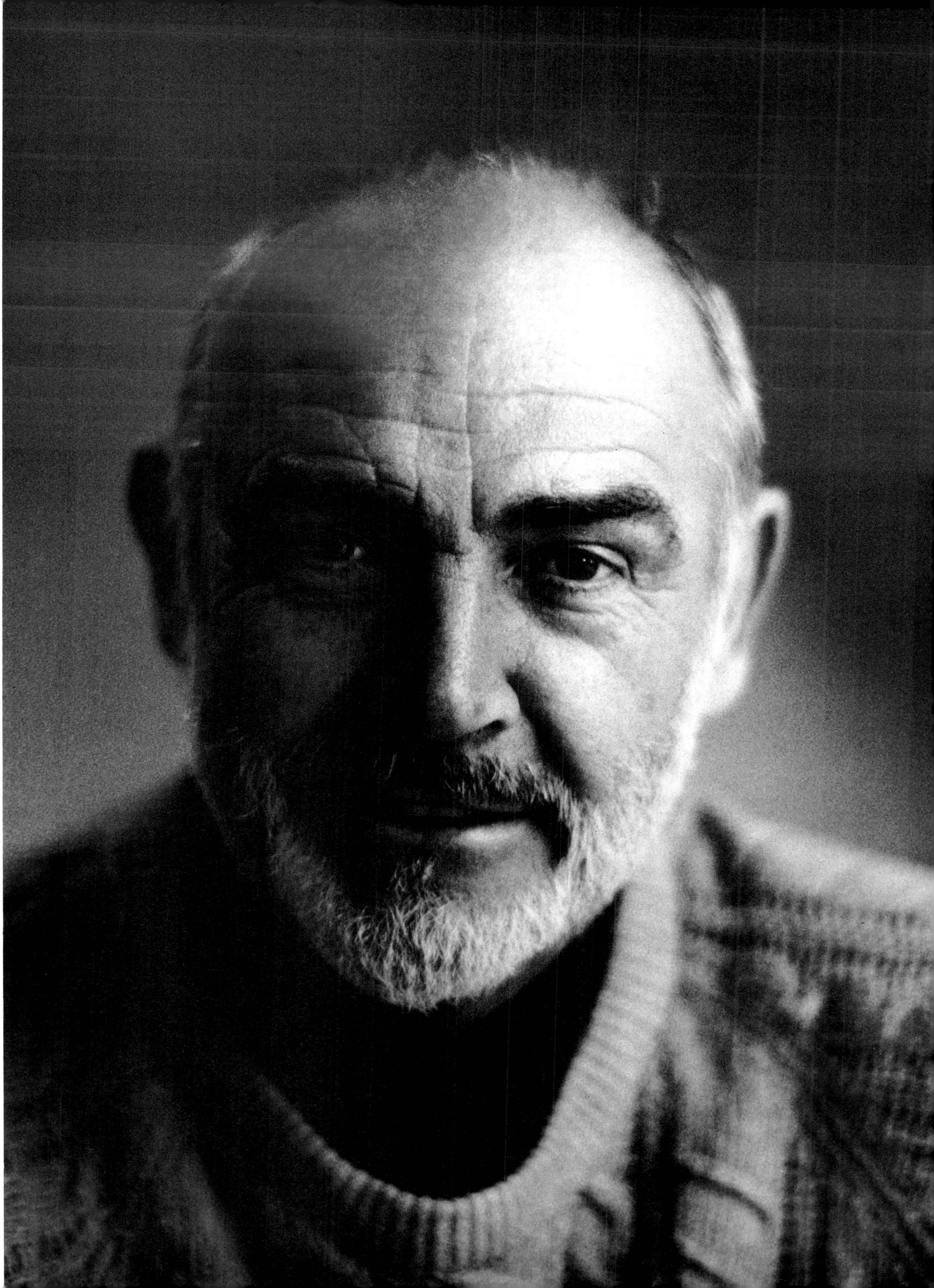

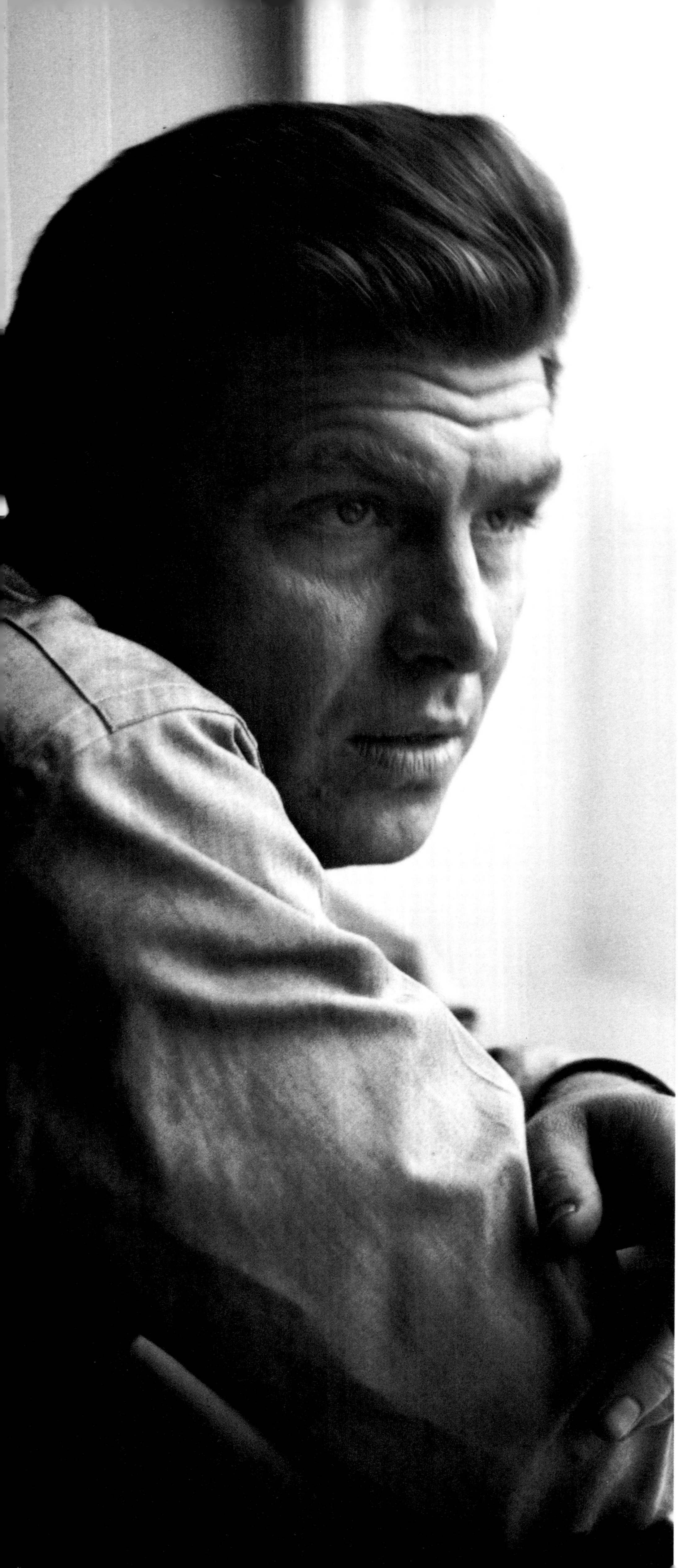

Andy Griffith
BY
Ron Howard

People always ask me if in growing up on *The Andy Griffith Show* (I went from age 5 to 14 on the program) I ever thought of Andy as a second father. Of course, I didn't . . . but in many ways Andy does fit the description of a close uncle . . . the fun kind. The kind who never disciplines you or negatively judges you. The kind who is easy to laugh with but also impressive in his accomplishments, his talents, and in the way he carries himself. The kind you see a lot of so that you are very comfortable with him . . . but not so much that you could ever take him for granted.

Andy established an environment on our set that made me want to be there—just hanging out, listening to music, hearing stories, and watching the work when I could've been at home playing whiffle ball, army, or trading baseball cards.

I learned from Andy how to be committed while making the creative process collaborative and fun. I continue to learn from him with every get-together and every performance of his I see.

He obviously made a great impression on me when I was a child and as an adult his candor, integrity, warmth and sustained creative energy make him one of the more extraordinary and interesting people I know.

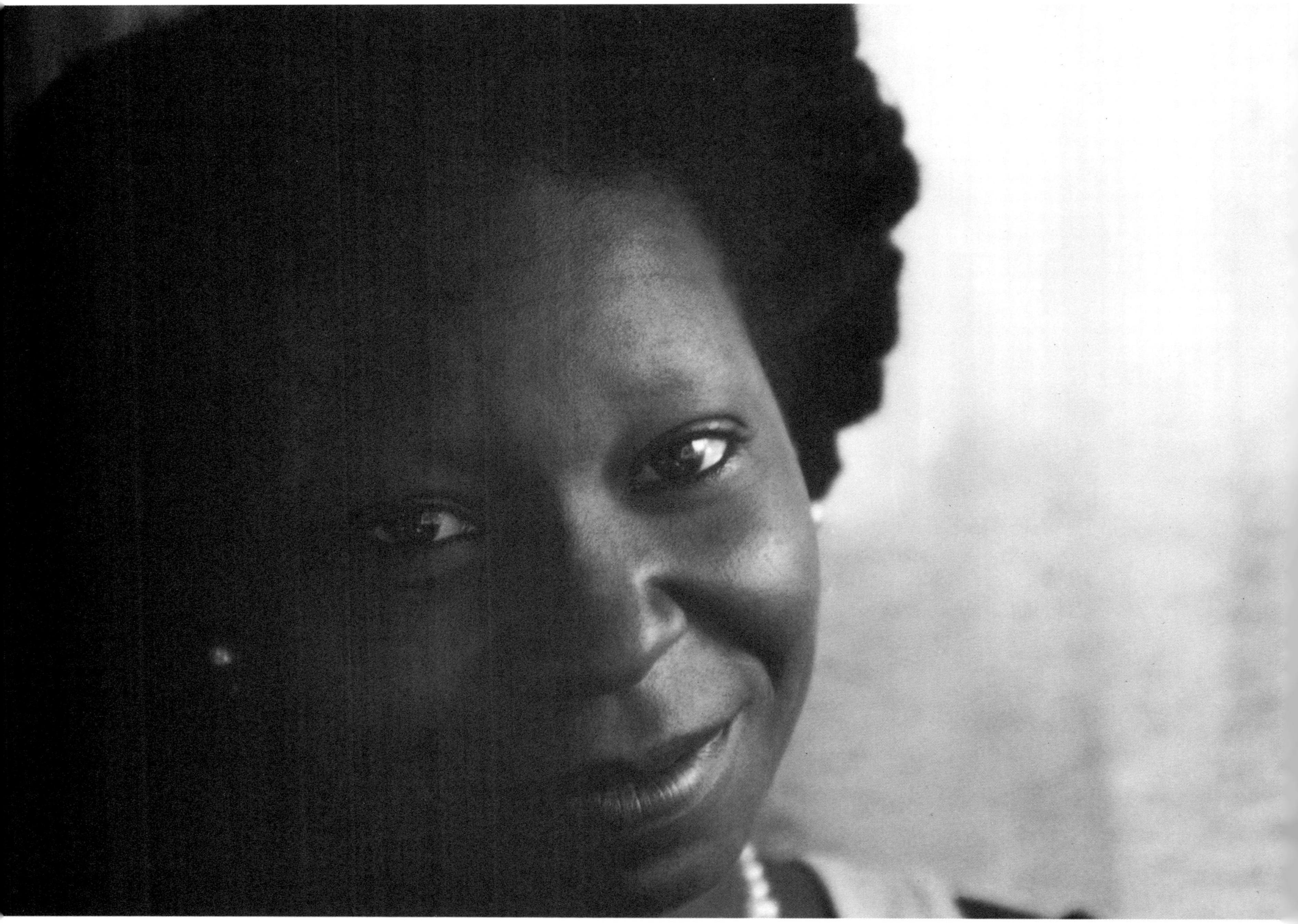

Whoopi Goldberg
BY
Maurice Sendak

With a child's ferocity, Whoopi boldly steps forward, clicks her magic heels together, and spirits herself off to LaLaLand, spreading the good word as she goes and offering herself up as artist and *mensch* first class. And like her brave sister Dorothy, Whoopi stays—against all odds—tangible and tough, always peering over the top of whatever she's doing and laughing her blessed head off.

New York City *1990*

Gene Autry
BY
Ringo Starr

In my brain it was around '47, '48. I was in the Saturday morning cinema where they'd show lots of movies, and what was great when you were a kid was that whatever the movie, you would go home in that character—a pirate or a cowboy, or whatever. They were showing this Gene Autry movie and he was on his horse with two of his pals and he started singing "South of the Border" and shivers went up my spine. You know, I was into music even then and it just blew me away. It's stuck with me all my life: Gene Autry, when he sang "South of the Border."

Griffith Park, California *1990*

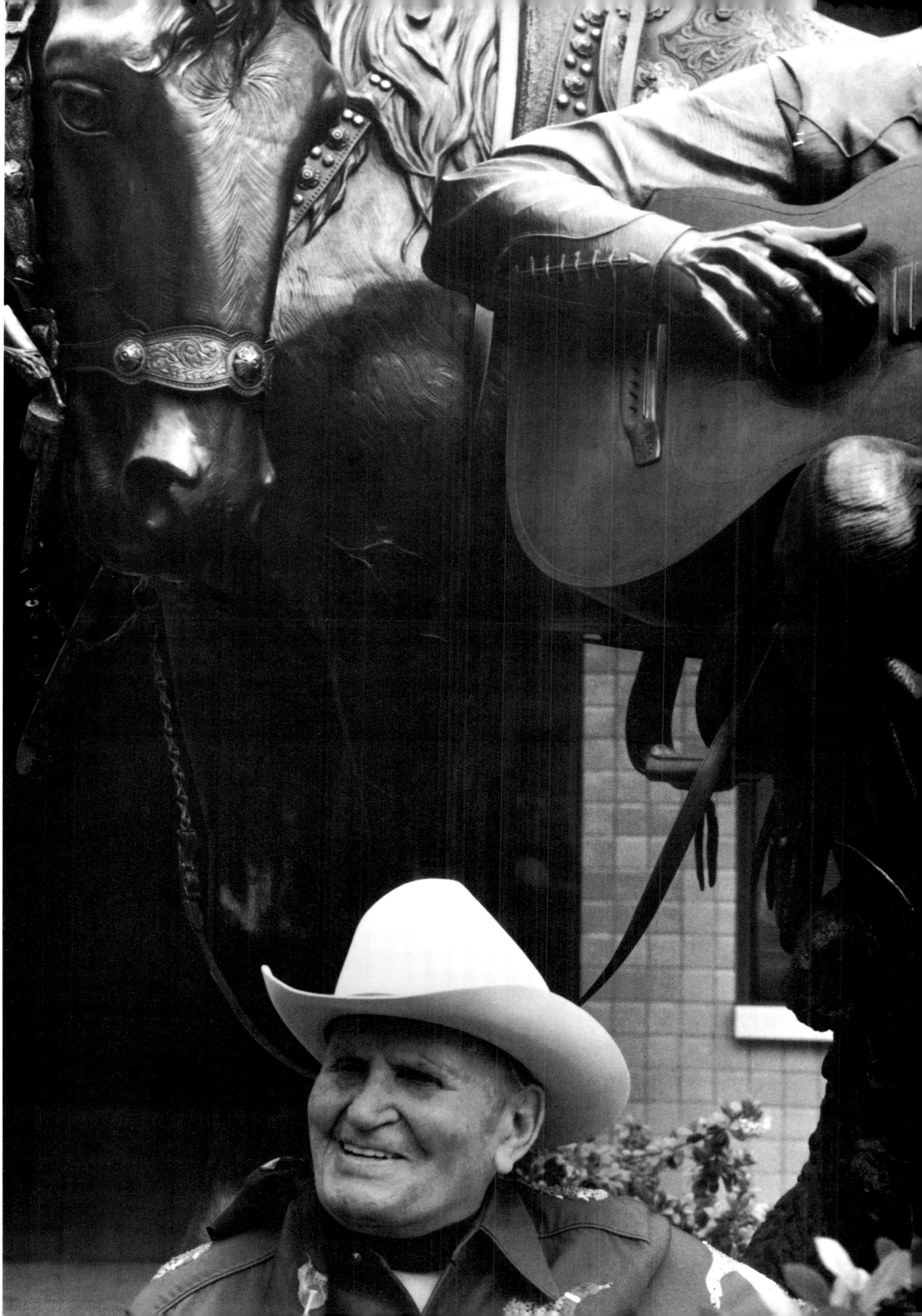

Anjelica Huston
BY
Stephen Frears

I first met Anjelica when I had dinner with her and the painter Anne Rothenstein with whom I live. They had been at school together and there had been a lot of jealousy behind the gym because Anjelica knew Mick Jagger. When I first read *The Grifters,* I immediately thought of Anjelica and Cher, but then *Moonstruck* went through the roof and Cher stayed a dream. I refused to approach Anjelica, although I remember walking back with her from a party on the Upper West Side to her midtown hotel, and staring at her all the way. When I decided to make the film with another actress, I had to ring Anjelica to tell her I was not going to offer her a part we had never discussed.

Actresses drop out as they do, and I came to Los Angeles to make the film with the part of Lily uncast. I sat with my producer, Martin Scorsese, in the Chateau Marmont waiting to meet two actresses. After the first left, I said that she would give the film a strong sense of reality. Marty thought that was very important. I said, what if you want to make a different kind of film? He said he'd seen little of Anjelica's work. I said, what about *Prizzi's Honor*? He said he loved John Huston's films, but he'd seen the trailer and it was the Irish making fun of the Italians, and I wondered what crazy country I had come to where people could have such mysterious passions. He talked about Bensonhurst and Spike Lee's work, until, all unsuspecting, Anjelica walked in. For twenty minutes she was like Princess Margaret, and I thought I would throw myself out of the window, but then I went and sat beside her on the sofa, and she became very animated and intense and powerful. Hypnotic and magnificent. The decision who to cast in the part had somehow been taken out of our hands.

I have often wondered why it took me so long to get back to my first instincts and approach Anjelica. In part I was trying to find out what film I was making. But I also think I knew she would play Lily with that full-bodied note of tragedy, and I needed to screw up my courage to breathe the same air as her. On days when we had to film bad scenes, she would say in her father's voice, "Just do it, honey."

The Grifters had two pretty women in it, and that always doubles the fun. After a couple of weeks, Anjelica got the bit between her teeth, and I discovered how to photograph those wonderful legs of hers. She's coming up on the inside rail, the cameraman and I would say. Aren't men awful!

Studio City, California 1990

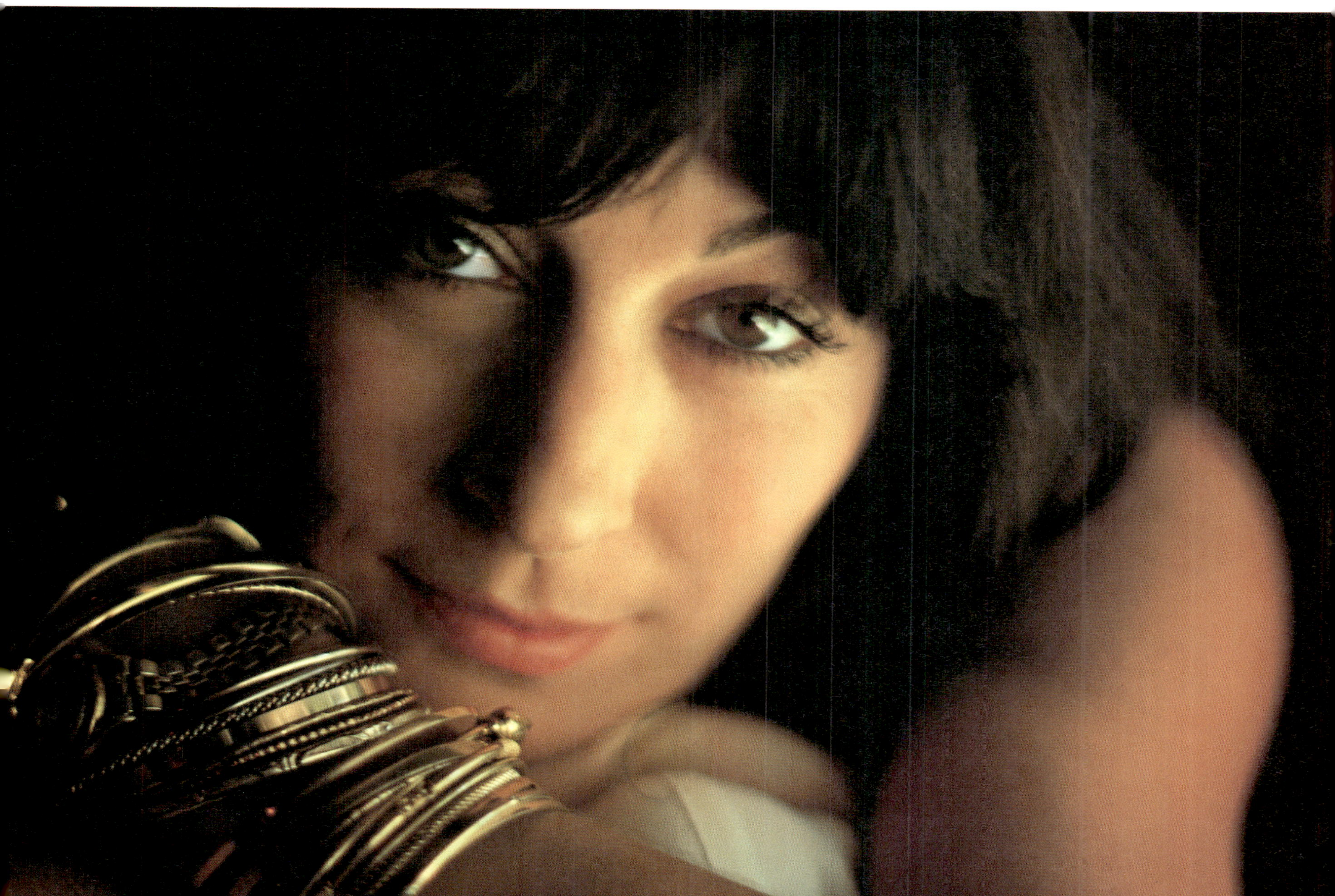

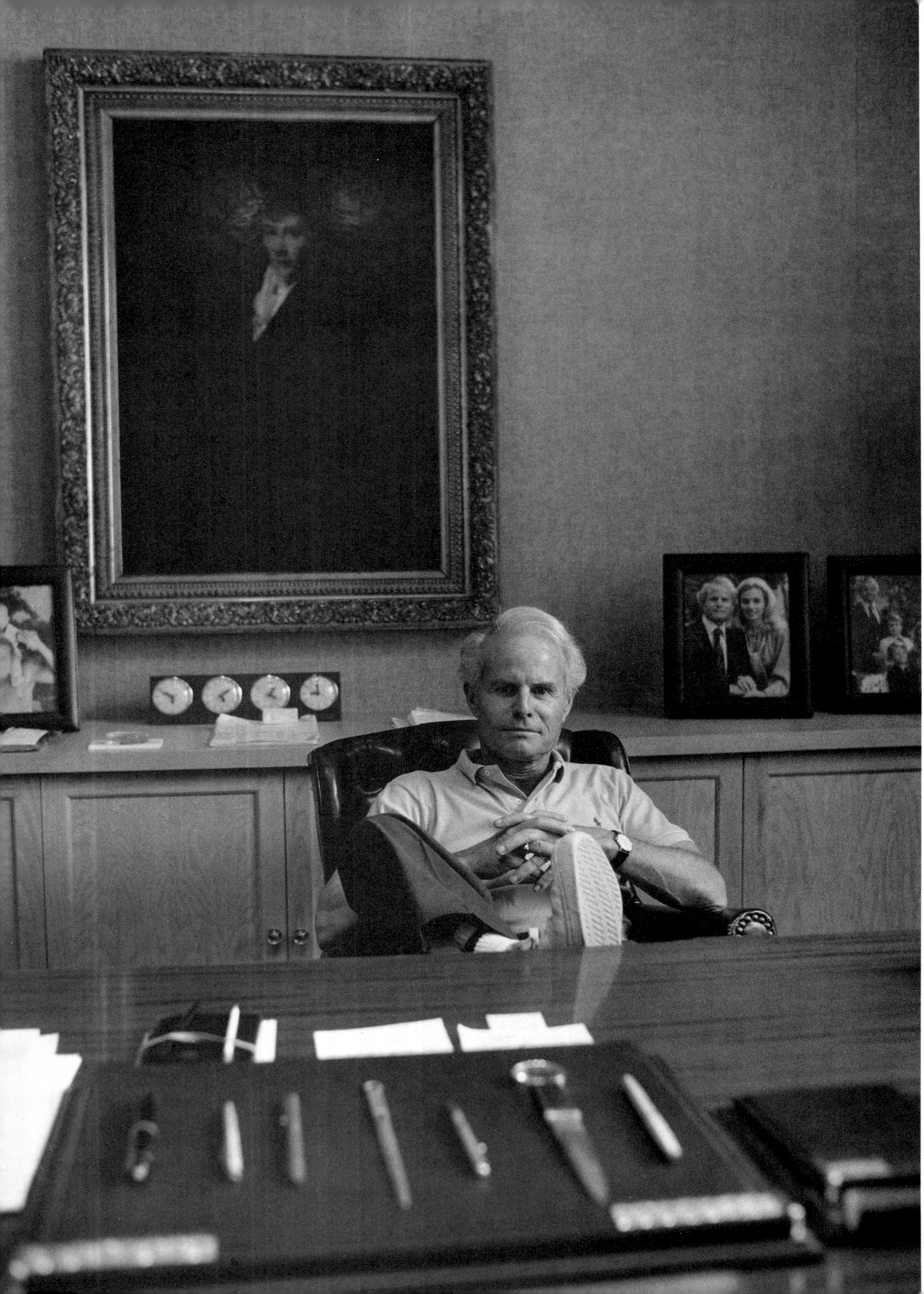

Richard Zanuck
BY
Alan Ladd, Jr.

What can I say? I've known Dick Zanuck for over 30 years. He's loyal, honest, talented, a brilliant businessman, extraordinary athlete, good husband, good father, great friend, an all-around even-tempered guy.

. . . Did I say even-tempered? Only in his movies. And, by the way, he makes great movies!

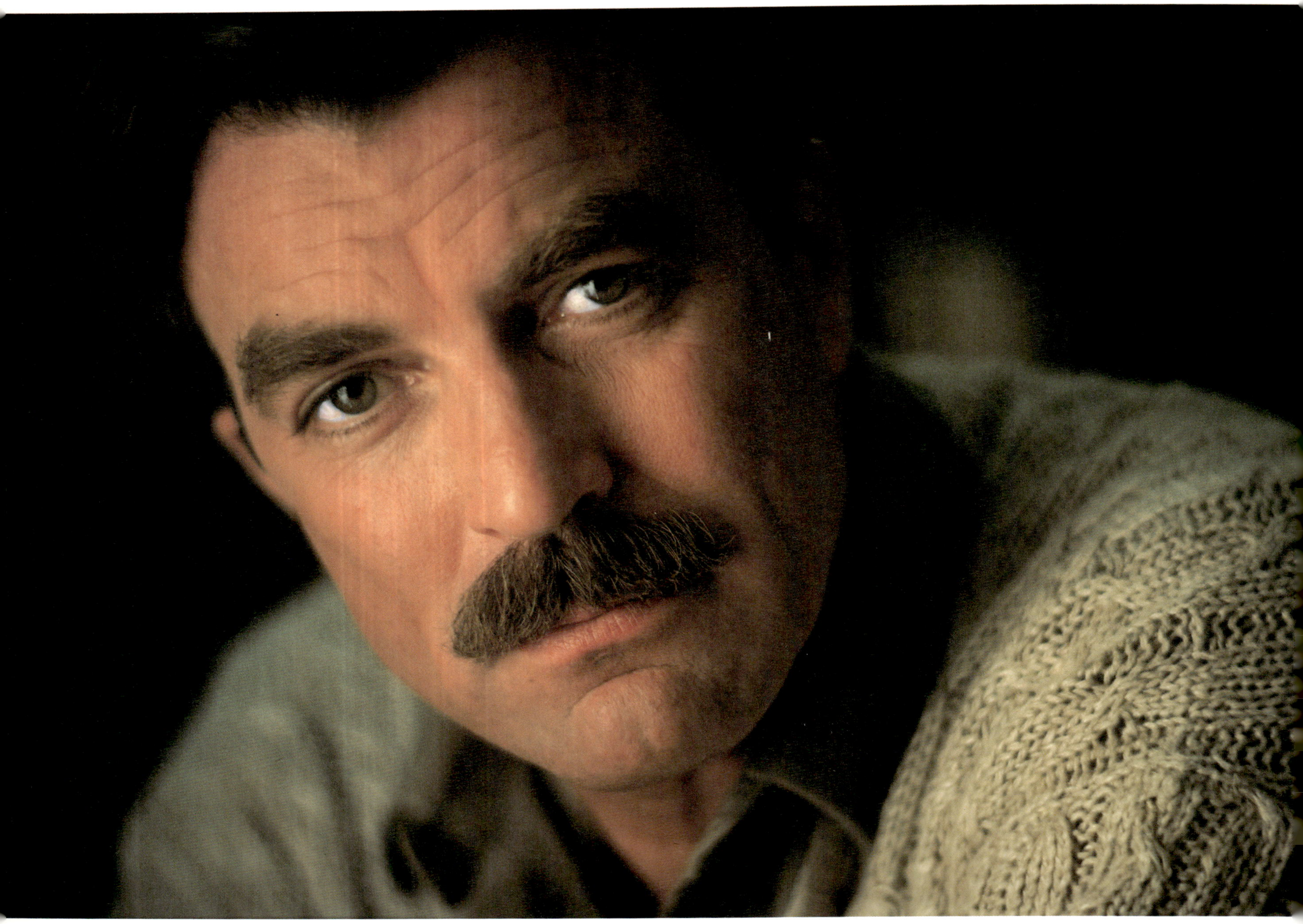

Tom Selleck
BY
Carol Burnett

When I was asked to write something about Tom as I know him, I jumped at the chance.

I tried a paragraph or two and thought that maybe I said "yes" too fast. The problem was that he is *nice* and that's not what a lot of people want to read about. Then I figured that those folks can always go out and throw away good money on a tabloid . . . you know, one of those magazines that would feature the outbreak of World War III on the back page . . . (if at all).

I also remembered that the first thing people usually ask about So-and-So is: "Is he (or she) *nice*?" They want to know.

So here is my view of Tom. Cynics, take a hike.

I met Tom at a People's Choice awards show many moons ago. He had won one (I think as Favorite New Star) and because we both had homes in Hawaii, somebody (probably a PR person) covered us in leis and threw us together backstage where we smiled for the photographers exuding true Aloha spirit which made for good photos. Even though we had never met before, he made me feel as if we surfed together on a regular basis. He was gracious to me, to his fans, and to the photographers. I remember that he was genuinely pleased about the prize he had won and at the same time totally unassuming. Let me put it this way, he handled it *well.* I also remember thinking, "If I could look like that, I would grow a moustache."

A few years later I guested on *Magnum.* I had the most fun I ever had guesting on a show. The crew was happy. Nobody had a gripe. I remember a lot of laughs. One afternoon when we were working, someone (probably a PR person) came on the set and announced that Tom's movie *Three Men and a Baby* was the top picture in the country. The public and the critics were delighted with his performance. Everybody cheered, and Tom's expression was . . . I don't know how to describe it. He was pleased, of course, but he wasn't that . . . *impressed.* Again, he handled it well.

I doubt that he ever has, or ever *could,* come down with the dreaded "I'm-A-Big-Star" disease. It's simply not his thing.

On *Magnum,* he helped with the scripts, the direction, and the production without the blowing of whistles or the waving of flags. He knew about cameras, lighting, and special effects. He was able to get his opinions across without stepping on anyone's toes . . . and he played darts with the crew during the breaks. The people who worked for (I should say *with*) him have been with him forever.

Burbank, California 1990

He adores his family . . . his folks . . . his siblings. He is married to a terrific woman. He has a son and a baby daughter to whom he is utterly devoted. He talks about them nonstop and carries pictures . . . *up-to-date pictures.*

His acting (like the best of them) seems effortless. He is gifted with the comic touch. He's not afraid to make fun of himself. He's one of the chosen few who can play a sexy buffoon.

He has a great giggle.

He can also pass a mirror without looking in it. He's that secure.

And boy, is that nice.

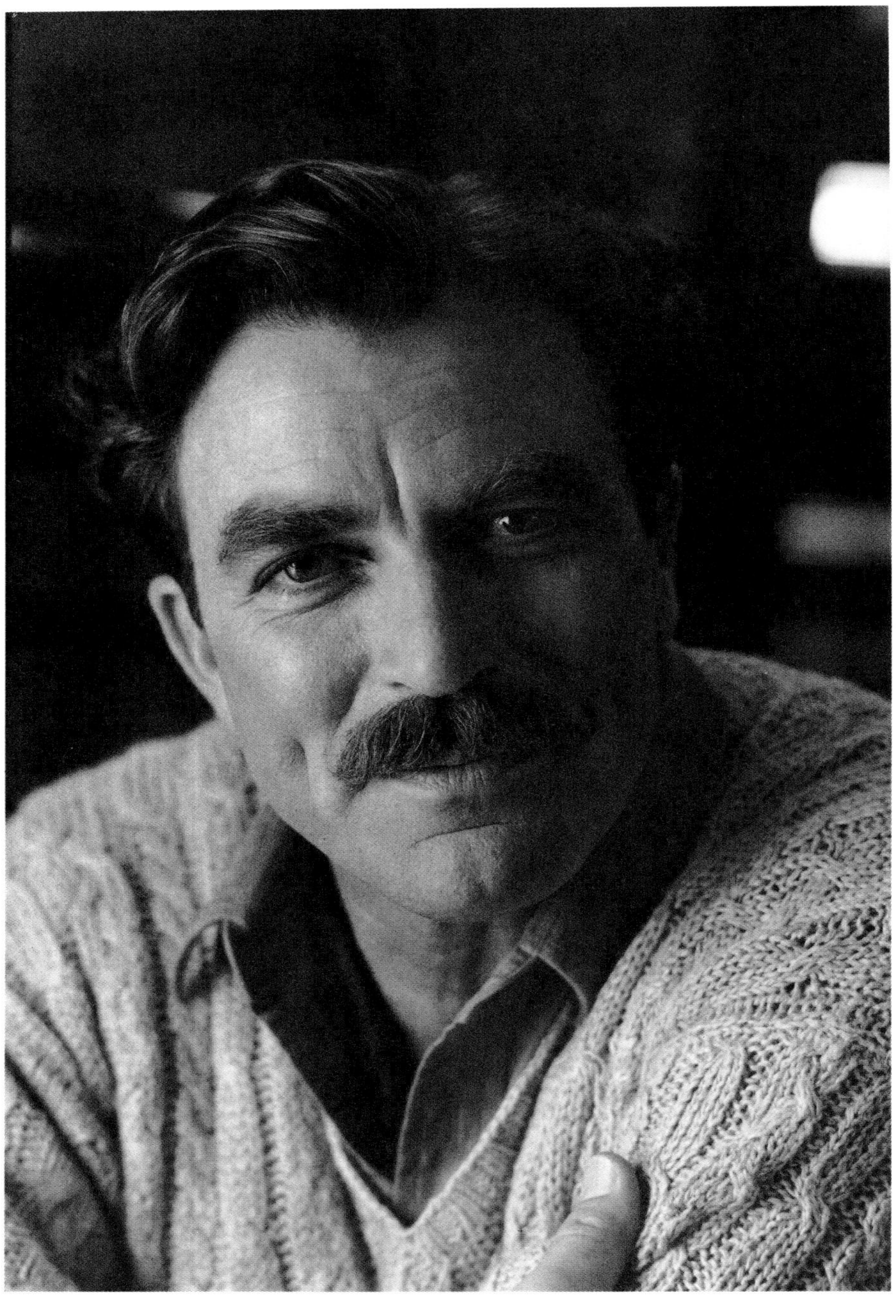

Burbank, California 1990

Garland/Merman/Streisand
BY
Norman Jewison

We called them "The Belters."

"Judy . . . wouldn't it be fantastic if I could book Streisand on the show? Just the two of you? And then just before the last number, as a surprise . . . Ethel Merman comes out of the audience . . . And for one historic magic moment the three of you are belting out a song together! Wouldn't that be a once-in-a-lifetime happening?"

God they were sublime!

Hollywood *1963*

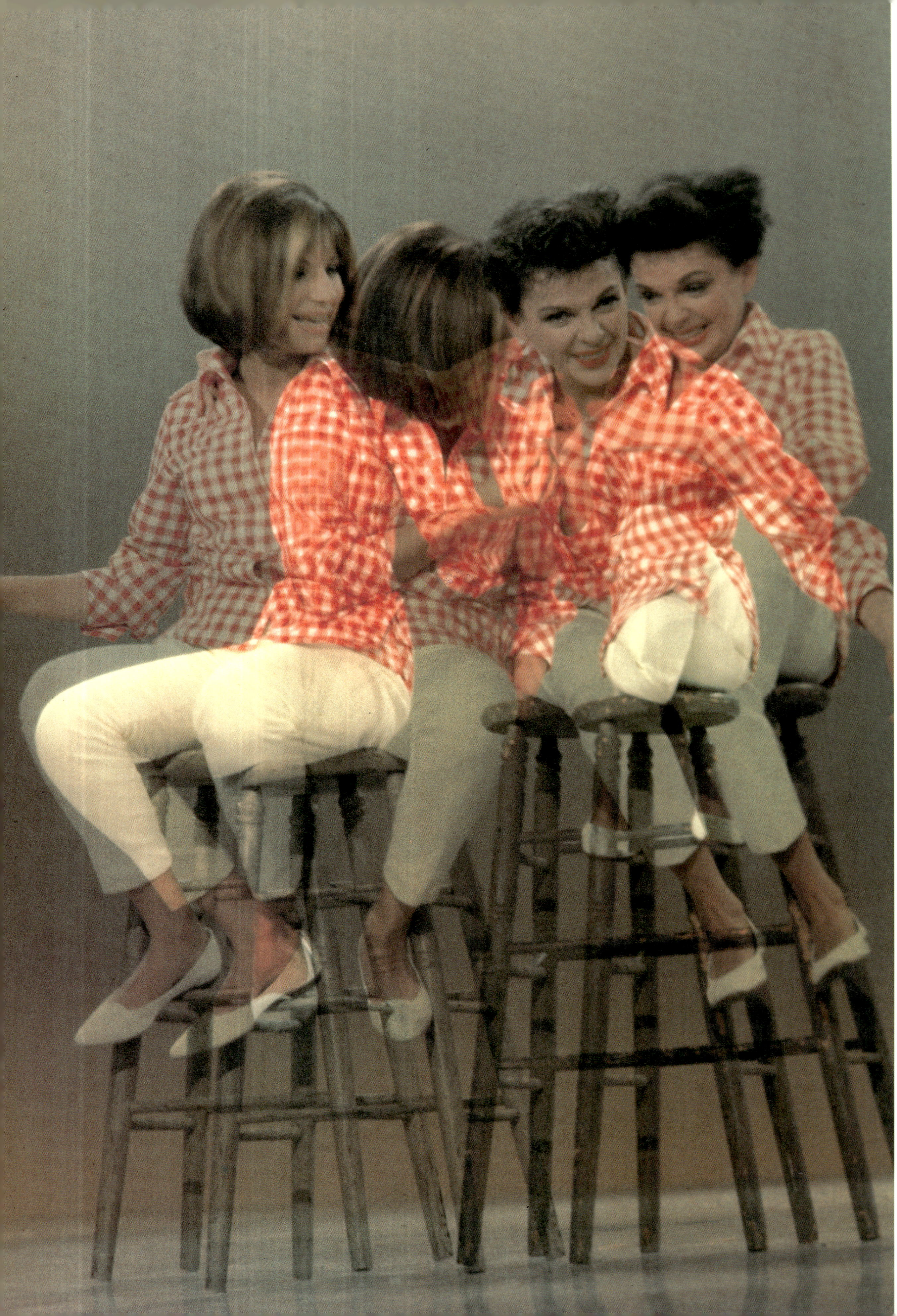

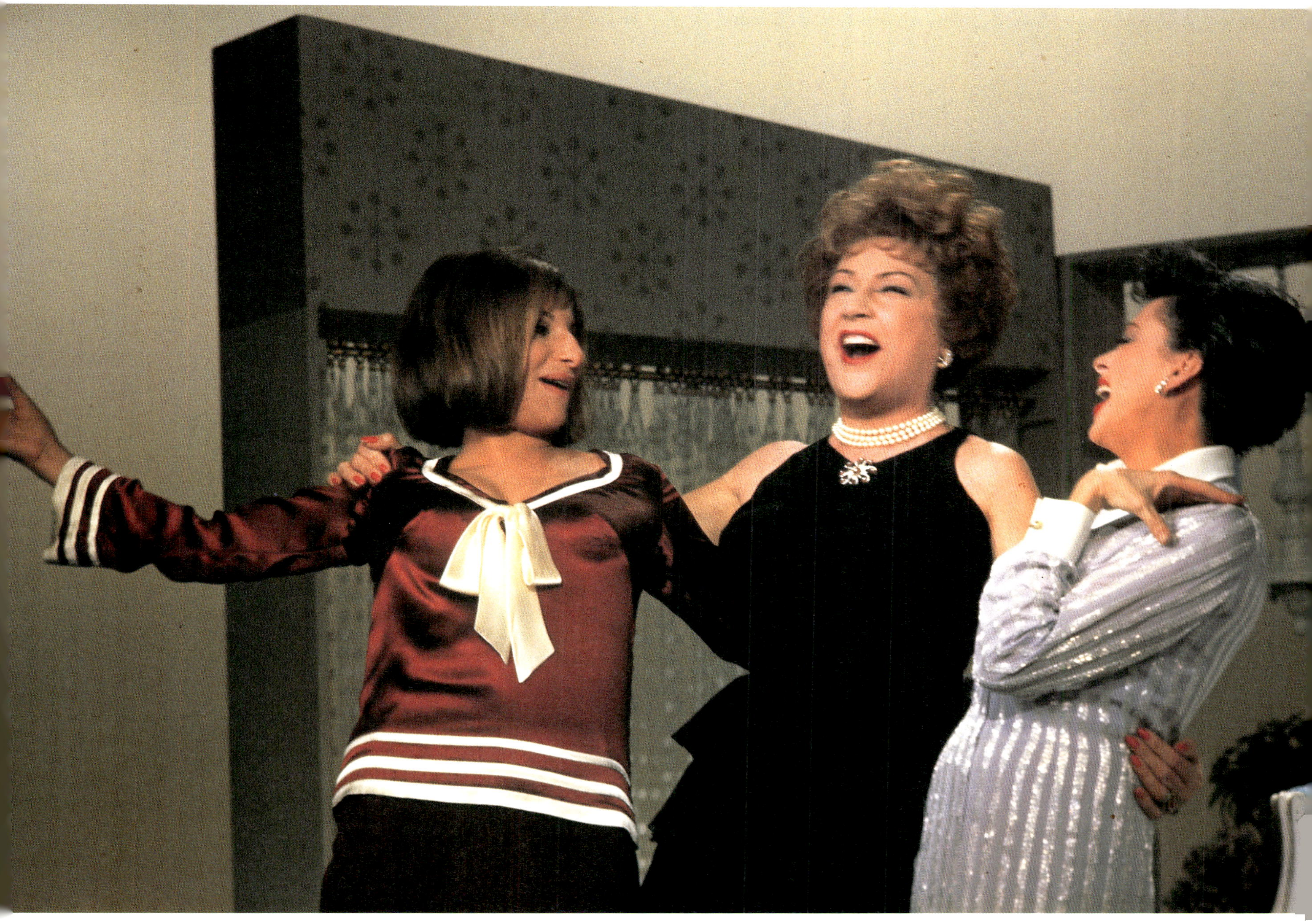

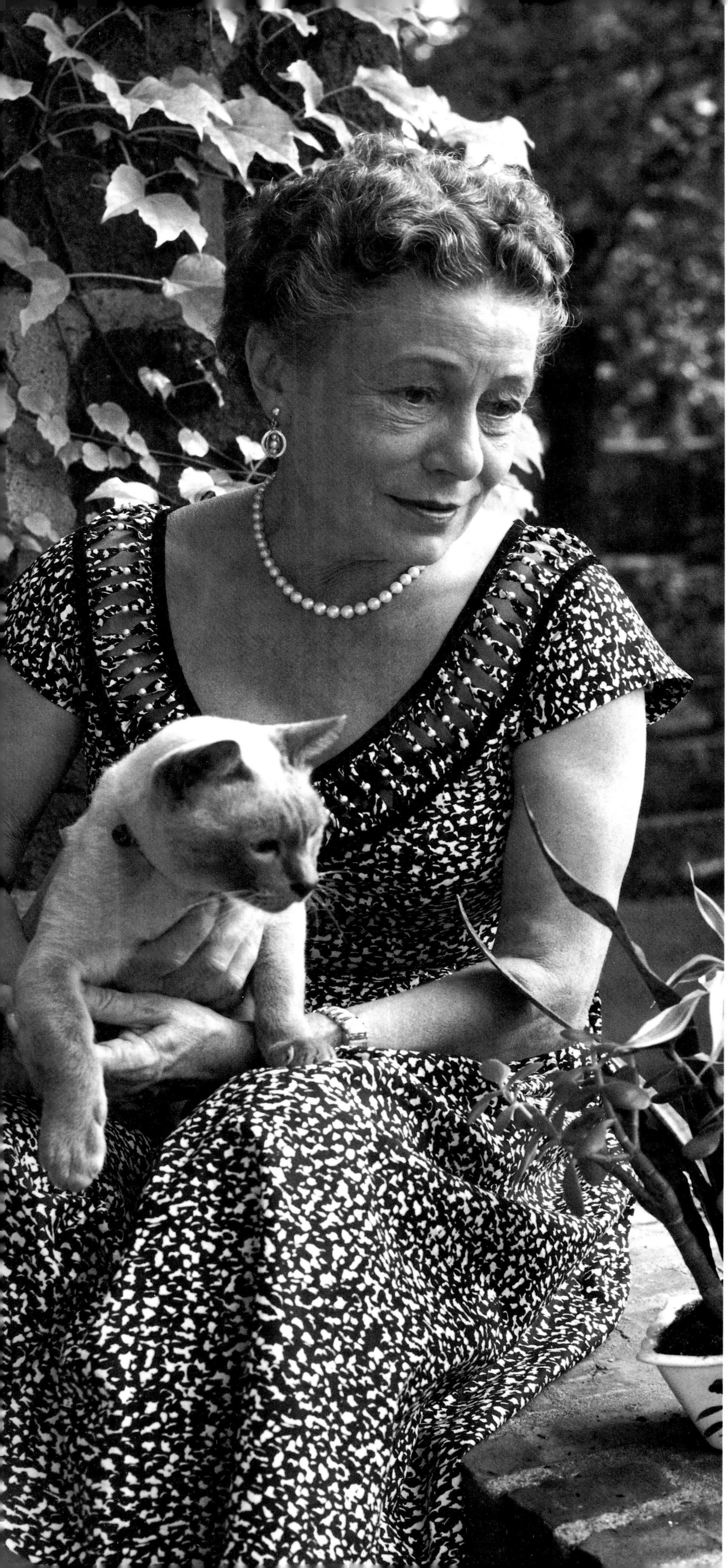

Thelma Ritter
BY
Nancy Walker

Thel . . . Thelma Ritter . . . Mrs. Joseph Moran.

My darling friend answered to all of the above and enjoyed the fruits of life that each title brought her. She preferred the life of Mrs. Moran, but we all have to get away from our spouses and children now and then, and she made the most glamorous getaways of all. To Hollywood and films.

She was my sweet and strong Irish friend and one of our finest comediennes. For perfection see *All About Eve.* In three or four lines she sets the scene. We are given insight to her feelings for her employer (played by Bette Davis) . . . her disgust with the invited guest and the disdain she feels for the world in general. It's a lesson in humor that shows years of commitment to learning one's craft.

I always found her a tower of strength. A mentor with laughs. She balanced her family life and career with ease and love . . . she wisecracked her way through troubles and sorrow with an attitude that said . . . "That's the way it goes, folks."

Years into our friendship I directed Thelma in a play. I found, suddenly, a lady full of fears and concern for her work on Broadway. She was vulnerable and shy and I saw for the first time a different Thel. Which did I prefer? I loved every lady that went into the composing of Thelma. They were all equally true and dear.

At Thelma's funeral . . . the good Father, who was presiding over the proceedings, looked out on a group of friends who had struggled their way on foot through the worst blizzard in the history of New York to get to the church on Long Island. He took his time . . . gazed at us and in a very somber, respectful voice said . . . "I know that our dear friend Thelma is looking down on us now and saying . . . 'What the hell are those silly bastards doing out on a day like this?' And that last remark is exactly why we're here. We came to make sure she knew we loved her."

That about wraps up my thoughts on Thelma.

Forest Hills, New York *1956*

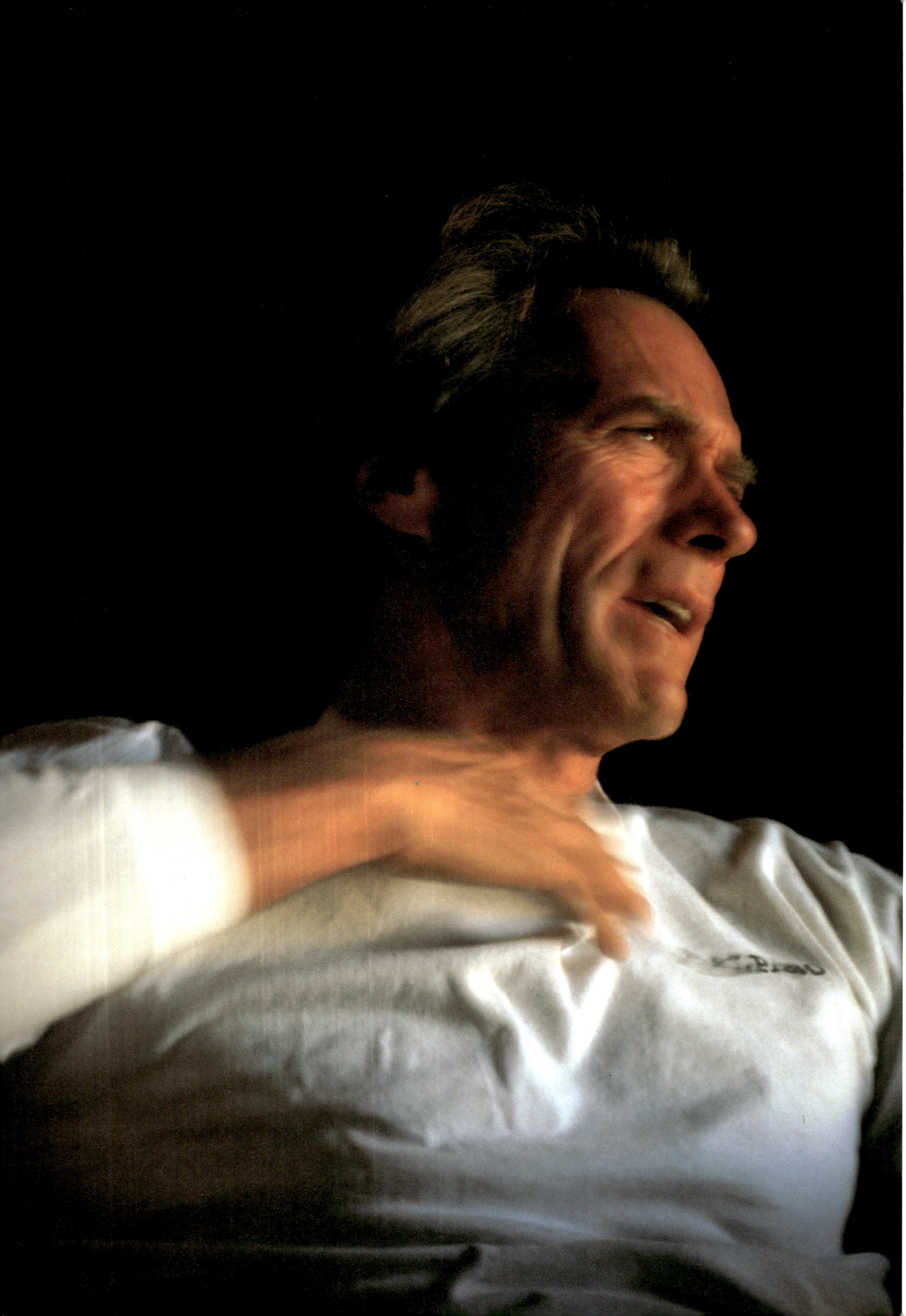

Clint Eastwood
BY
Arnold Schwarzenegger

Back in the 1960s, as a teenager in my town of Graz, Austria, movies were still a fantasy to me. Like everyone else of that age, I had my favorite stars. And what boy wouldn't have been impressed with the total cool and quiet menace of Clint Eastwood's "Man With No Name"? From Clint's performances, I learned that silence can be golden ... and deadly. I learned that what can be conveyed on-screen with one look is sometimes worth a thousand words (especially early in my career, when those words were still being spoken in a thick Austrian accent!). I admit it . . . if you stare very, very closely at *The Terminator,* you may see a little bit of the "Man With No Name" staring back at you! And even though Clint is now my friend, whenever I watch him on-screen, I can only see the character he's playing. And I begin to feel like that teenager in Graz all over again . . .

Burbank, California *1990*

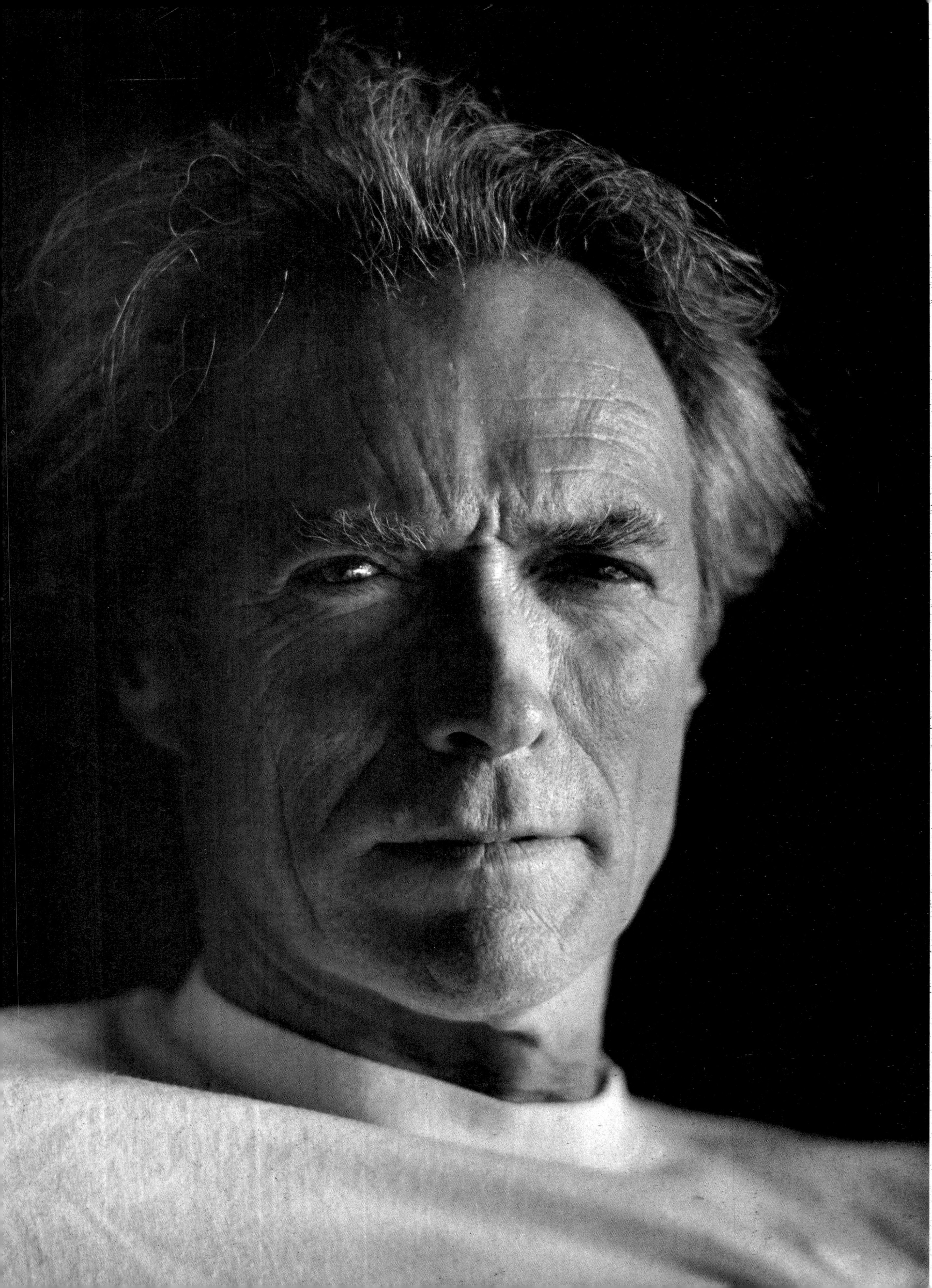

Alexis Smith
BY
Dirk Bogarde

A. is for Ace. Apple and Alexis. And Alexis IS Ace.

A lot of Firsts going here. She was my First Hollywood Leading Lady. Miss Iceberg (sic) from Warners arrived, in 1953, to play opposite me in a whole bundle of rubbish called *The Sleeping Tiger* to be directed by one Victor Hanbury (in fact Joseph Losey.) written by Derek Frey (in fact Harold Buchman and Carl Foreman.) The first European movie to be made by this sad group of American moviemakers sent into exile by the McCarthy witch-hunters. All unaware of this deception, Alexis arrived in London, jet-lagged (except there were no jets then. Only propellers.) and ill with a tummy bug. In a heavy mink coat, with an ashen face, she arrived at my house in the country to meet us all for the first time, and to read the perfectly terrible script.

It was, at first sight, clear that Miss Smith needed assistance, bed, hot-water bottles, and sleep.

She was sent to the guest room and only surfaced, good pro that she is, when rested; secure in the knowledge that whatever she might require was not far away.

Her astonishment, not to say appalled shock, when she discovered that poor Victor Hanbury was not who he was supposed to be, and that Derek Frey was two quite other people, cowering in the more unfashionable parts of London, was amazing to behold.

Faced with this terrible dilemma, to return to the U.S. and junk the movie or to stay and throw in her lot with a bunch of expelled, and respected, filmmakers from her own country; she discussed it at some length with us all. I was going ahead with the project anyway. I was a European so no skin off my nose, but I liked the exiles, liked their ideas and had decided to work with them. She took an immense risk, and spent a fair amount of time avoiding various members of the DAR who were, for one reason or another, hovering about London and the Studios.

So did Losey, Buchman, and Foreman. But we managed, and Victor Hanbury, who actually *did* exist, sat in the director's chair on set and gave every impression of being in charge. He was a good guy: knew the form, and carried us all through many problems without a word.

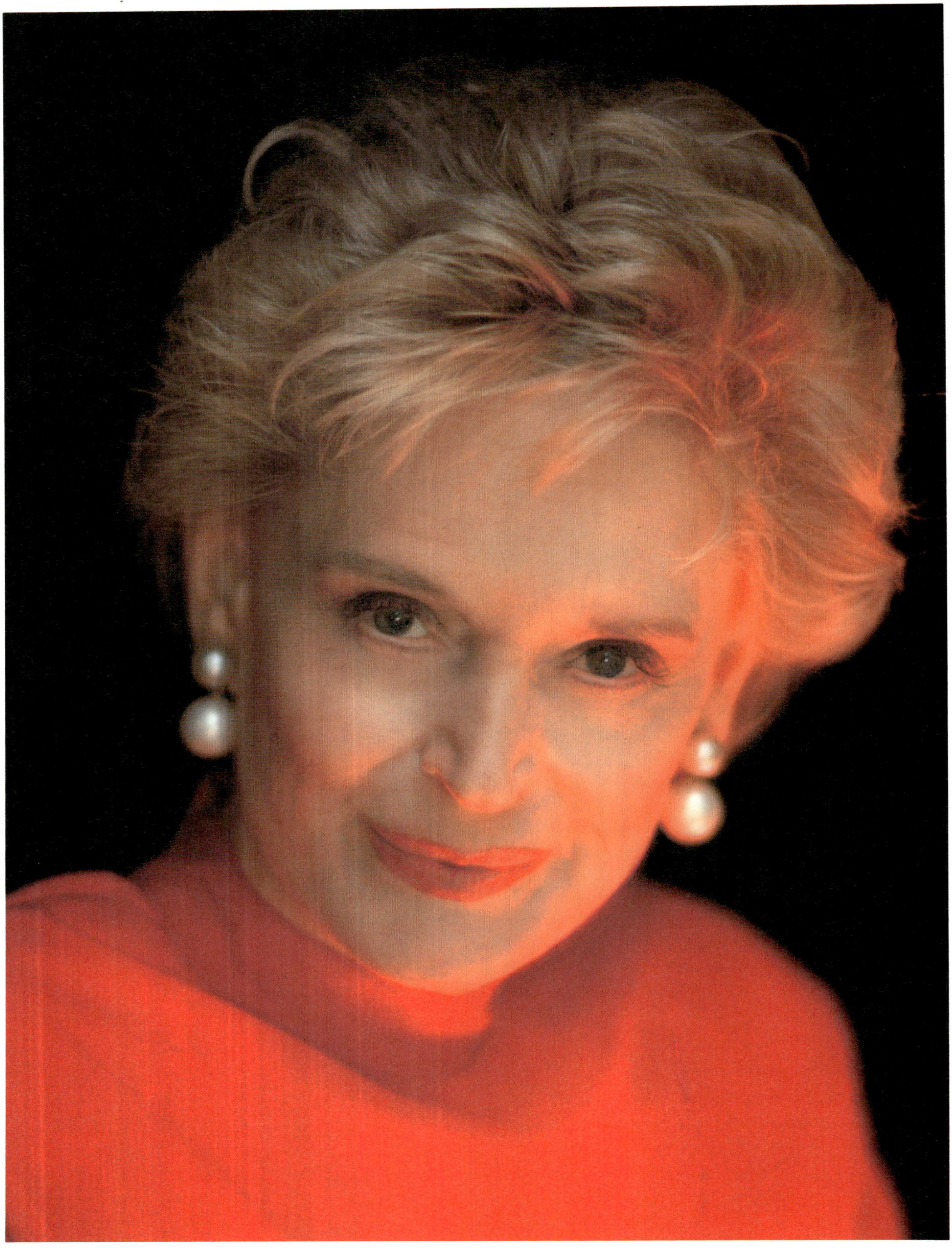

One day Alexis watched me on the set, and when I had finished giving "my all" said, in her quiet, considered, gentle, voice:

"Dirk, what were you doing then?"

"Acting," I replied loftily.

"Is it fun?" said Alexis.

"Great fun."

"Can I try?"

She did. And we have been devoted and loving friends ever since. Her fun, her total professionalism, her energy, her loyalty, and above all, her courage remain as they always have been. First in her life. In bad days, not-so-good-days, in days of triumph, like *Follies*, she has remained my chum. Steadfast, willing to take a chance, brave and compassionate. She has even forgiven me for passing out, face down, in her special avocado dip in her ravishing house last time I arrived in L.A., jet-lagged from the Concorde and a brutal flight across America. You don't get a better friend than that. There is a strong promise, on the familiar yellow letter paper, that she might be back in Europe in the summer.

I'm polishing the silver already. No need to dust off the Welcome Mat . . . she knows that she is, and always has been. The days are the brighter for knowing her.

Hollywood 1990

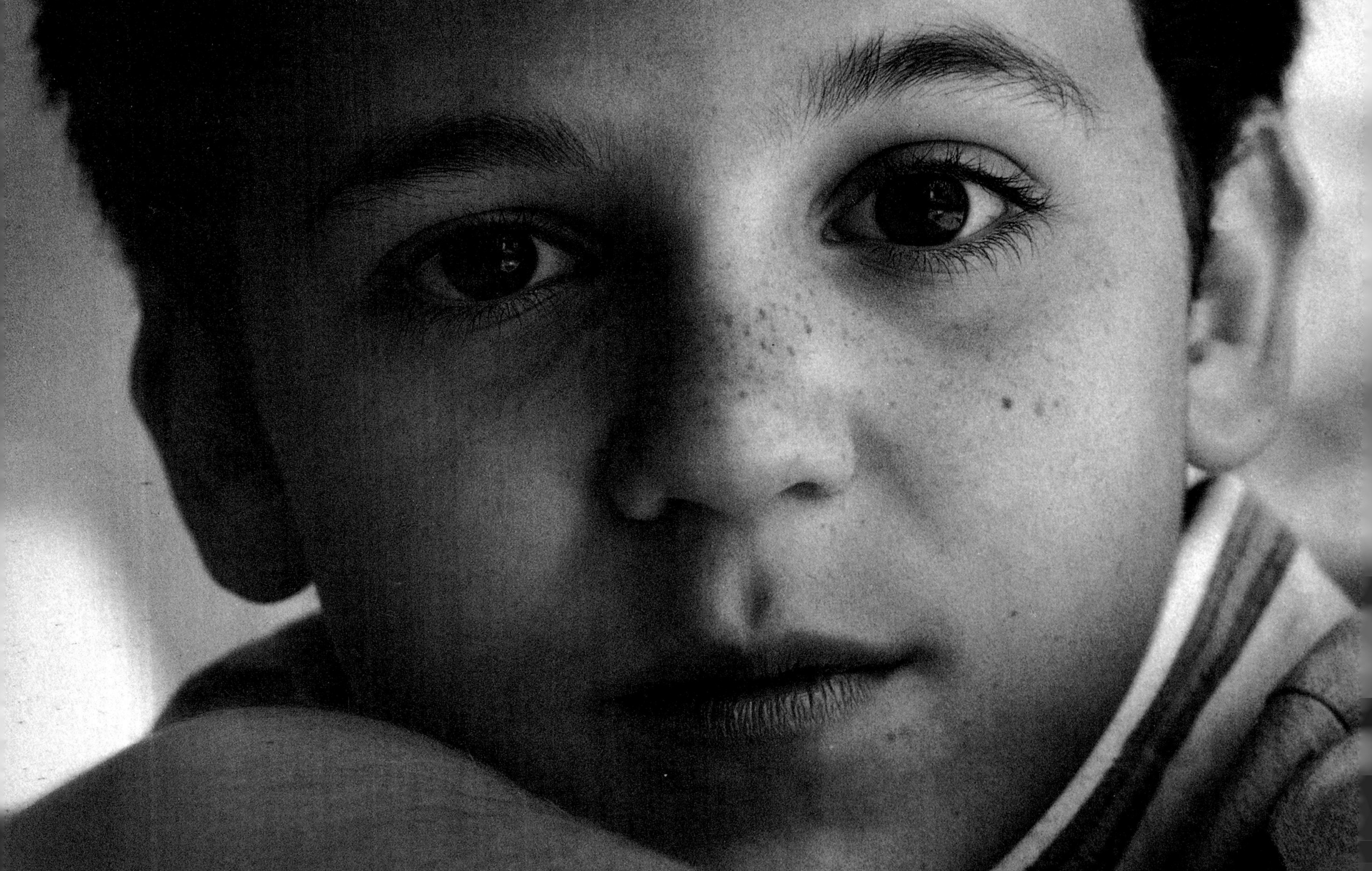

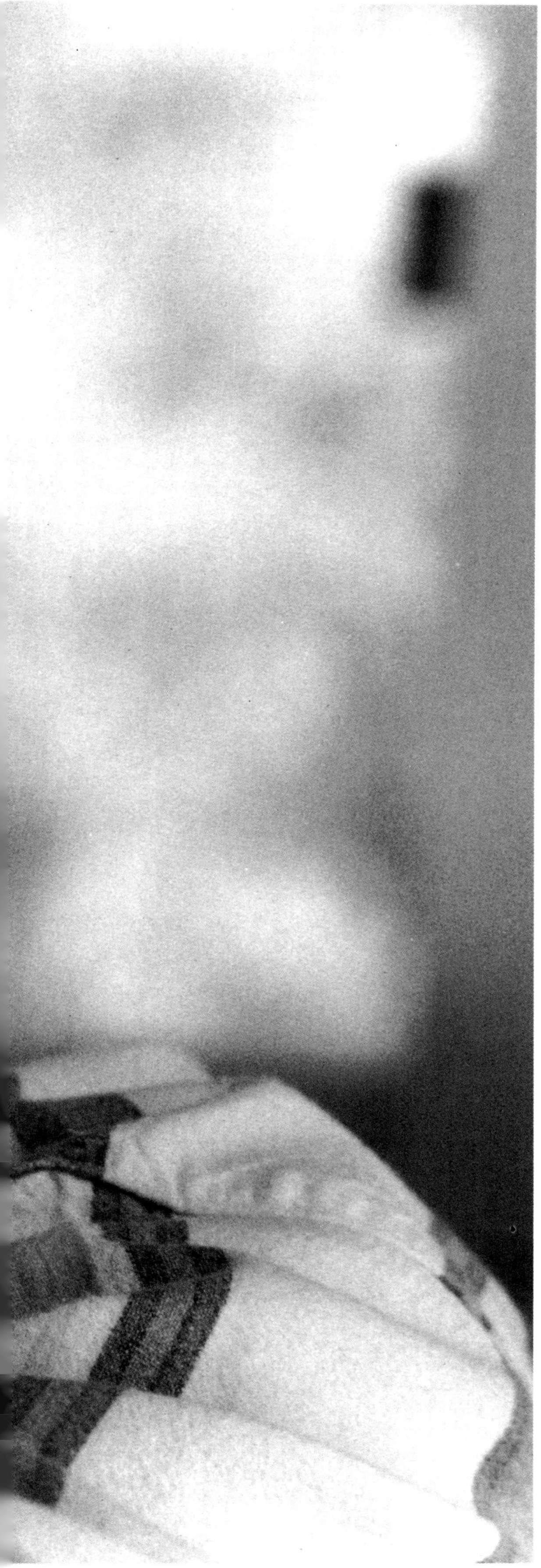

Fred Savage
BY
Kurt Russell

Perhaps the single most enjoyable performance for me to watch is given by a child actor whose on-screen persona is adult but not precocious. The actor is working at an age when innocence and awareness count for equal measure which allows for the best opportunity to most believably create an unpredictable, yet totally honest, spontaneous reaction.

Shirley Temple, Freddie Bartholomew, Billy Gray, Ronnie Howard, Jodie Foster, and, yes, the very young Roddy McDowall combined all those qualities in many of their childhood performances.

Fred Savage can stand up and take a bow alongside those memorable and terrific young actors. He is that good.

Tarzana, California *1989*

Joan Sutherland
BY
Marilyn Horne

As I stood on the stage of the Royal Opera House on New Year's Eve, 1990, celebrating the farewell of the great Joan Sutherland, I could not help but reflect on the first time I heard her glorious voice. Those silver tones came to me via the *Westdeutsche Rundfunk*. It was 1959 and her operatic career was going into orbit. I remember sitting there in utter amazement at the extraordinary beauty and agility of her instrument. Two short years later we were making our New York debuts together! Needless to say it was an enormous thrill for me to be singing before the New York public with "The Best." For thirty years she has given us unmatched singing, pure professionalism, and to me a warm and personal friendship.

I salute you, Joan, as the greatest of our time.

New York City 1965

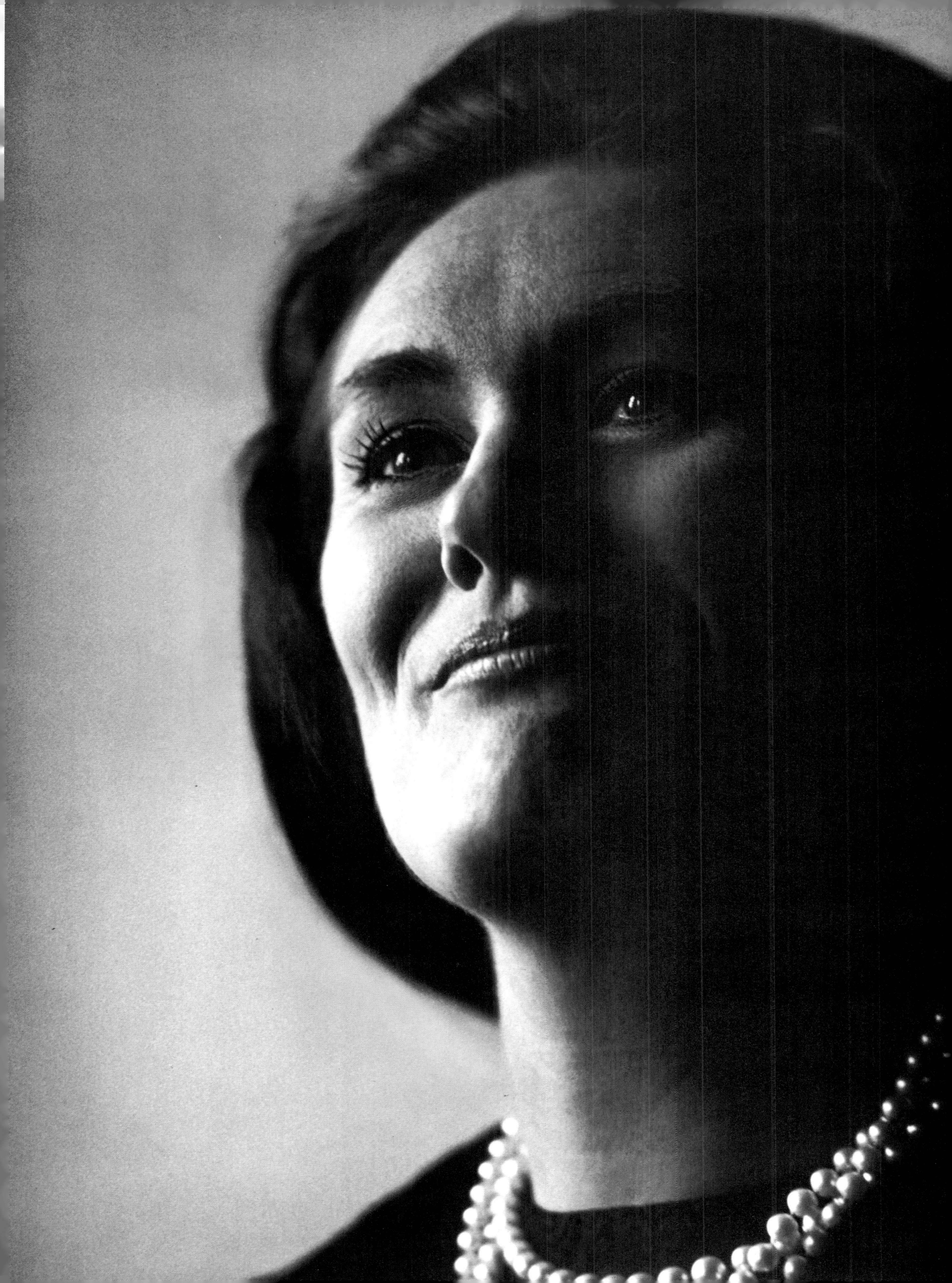

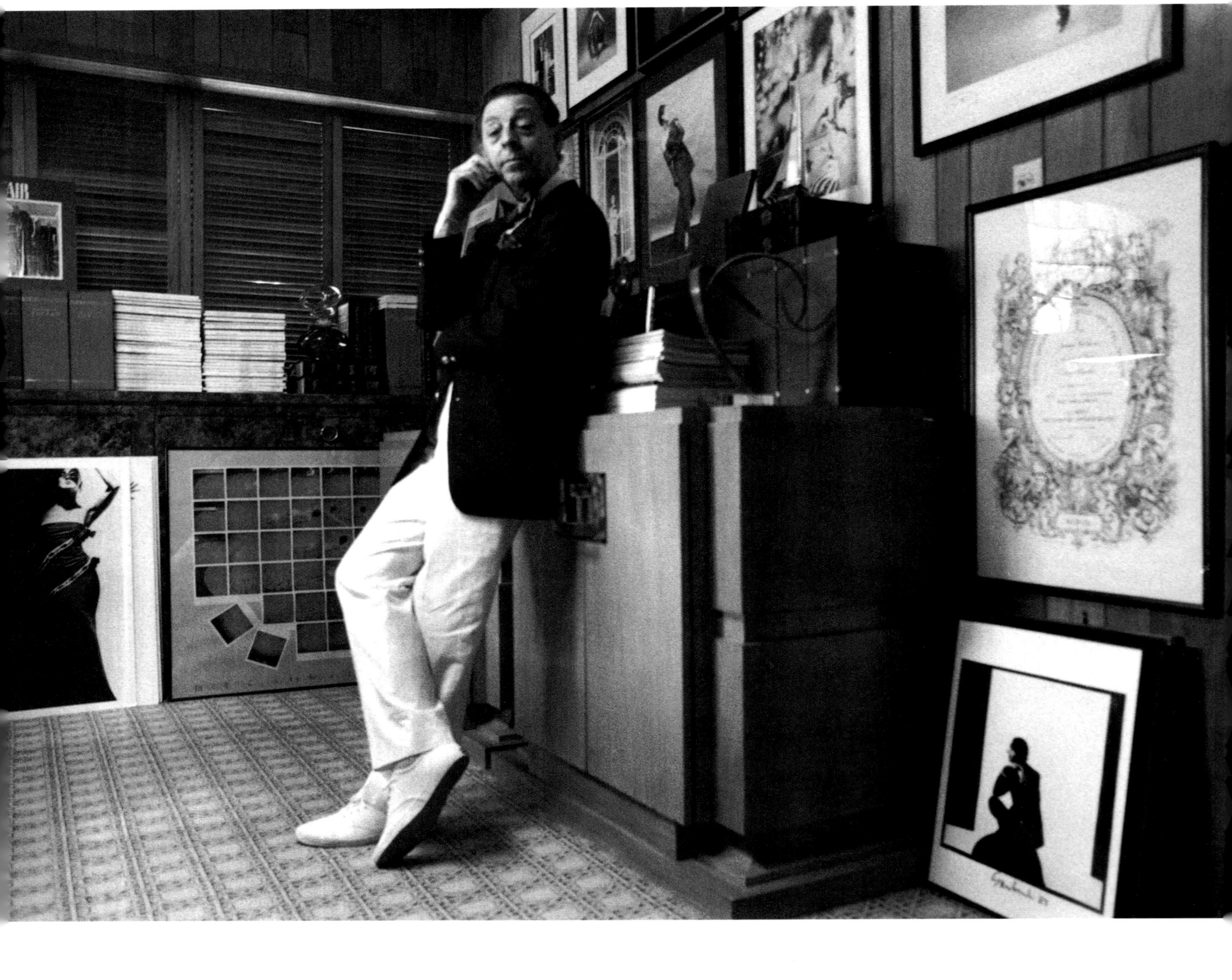

James Galanos
BY
Nancy Reagan

I met Jimmy when I first came to California under contract to MGM. Amelia Gray, a mutual friend, introduced us and I became his devoted fan from that moment on. I think it's probably difficult for most people to know him well, perhaps because he's unassuming and I suspect, underneath it all, a little shy. However, there is nothing shy about his talent—his clothes are absolutely beautiful—made with an extraordinary eye for detail, magnificent fabrics and workmanship. The first dress I had cost $125 if you can believe it. However, at the first State Dinner in 1981, I wore a dress of Jimmy's which was 12 years old at that time. It looked great and I'll probably wear it again some time.

As you can see, he wears well—not only his clothes but as a person. I'm so happy we're friends. He deserves every accolade that comes his way.

Los Angeles 1987

Debbie Reynolds
BY
Carrie Fisher

When I was a child, my mother seemed to me to be something like a miracle. Not my mother, surely. Too beautiful to be any mother of mine. She has always had some . . . impish kind of poise that is so endlessly, effortlessly *lovable.* Yes, there was no other explanation. I was not the child of this darling beauty, but some end-of-shoot remembrance sent to her from the prop department. A put-together thing complete with parts spare and missing.

I worshipped my mother from the nearest possible side of afar. This woman smelling of White Shoulders, Albolene creme and El Paso. She's a force of nature; an undeniable fact, like gravity or Greenland. Ubiquitous, lovable, and as it turns out, my actual mother.

Thanks be to God and Louis B. Mayer.

New York City *1953*

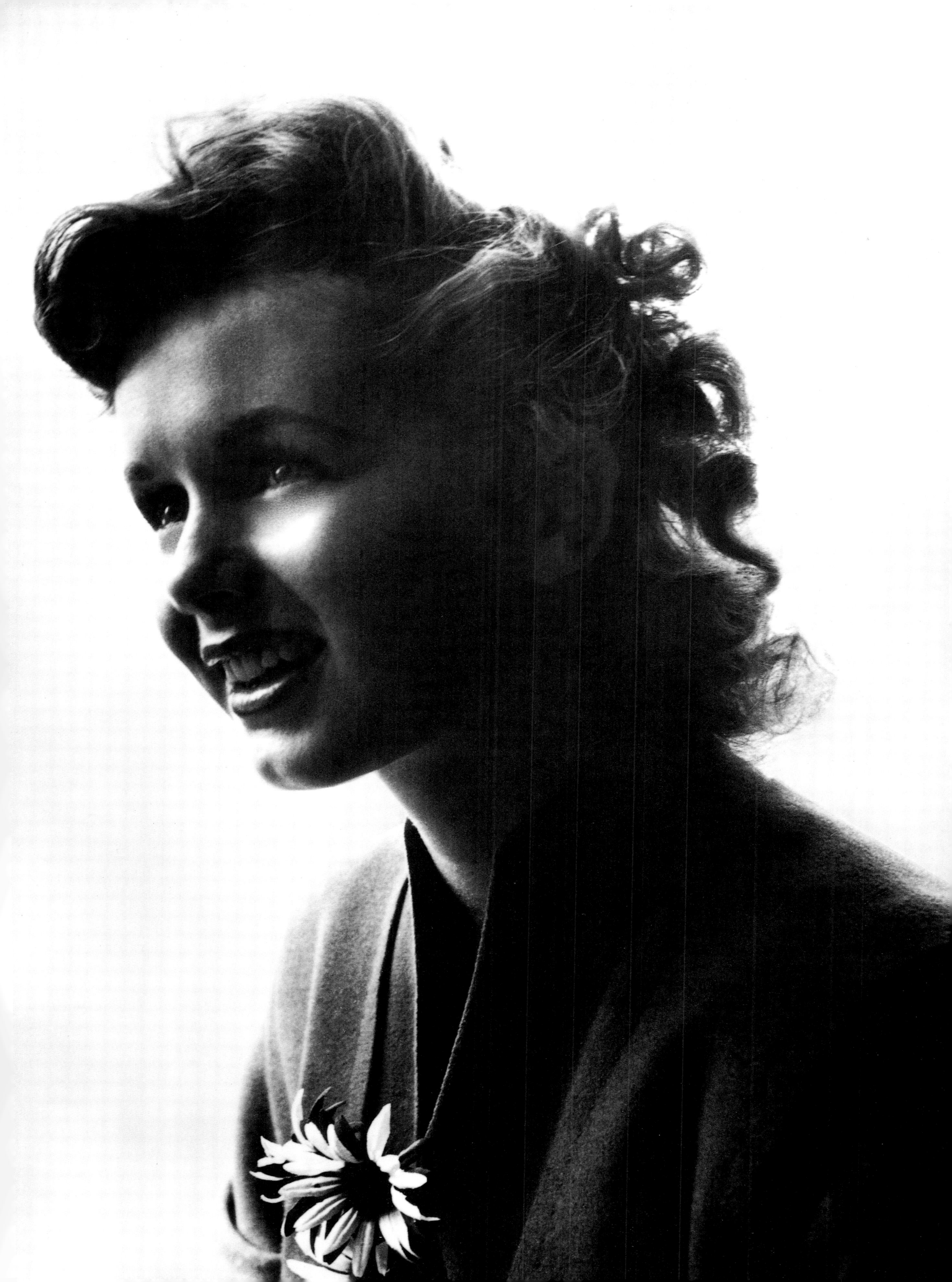

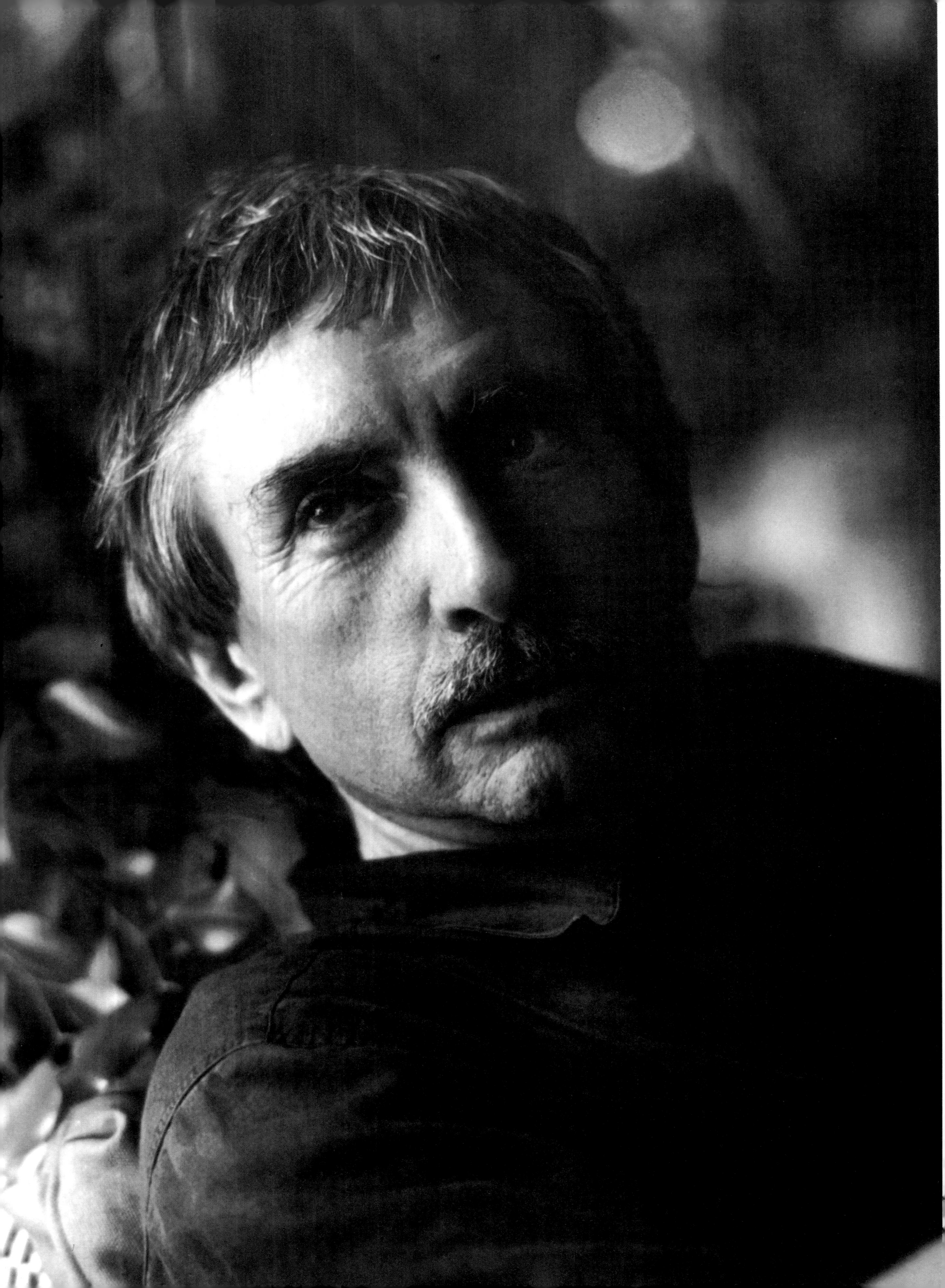

Edward Albee
BY
Colleen Dewhurst

Edward. Always listening, always observing. Yet distant, cool, and in control, as if to protect himself from the multitudes.

When I see Edward, I want to hug him. When I do, it is first like embracing a ramrod. But if I keep my arms around him long enough, there is finally—for seconds only—a giving in, a melting, lasting just long enough to see forever the boy lurking behind the man.

What makes Edward Albee one of America's greatest playwrights is the incredible beauty of his writing. But he is dangerous. He sees the world from a perspective that demands, indeed compels, an audience to reach beyond themselves. He forces us to see past lines that have been drawn as the boundaries of our everyday existence. He dares us to witness what may happen when we ask life to be all that it is, illuminating the passions that are unleashed when we finally give up the facade of good taste and propriety.

When Edward directed the 1976 revival of *Who's Afraid of Virginia Woolf?* he said to us in the cast, on the first day of rehearsal, "I'm directing this play because, after fourteen years, I now understand what I wrote." An actress, like myself, thanks God that there is a playwright, like Albee, who allows you to show the fullness of what it is to be a woman, when all is exposed and both beauty and horror are stripped naked.

Studio City, California *1989*

Gracie Fields
BY
Leslie Bricusse

"*Now* you know *why*," said Bea Lillie as the huge flying boat headed straight for the massive rock. Lower and lower, until it hit the choppy blue water as smoothly as it could under the circumstances. We coasted slowly into the safe harbour of the Marina Grande. My first view of Capri was heart-stoppingly impressive. It was April, 1955.

"There's nothing to fear," Auntie Bea had said with infinite wisdom a few hours earlier as we took off from the Solent near Southampton, "*provided* you get drunk in Marseilles!"—which we had all obediently done during the lunchtime refueling stopover. "Drink!" she had said, mysteriously but firmly, "I'll tell you why later!" So we drank, and she spent the second half of the journey blissfully and immovably asleep on the spiral staircase connecting the two levels of the flying boat. She awoke five minutes before landing and regaled us with a chirpy few bars of her currently favorite Lillie lyric—"I've Got You Under My Sink!"

Gracie owned the famed Canzone del Mare (Song of the Sea), Capri's most glamorous swimming pool-restaurant-hotspot on the Piccola Marina side of the island, where love came to Mrs. Wentworth-Brewster. It was protected by Emilio Pucci's boutique to the north, disused German World War II gun emplacements to the east and west (still there in 1990!), and the sea itself to the south.

Gracie lived simply and well with her, I think, fourth husband, a charming Italian ex-electrician called Boris, atop a high rock that towered over the Canzone del Mare. We went up to see her the next day for tea. We laughed till we cried, and we smiled when she and Bea sang fragments of bygone silly songs.

Gracie seemed both completely content and completely out of place. It was like being in Rochdale-Sulla-Mare, unfettered Lancashire in deepest Italy, except there wasn't an aspidistra on the whole island, and no cheering shiploads of British troops to remind me that this was "Our Gracie." The great inspirational singing heroine of the darkest Dunkirk days of the war, second only to Winston Churchill in British national affection.

Gracie and Bea and Noël and Gertie and Vivien Leigh and Vera Lynn and the rest of them had entertained the troops all over the place during the war. And then, unbelievably to us at the time—was it 1942?—Gracie suddenly married this Italian-born actor-singer called Monty Banks, who was no doubt a perfectly nice chap. But this was Our Gracie, and this was war, and we were fighting the Wops, and deep in our suspicious, insular, how-dare-you English hearts we felt somehow betrayed, as though behind that adored Lancashire lass's singing facade, with the easily reached high C, lurked some sinister Rochdale femme fatale, a North

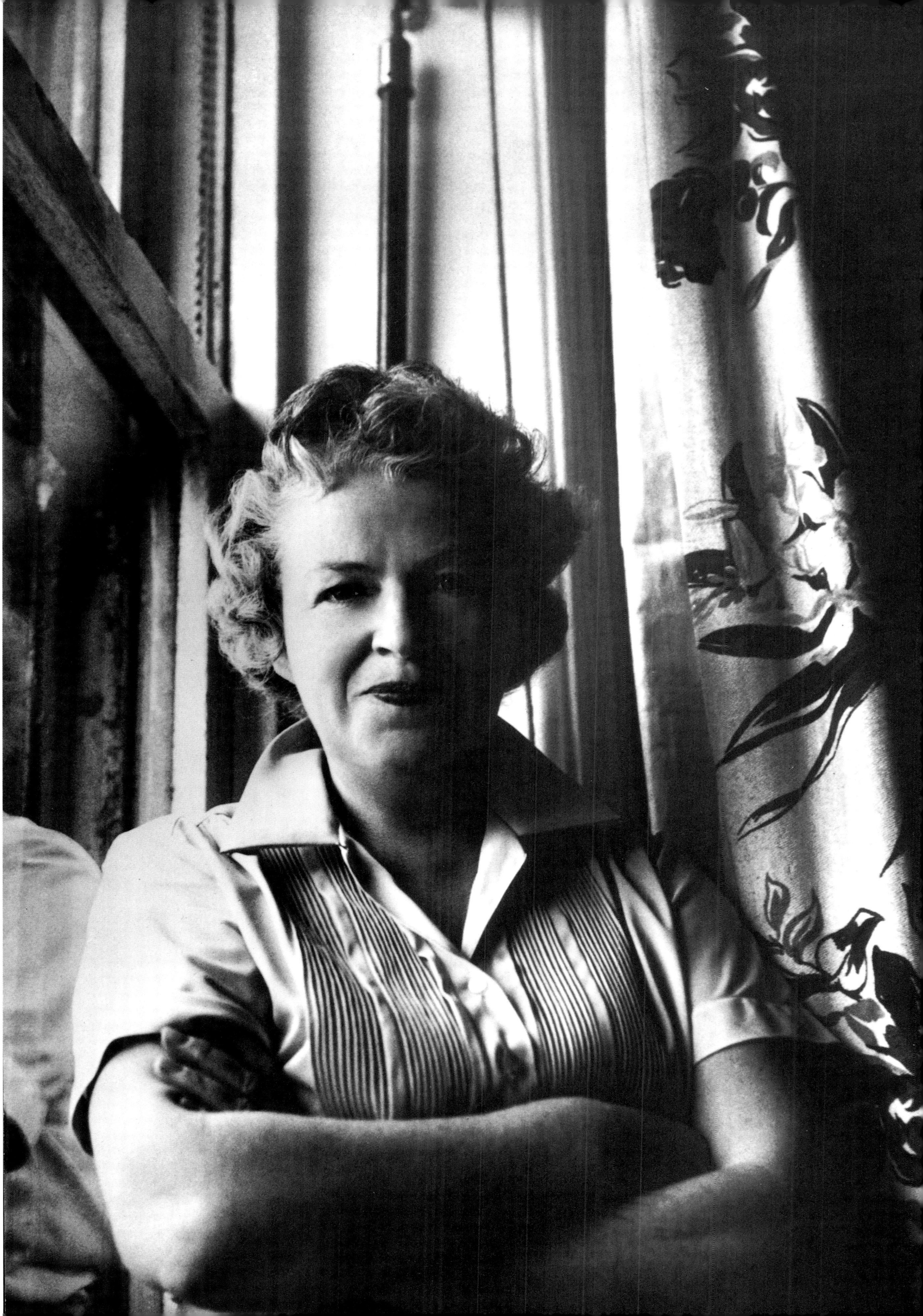

country Mata Hari. And as only the English can do, we turned our backs on her, and pretended we didn't.

How small we were, how big she was! All her life she went where her heart led her, did Gracie. She gave her all, be it to the British Expeditionary Force before and after Dunkirk, or to Monty Banks in 1942, or Boris the electrician in 1955, or me and Auntie Bea for afternoon tea!

Our Gracie was a wonder—and she made a bloody good cup of tea!

❑

Carl Sagan
BY
Arthur C. Clarke

It's quite a shock to realize I've known Carl Sagan for almost a billion seconds. One of our earliest and most memorable encounters was in 1964, soon after I had introduced him to Stanley Kubrick. We'd all planned to get together for a second meeting, but for some reason Stanley couldn't make it. So Carl and I suddenly had an empty morning—something that seldom happens to either of us these days.

No problem—the World's Fair was on just across the river, so we took the subway out to Flushing and mingled with the (rather thin) crowds of sightseers. However, before we had finished our "Grand Tour" it started to rain, so we scurried into a large tent which was featuring a movie on the wonders of the universe. It was very enjoyable and well made—but as the exhibit was the showpiece of a religious organization, it ended with a commercial for God . . .

On my way out, to my amused embarrassment, Carl button holed one of the attendants and started to lecture him on the intellectual dishonesty of the movie's concluding message. As it happened, I largely agreed, but felt constrained to point out to Carl that:

1) We'd been kept nicely dry, and for free;
2) We'd enjoyed an interesting movie;
3) The gentleman who'd ushered us to our seats was unlikely to have been the scriptwriter. (Though now that I've seen Hollywood in action, I'm no longer so sure of this.)

I do not recall if Carl showed any contrition, but have sometimes wondered if this was the initial seed of *Cosmos*. Let me say at once that I consider this series one of the most superb jobs of education/entertainment that has ever appeared on TV, and I'm happy that it's still going strong in various incarnations. We need more programs of this kind to counter the mind-rot now being injected into the U.S. public by press, radio, movies, and TV—astrology, pyramid power, reincarnation, the paranormal, UFOs—you name it, someone is making money out of it . . .

My last encounter with Carl was at considerably longer range. On a recent transit through London I had the privilege of joining him in a discussion with the brilliant cosmologist Dr. Stephen Hawking, author of the record-breaking bestseller *A Brief History of Time.* Carl joined us *via* satellite from the U.S., and we had a free-swinging debate for almost two hours. Some day I hope you'll have a chance of seeing the resulting T.V. special, "God, the Universe, and Everything Else."

After a quarter of a century, Carl hasn't mellowed much. I'm sure he'd still be happy to give God a little helpful advice on how the Universe *ought* to be designed.

Ithaca, New York *1990*

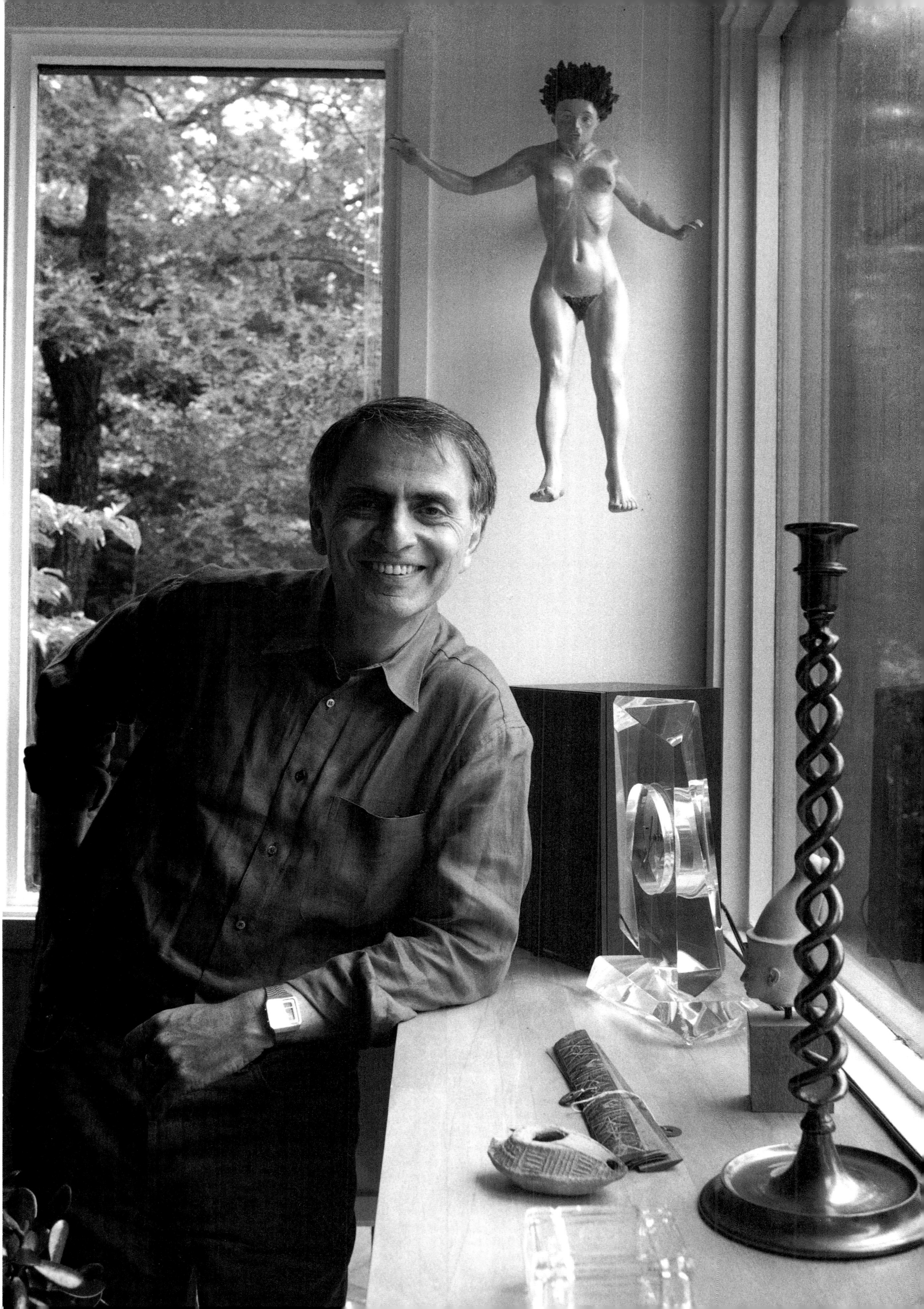

Andy Garcia
BY
Francis Ford Coppola

Deep brown eyes, smoldering with passion. At the core of this man is honor and tradition. After being with him a few moments you understand his priorities, nothing is more important than his heritage and his family. He is Cuban, and very aware of that noble country's culture and history. He is his father's son and his daughters' father.

Yes, it is his sweet way and kindliness that you first encounter; helpful, with a nimble imagination and a very constructive attitude. Andy is an artist, filled with the enthusiasm of being an actor. He follows the work of other actors with an involvement that the best of them have. He constantly works to develop his own talent and facility. He hones a taut edge of sudden tempestuous violence against a warm, understanding love that he has for all beautiful things and people. He is a complete man.

Studio City, California 1991

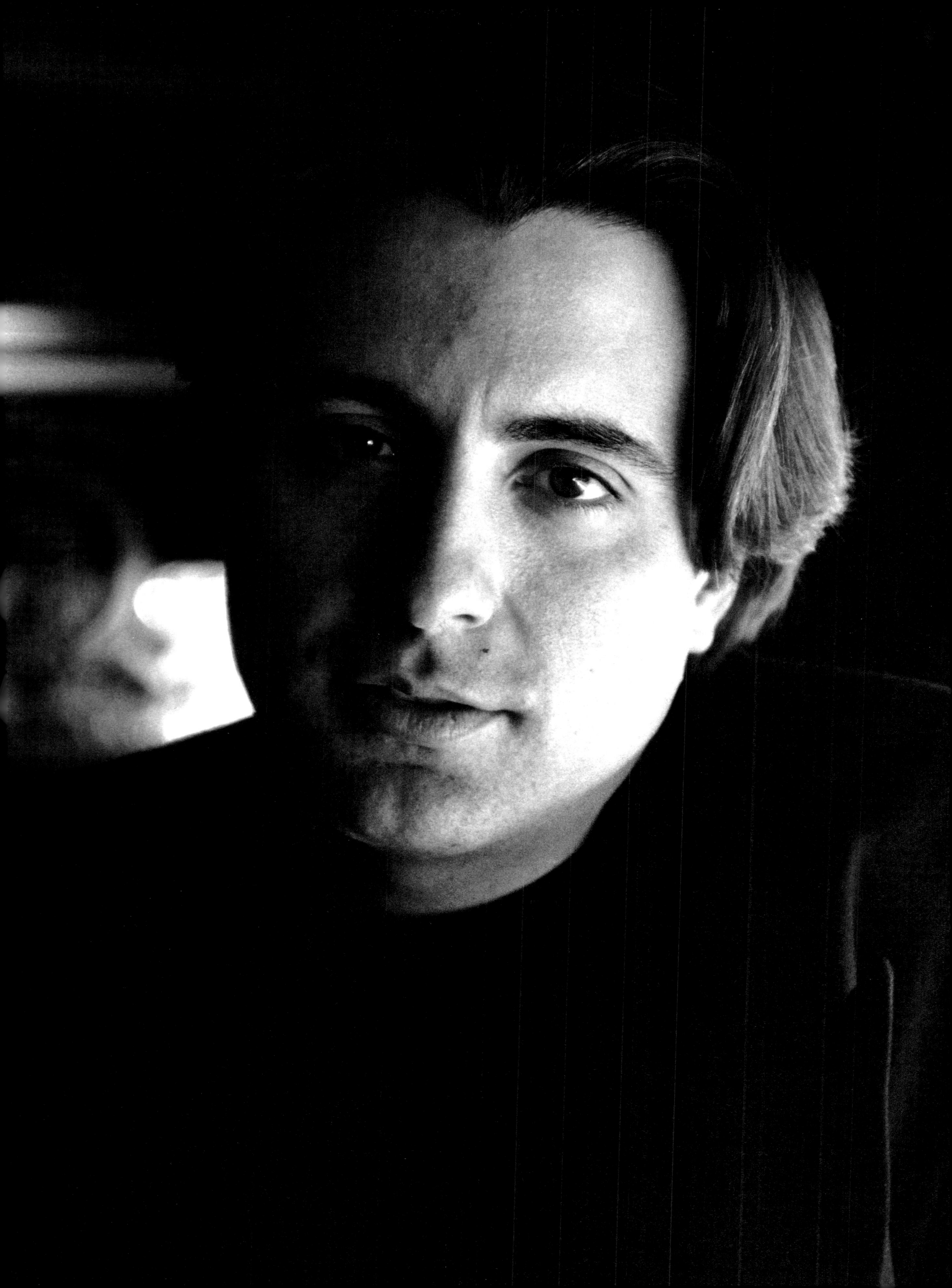

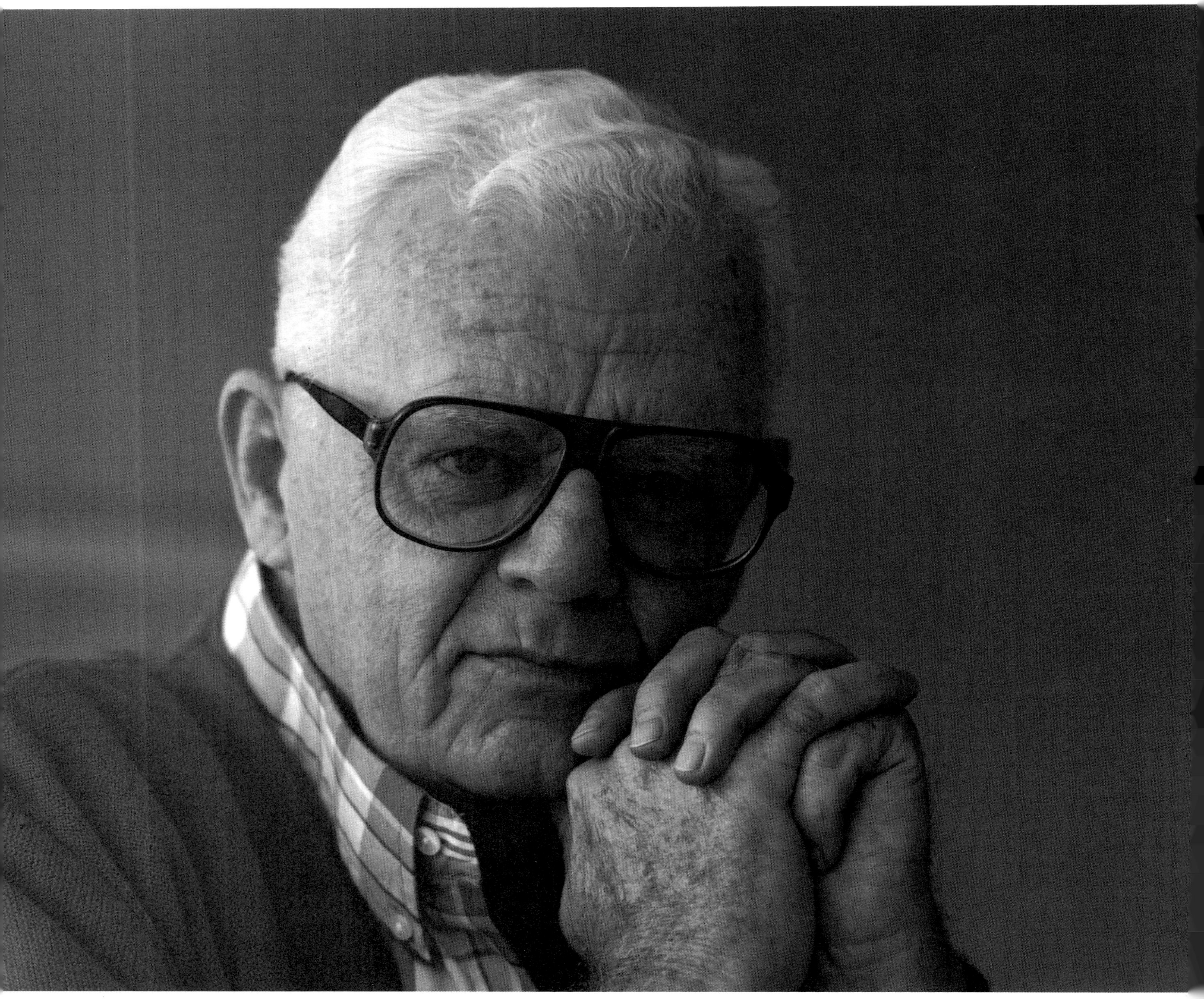

Freddie Bartholomew
BY
Comden & Green

As two heavily native New Yorkers born and bred in Brooklyn (Comden) and the Bronx (Green), we feel supremely qualified to write with warm, familiar feelings about the career of the wonderful young British star—Freddie Bartholomew.

But, his appeal to us is real and his image forever a shining one. He evokes the world of Charles Dickens' David Copperfield as no other child actor could have done. Early nineteenth-century England radiates from his eyes with a feeling that no history book can convey and his gentlemanly sensitivity and charm are heartbreakingly appealing—a heroic little figure, vulnerable but all man.

These same qualities continue to shine through in *Captains Courageous*, in which he portrays the spoiled rich brat unceremoniously hurled into the world of the sea and regenerated by his pre-adolescent love of a Portuguese fisherman played by the great Spencer Tracy, two performances of unforgettably grand proportions.

Little Lord Fauntleroy, Tom Brown's School Days, The Swiss Family Robinson—in all of these films he shone with his unique image. He occupies his own special niche in movie history. Thank you, Freddie!

Kate Burton
BY
Amanda Plummer

Kate—Hello, Kate. Probably you could be the first baby I knew—we must have spoken somehow to each other in the crib we shared. Our noses mushing together. I look for that baby knowledge in her face when I see her now and then, now. Gorgeous face. Unlike any visage in the world, even Dad's. Without asking, her face cries to be looked at into. AHH. But it is a secret. You search around this woman. Up and down her movement, up and down her stillness, and your imagination flies.

Rome, Italy 1961

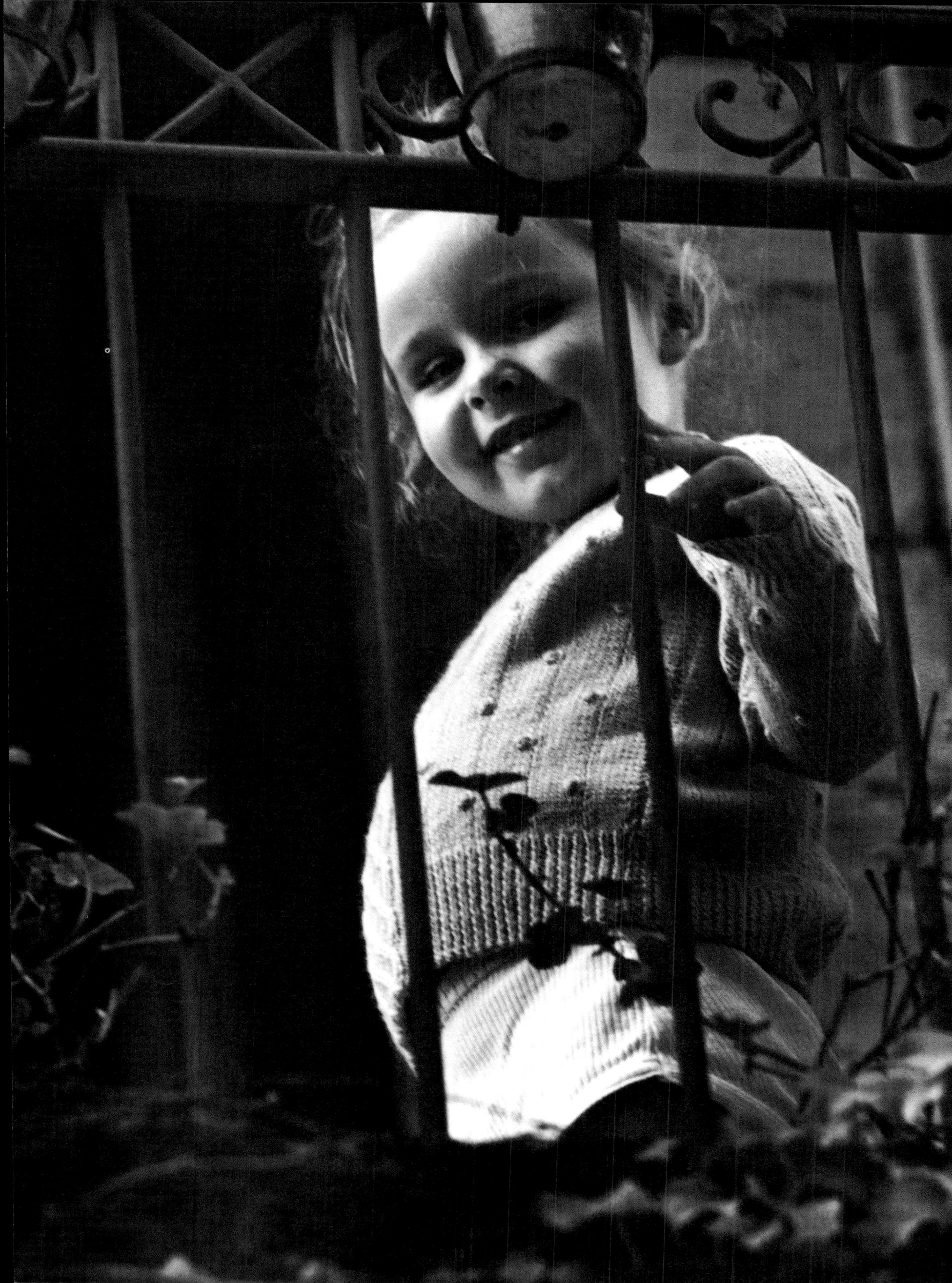

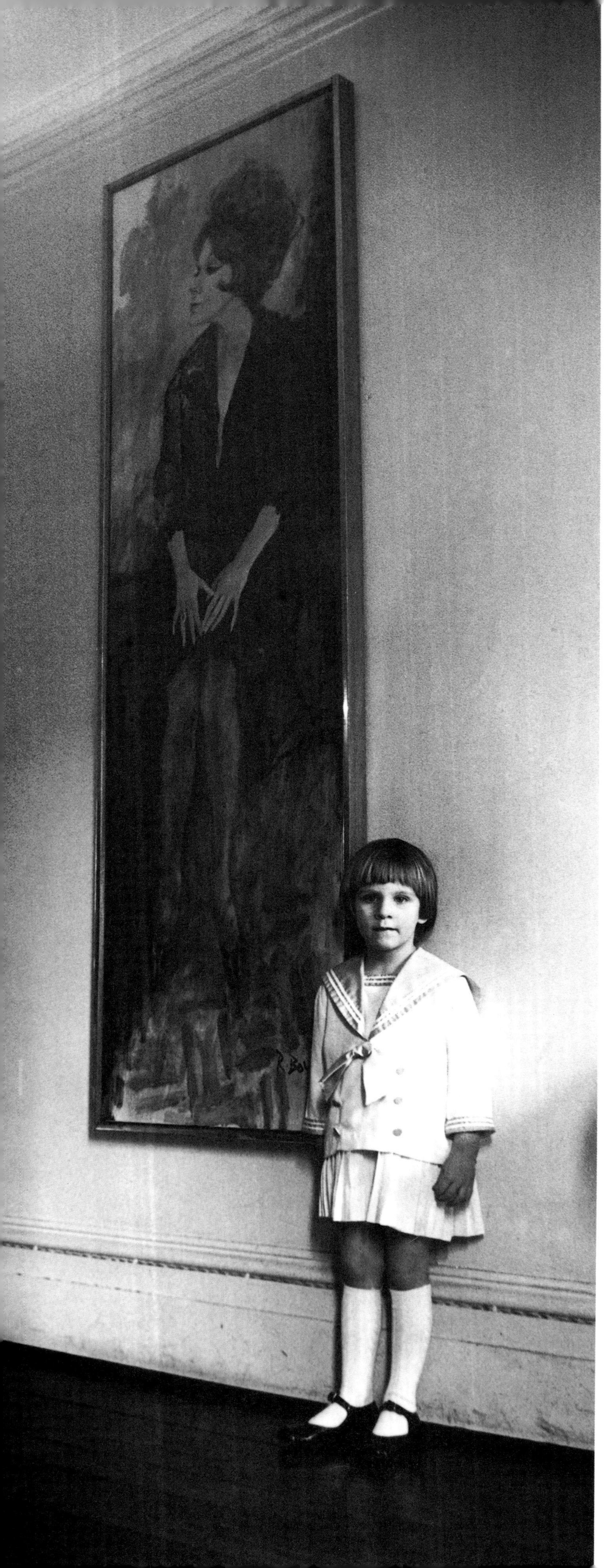

Amanda Plummer
BY
Kate Burton

Amanda and I met when she was nine months old and I was born. It was September of 1957. We were referred to as two baby Hamlets because of our remarkable resemblance to our fathers.

We grew up together. Amanda spent quite a lot of time at my house and I at hers. Thanksgivings. We went to the same schools in New York for almost all of that time; Fleming for grade school and "junior high" and the Union Nations International School for high school.

It was at Fleming that we appeared together in perhaps our first play: a sixth grade production of *You Can't Take It with You,* Amanda as the drunken actress, myself as the male ballet teacher (very few boys in the school).

She was an original. Often found wearing a Pippi Longstocking hat, incredibly athletic, devoted to animals, long hair down her back, wanted to be a veterinarian. We were as different as possible, yet we shared a great love and mutual respect. Although I knew then how unlike anyone else she was, I realize now it was Amanda in the process of discovering her brilliant gift.

New York City *1961*
Studio City, California *1990* (page 74)

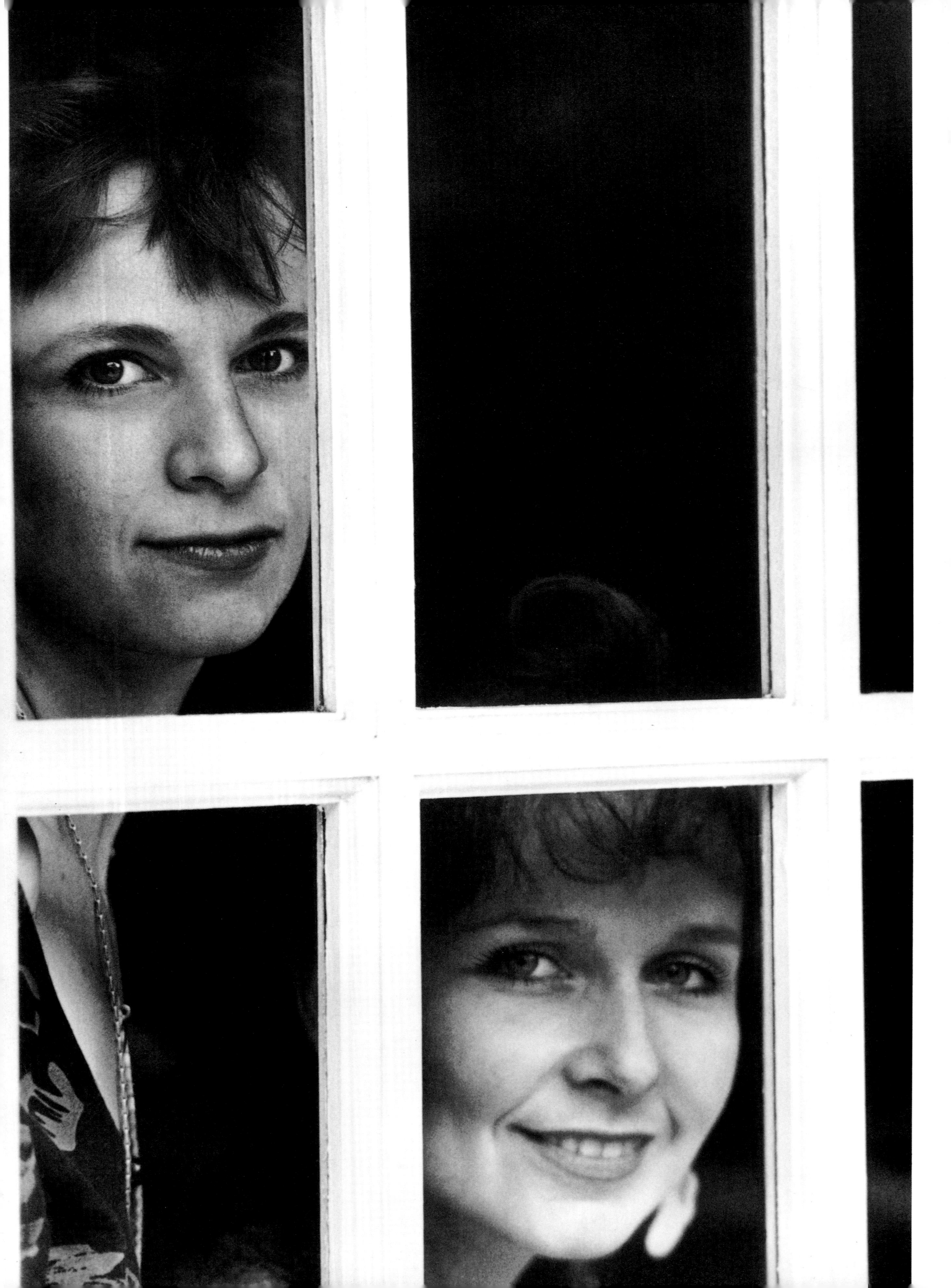

Gordon Davidson
BY
Adam Davidson

Roddy McDowall sent me this photograph and asked me to write about his subject . . . Hoping this would not be the last thing I would ever write about my father I set to the task, but fell asleep and had this revealing nightmare:

INTERIOR—POLICE STATION.

INSPECTOR C: (holding the photograph) Can you identify this man?

A: (seated in a high chair) Yes, yes that's him! That's him, Inspector Cornelius! . . . That's the man!!! I'd recognize him anywhere!

INSPECTOR C: Who is he?

A: Well, he's my father!

INSPECTOR C: Ah. How do you know it's him?

A: Well, the chipped tooth! The monolithic eyebrows! And of course, the unmistakable deep left dimple, so distinguishing on him that when I was born it struck the doctor to declare to my mother, "It's a boy . . . and he has the dimple!"

INSPECTOR C: (biting apishly into a banana) Yeah, so, go on . . .

A: Well, that's him there too, with my mother. They've been married for over thirty years and are still very much in love. And there, next to them, is my sister, their second and more successful attempt at producing a child.

INSPECTOR C: Hmm, yes . . . go on.

Los Angeles 1990

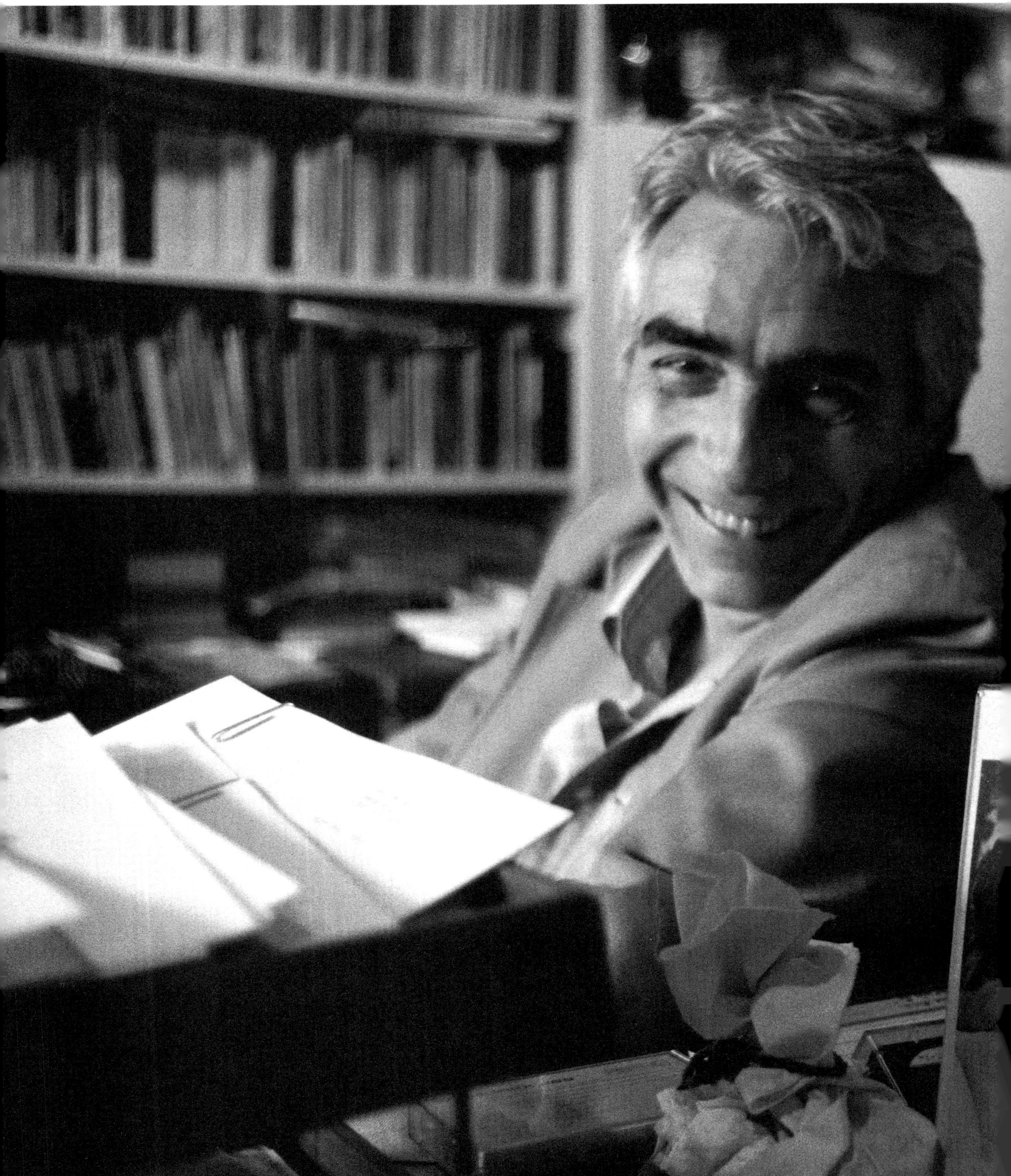

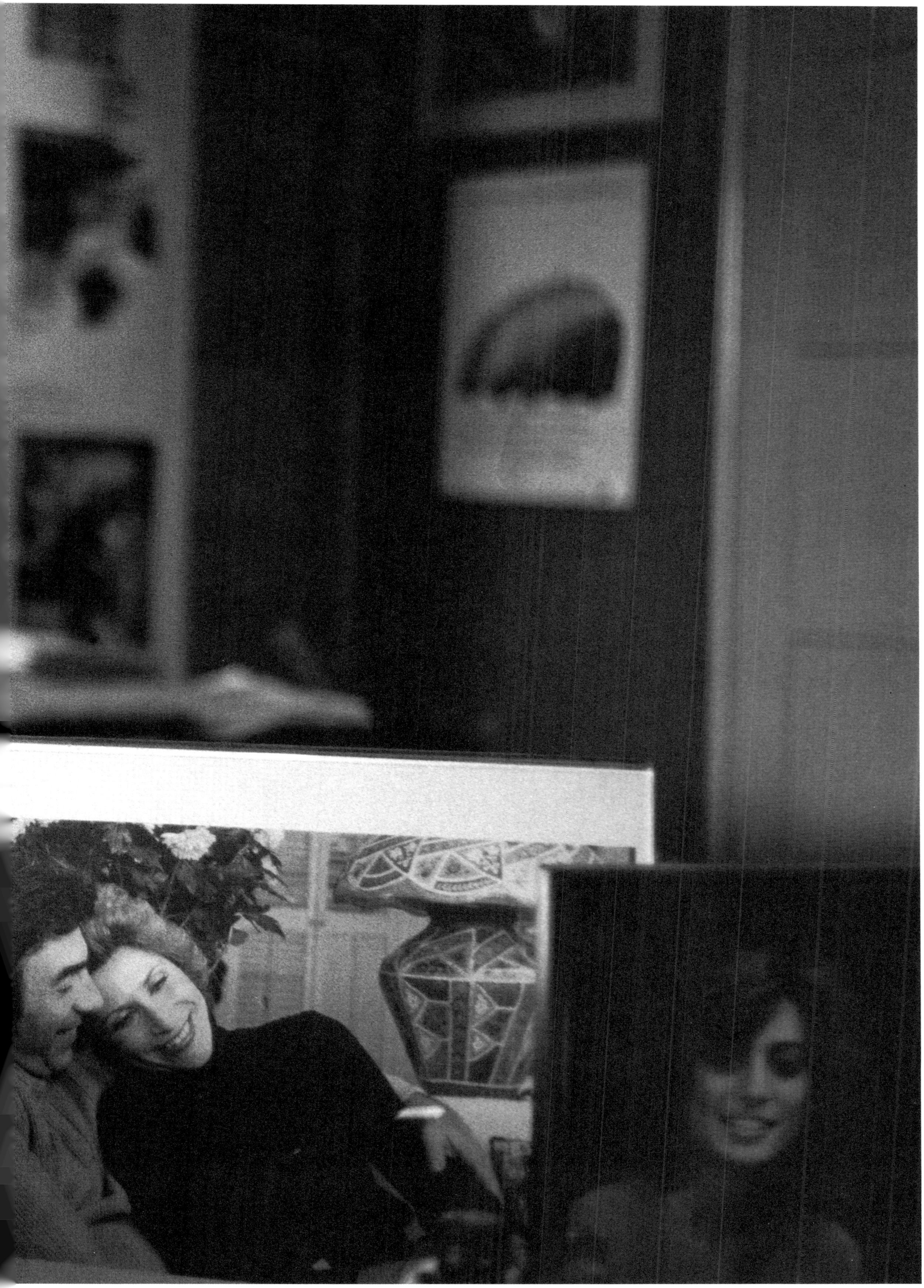

A: Well, this photo must obviously have been taken in his office at the Mark Taper Forum in Los Angeles where he spends most of his time, producing and directing some of the best theatre in the country. So much time that those bookcases you see behind him were installed and can actually swing open and fold into a bed!

INSPECTOR C: Does he sleep there?

A: No, he never uses it. In fact, he never sleeps . . . only a nap here and there during performance, but even then he's only half-sleeping, I call it "sleepwatching," for he still manages to laugh and clap at the right moments and, after curtain, to give his actors and staff incisive critiques. When we were very young, no matter how little sleep he had the night before, he still found a way to see my sister and me off to school in the morning.

INSPECTOR C: Why so much time? How does he do it?

A: Well, he loves his work. It's his passion. It's his life force. It consumes him but it feeds him as well. I feel fortunate to have been raised by a man with such drive, dedication, and commitment to the Arts, to the enrichment of community, and, to family.

INSPECTOR C: (scratching his head with his hairy opposable thumb) Ah, I see . . . But, where are you in the picture?

And there, friends, is precisely where I woke up!

❑

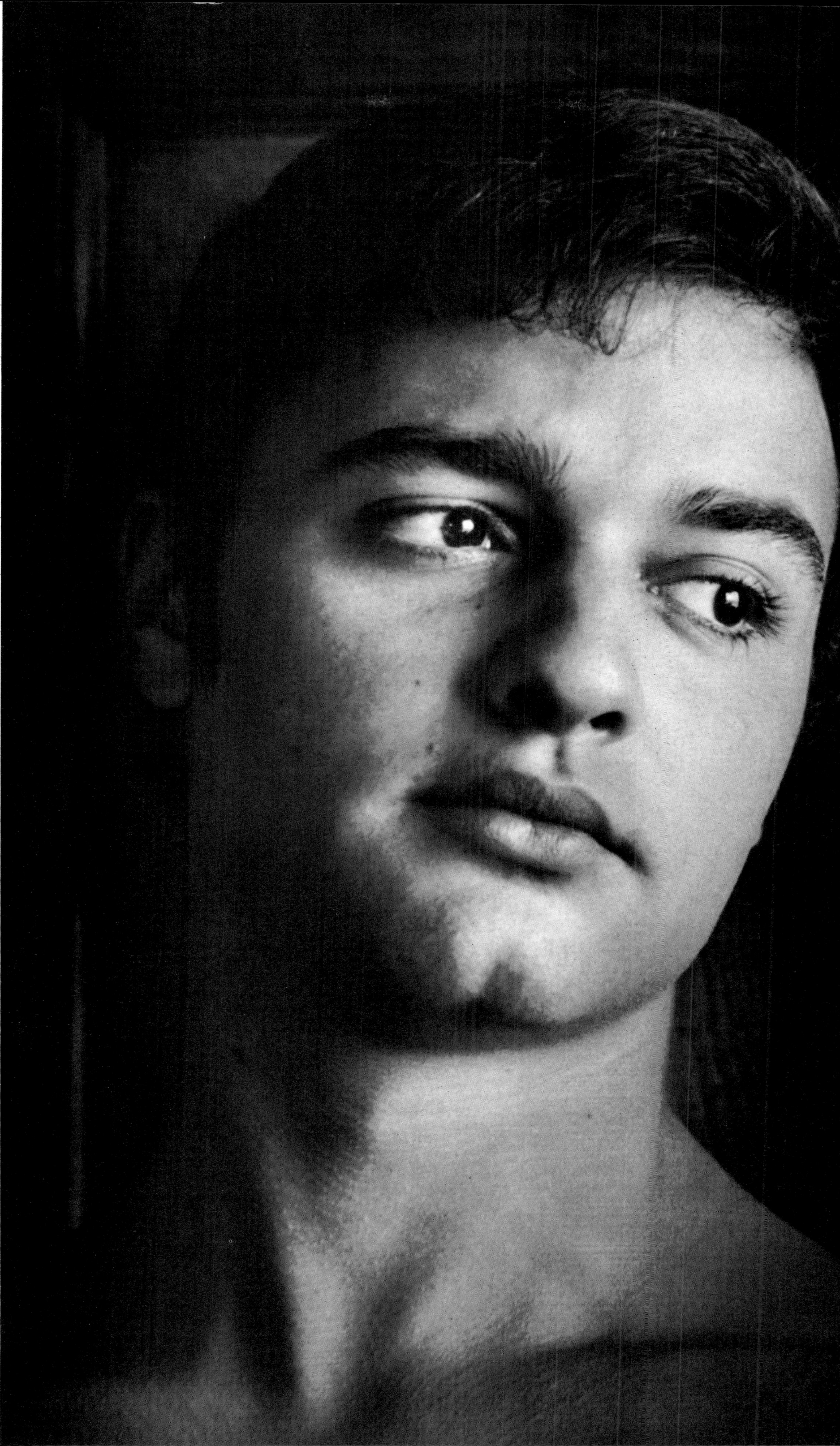

Sal Mineo
BY
Dennis Hopper

I didn't know Sal Mineo well. My only recollections of him are on *Rebel Without a Cause* and *Giant.* On *Rebel* I remember him as a young innocent with beautiful large doe like eyes, always with his schoolbooks coming to and fro from set to trailer where he and Natalie were tutored, not old enough to hang out with us gang members posing tough and smoking cigarettes in the parking lots or outside our dressing rooms. On the set he seemed to always be under the protective arm of James Dean, which was the relationship that Jimmy created and that their parts demanded.

I used Sal as a shill to distract the teacher so that I could get Natalie out of the trailer for a little hanky-panky. He always smiled and was good-natured about being my devious tool. I remember him later when we were making *Giant*, in his Army uniform coming to get Rock Hudson's blessing because, as Angel, he was the first soldier from Riata to go fight in the war.

I remember hearing about how well he directed a play that dealt with homosexuals in prison, I saw him in many gifted performances, I heard about the terrible way he died—stabbed fifty-eight times by a crazed killer. I remember his beautiful brown eyes, his innocence, and how proud he looked in his uniform that day on *Giant.* But maybe, in a strange way more appropriately, I remember a little Mexican boy throwing up the rock outside the church before the funeral in *Giant*, and how George Stevens had waited for two weeks in the blistering sun in Texas for the sky to cloud over so that the mood would be appropriate for the funeral. For the scene welcoming Angel home, the audience was baited as a train pulled out and mysteriously revealed a flag-draped coffin.

The big brown doe eyes and the innocence will live forever in *Rebel* and *Giant.*

Beverly Hills *1963* (page 79)
Page, Arizona *1963*

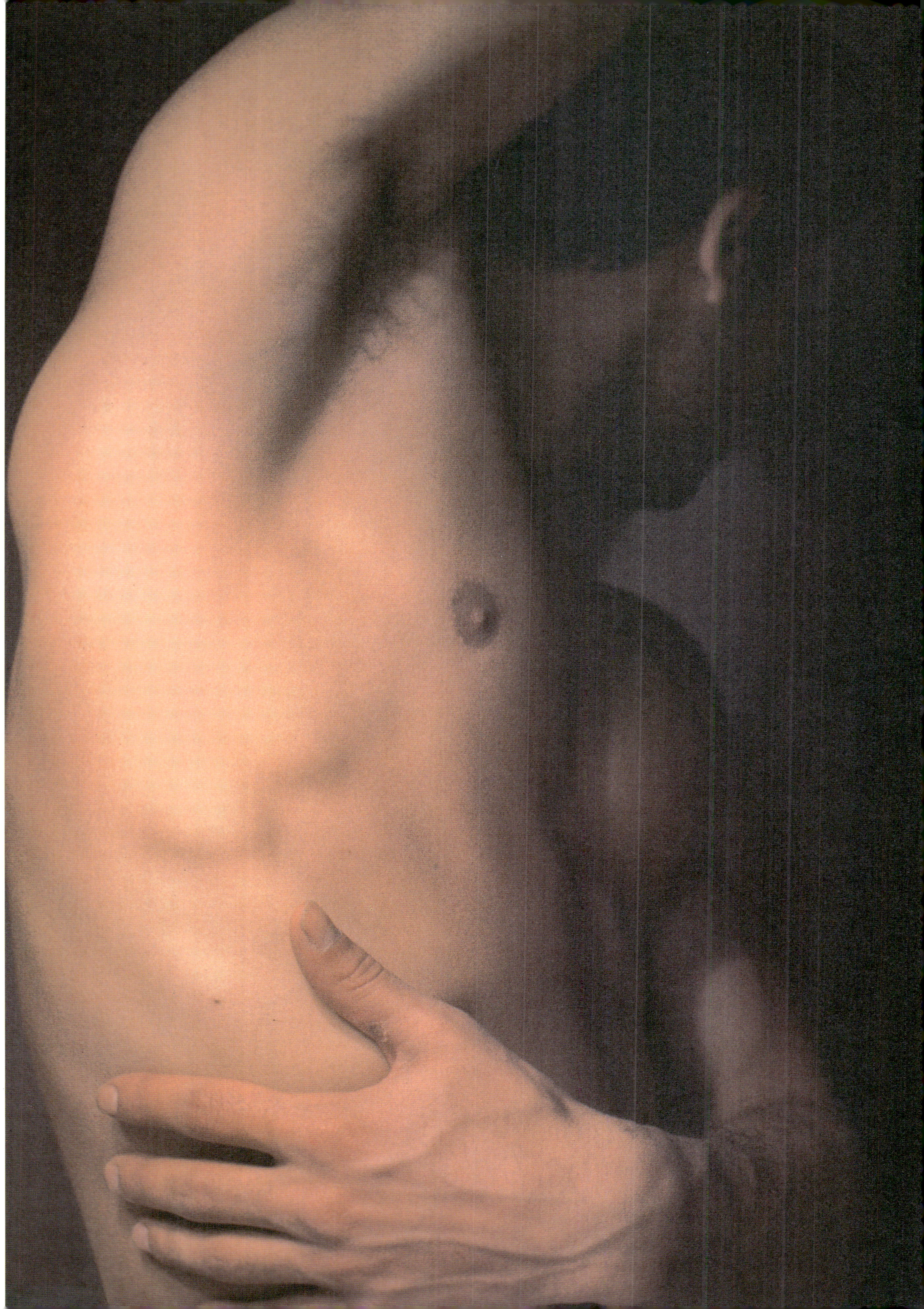

Charles Schulz
BY
Barnaby Conrad

Charles Schulz is, of course, Charlie Brown—an erudite, aware Charlie Brown.

Sensitive, quiet, modest, the most successful cartoonist in history, comes to our writers conference in Santa Barbara every year to give of himself to the students, even though he puts himself down thusly:

"Cartooning is a 'fairly' sort of a proposition. You have to be fairly intelligent—if you were *really* intelligent you'd be doing something else; you have to draw fairly well—if you drew *really* well you'd be a painter; you have to write fairly well—if you wrote *really* well you'd be writing books. It's great for a fairly person like me."

You can't pin "Sparky" down on his own favorite of the thousands of strips he's drawn, but he'll tell you about the Sunday one that drew the greatest mail response.

"The kids—Lucy, Linus, and Charlie are lying on a hill looking at some clouds. Lucy says: 'Aren't the clouds beautiful? They look like big balls of cotton . . . I could just lie here all day and watch them drift by . . . If you use your imagination, you can see lots of things in the cloud formations . . . What do you think you see, Linus?' And Linus answers, 'Well, those clouds up there look to me like the map of the British Honduras on the Caribbean . . . That cloud up there looks a little like the profile of Thomas Eakins, the famous painter and sculptor . . . And that group of clouds over there gives me the impression of the stoning of Stephen . . . I can see the apostle Paul standing there to one side . . .' And then Lucy says 'Uh-huh . . . that's very good . . . what do *you* see in the clouds, Charlie Brown?' And Charlie says, 'Well, I was going to say I saw a ducky and a horsie, but I changed my mind!' "

"Sparky" chuckles, a man who truly loves to create and loves his creations.

"People ask if I have an assistant to do my cartoons. The two things I like to do best are drawing cartoons and hitting golf balls; now if I hired someone to draw my cartoons what fun would I get? It'd be like getting someone to hit my golf balls for me."

Santa Rosa, California 1990

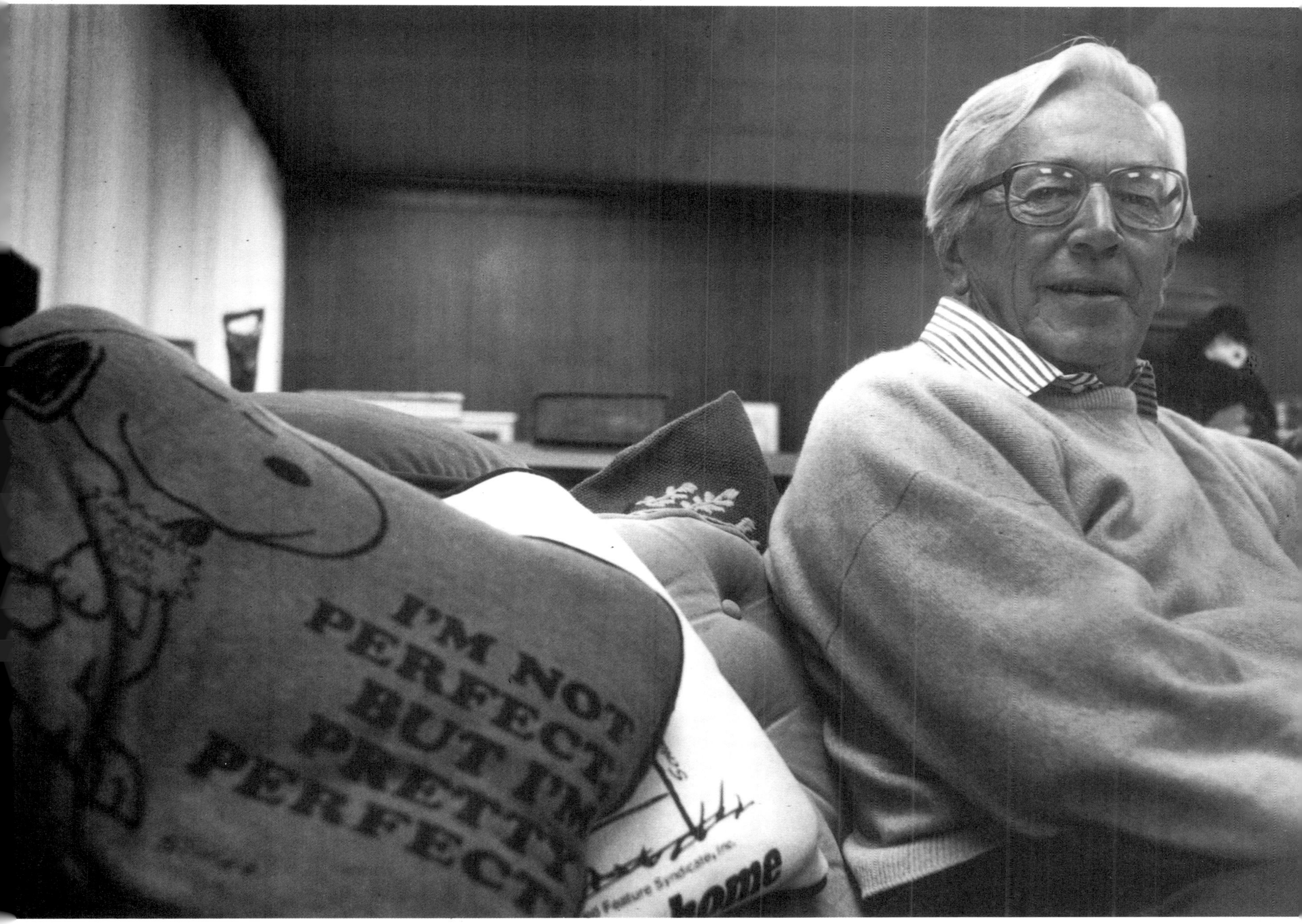
I'M NOT
PERFECT
BUT I'M
PRETTY
PERFECT

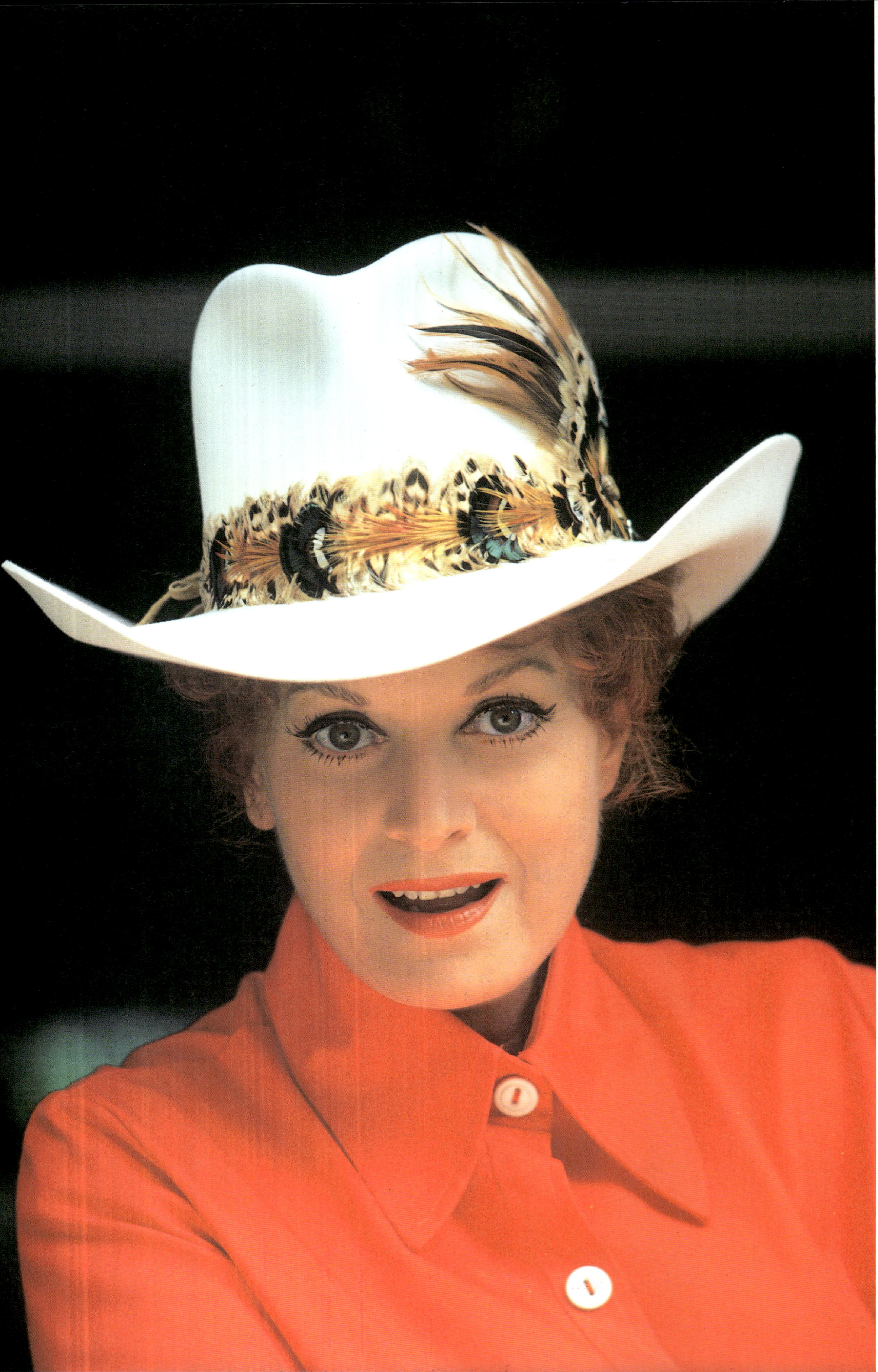

Maureen O'Hara
BY
Jean Negulesco

In the Spring of 1949, in London, I met Charlie Blair, a kind man, handsome, soft voice, a devil with the ladies and a great pilot. Maureen O'Hara was the star in the picture I was making then in England. I knew Maureen was the perfect match for Charles. I arranged a date, they met, they fell in love, they married, and now she remembers this as the best ten years of her life. Charlie was running a successful private independent airline, when a stupid accident—never to be explained—left Maureen alone and the head of an airline. Today she runs two profitable airlines.

Maureen can do everything, anything. As an actress, the miraculous trio—Ford, Wayne, O'Hara—gave us classic films, legends.

Maureen can preside smoothly and expertly over a noisy political gathering or a festival of kindergarten kids—as well as managing with the same sophisticated skill a chain of fun-loving ill-reputed clubs.

She can talk you into anything—no matter how strange and far from all your other hobbies, and you'll be grateful. Maureen talks sensibly, she talks forcefully. Maureen talks with the right thinking and somehow we accept her logic totally and completely without ever daring to stop her or have a chance to agree or protest.

As a woman Maureen is a juicy beauty.

It all sounds like a love letter . . .

It is.

Studio City, California *1980*

Max von Sydow
BY
Signe Hasso

England's Sir Alec Guinness is the only other great artist who comes to mind when talking about Max von Sydow. Although Swedish in looks and bearing—the temperament of Max embraces the entire world and he was destined to become part of its elite artistic community.

A treasured highlight of my own long career happened in the early sixties . . . when Max and I appeared together in Sweden at Uppsala Stadsteater in Pirandello's last play *The Mountain Giants.* I had been brought from Hollywood. Max had just returned to Stockholm after completing the film, *The Greatest Story Ever Told.* Brilliantly directed by our friend Frank Sundström—also head of the theatre—the play became a great success which was repeated in Stockholm that same year during the annual Summer Arts Festival.

The Mountain Giants remains a most inspiring memory and one moment each night during the run I shall never forget. The one when Max and I—just before curtain time—met onstage, took each other's hands, and silently asked the Powers to guide us through the evening.

I think audiences throughout the world as well as co-workers in the various fields of our entertainment industry would agree with me in saying that—aside from being a wonderful, generous friend and gentleman—Max von Sydow is truly a multitalented artist for all seasons.

Beverly Hills *1989*

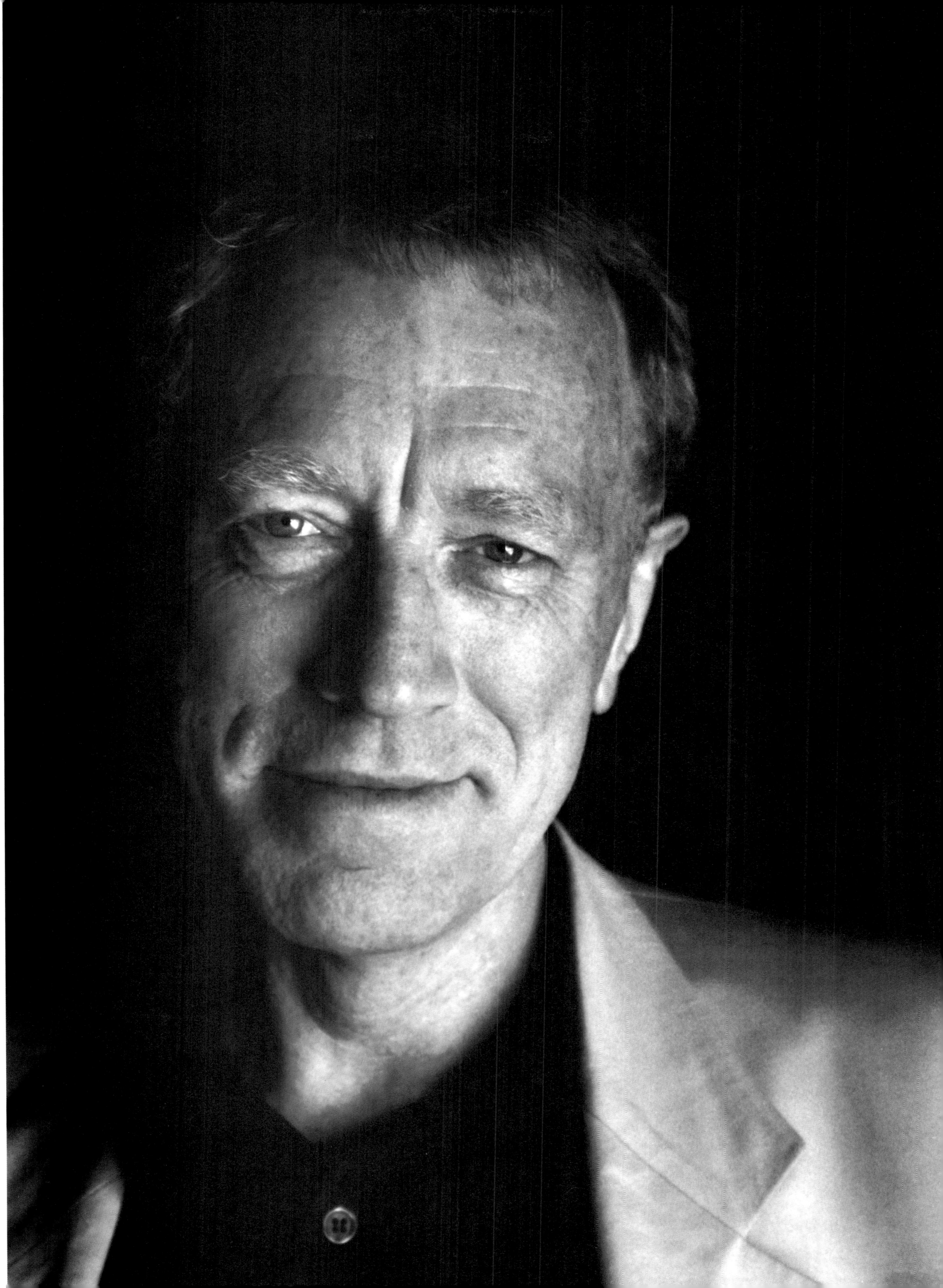

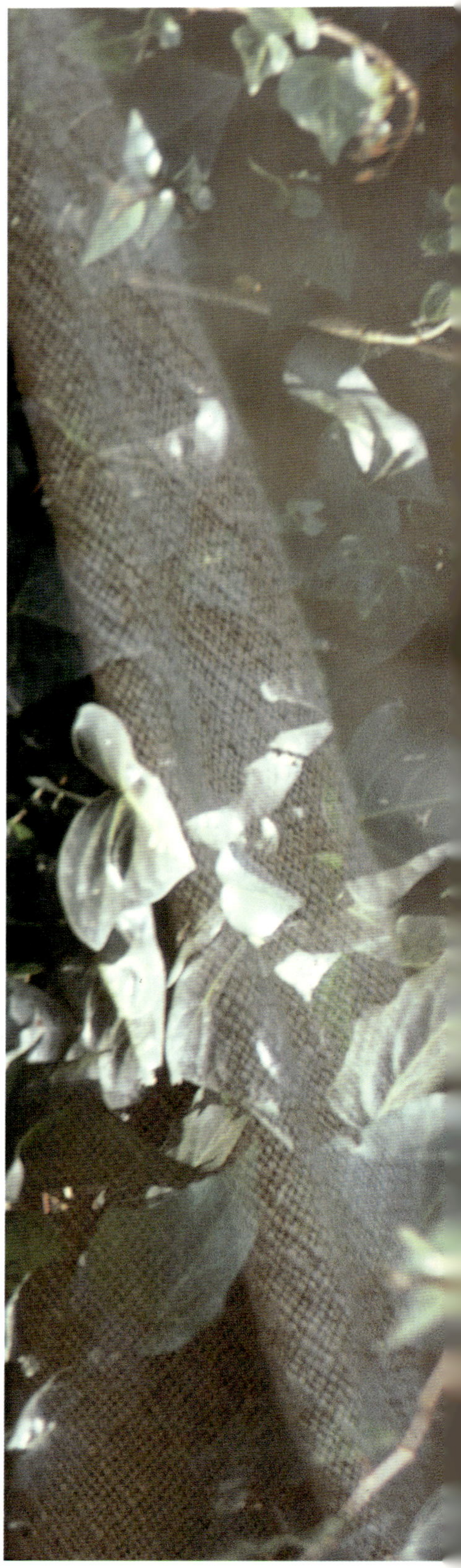

Page, Arizona *1963*
The Greatest Story Ever Told

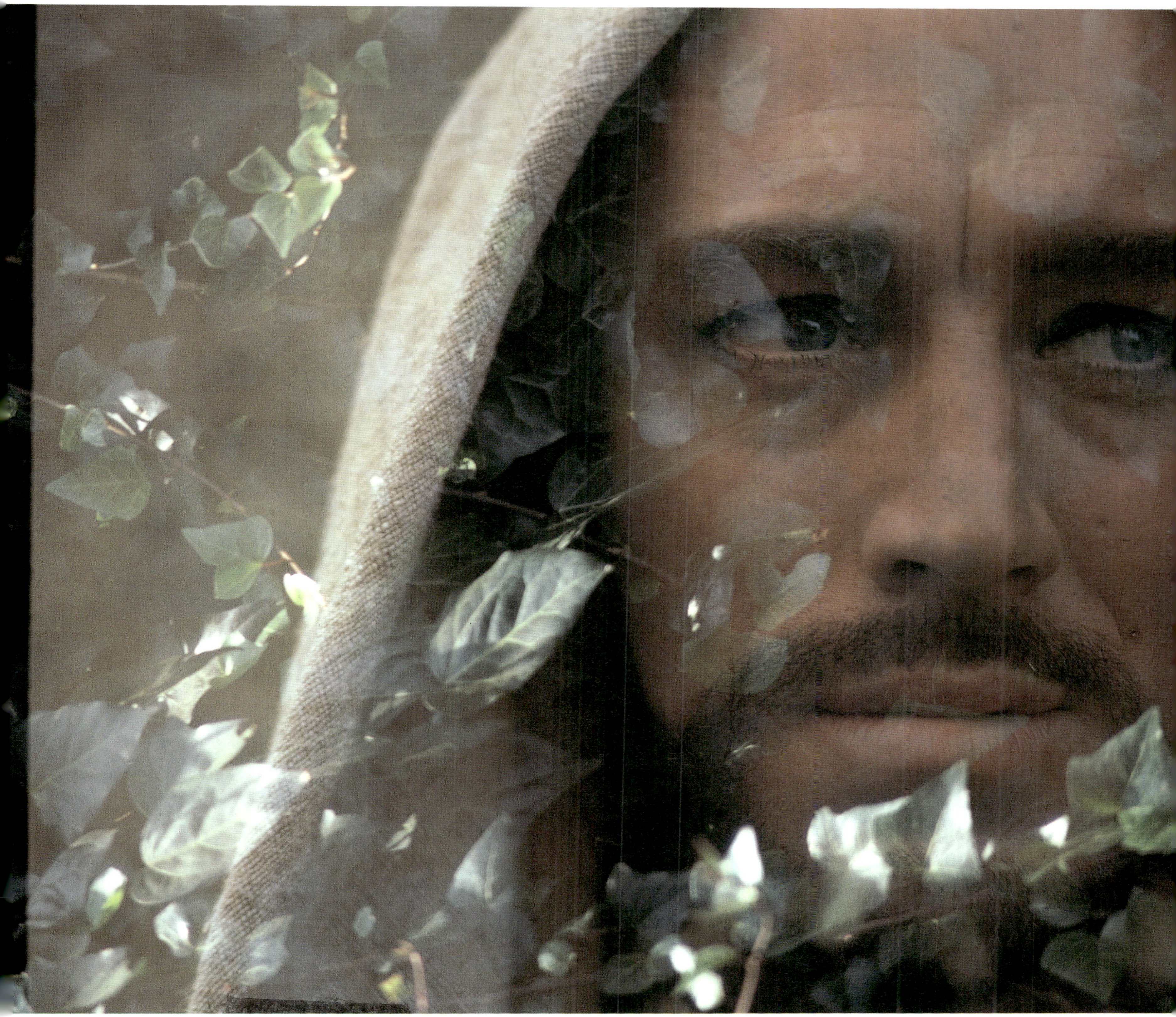

Arthur Penn
BY
Larry Gelbart

AP IN MY PHONE BOOK.
AP.
ARTHUR PENN.
AUTHORS' PAL.
ACTORS' PRAYER.
ACTION! PROCLAIMER.
AP.
AWESOME PRESENCE.
AGELESS PUNIM.
ALWAYS POISED.
ARISTOCRATICALLY PLAIN.
ARTHUR PENN.
ANTI-PHILISTINE.
ANGST-PROOF.
ANONYMOUS PATRIOT.
AUTEUR PIONEER.
AVERAGE PUTTER.
ADORES PEGGY.
AP.
APPROACHABLE PUNDIT.
APLOMB PERSONIFIED.
ALL-PRO.
AP.
ARTHUR PENN.
A PRINCE.

Toronto, Canada *1986*

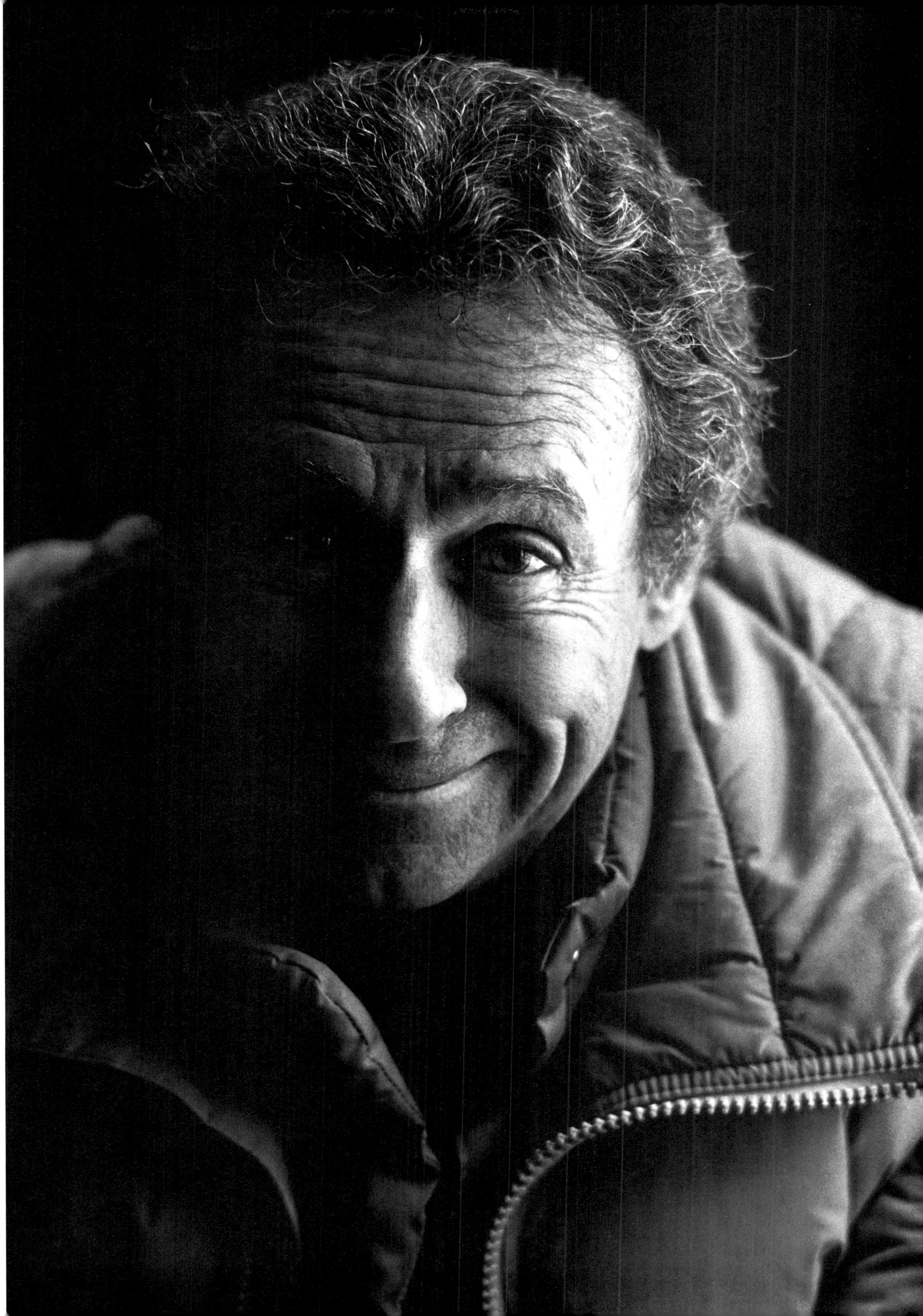

Winona Ryder
BY
Jason Robards

It is no surprise to me that Winona Ryder is at the top of her first peak. She is only twenty and I think of the many peaks she will climb and conquer in the years to come and what joys she will give us.

I am proud and happy to have supported Nonie in her first starring role in the motion picture *Square Dance.* She was only fourteen and yet had such depth, understanding and natural ability that I was awed. I would look into her eyes and see her vulnerability, her ageless beauty and think—she has been here before—and knows and understands more than I ever will. I only wish I were younger so I could be around for another fifty years to see the wonders she has in store for us all. You see, Nonie, your grampa really loves you.

Studio City, California 1991

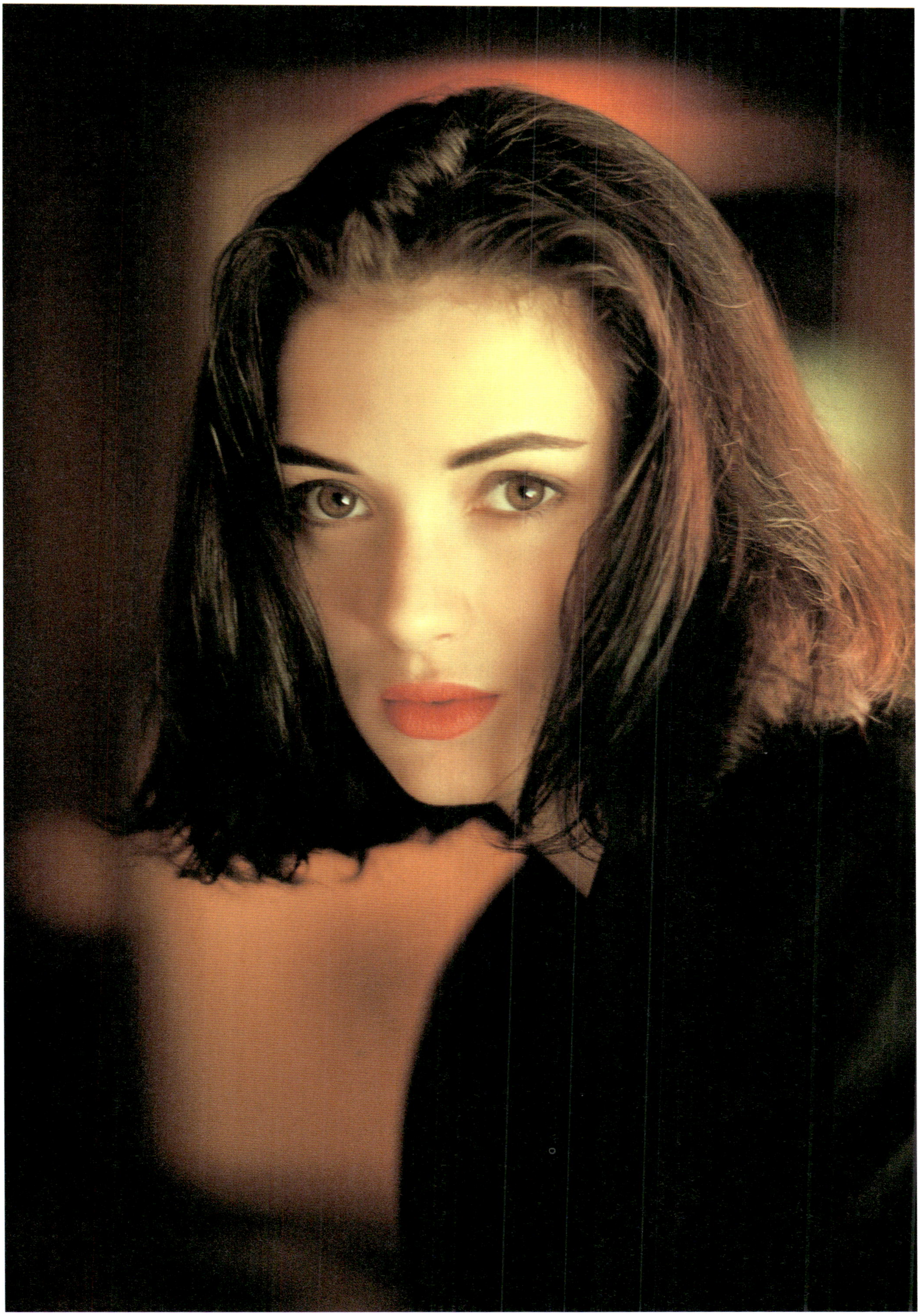

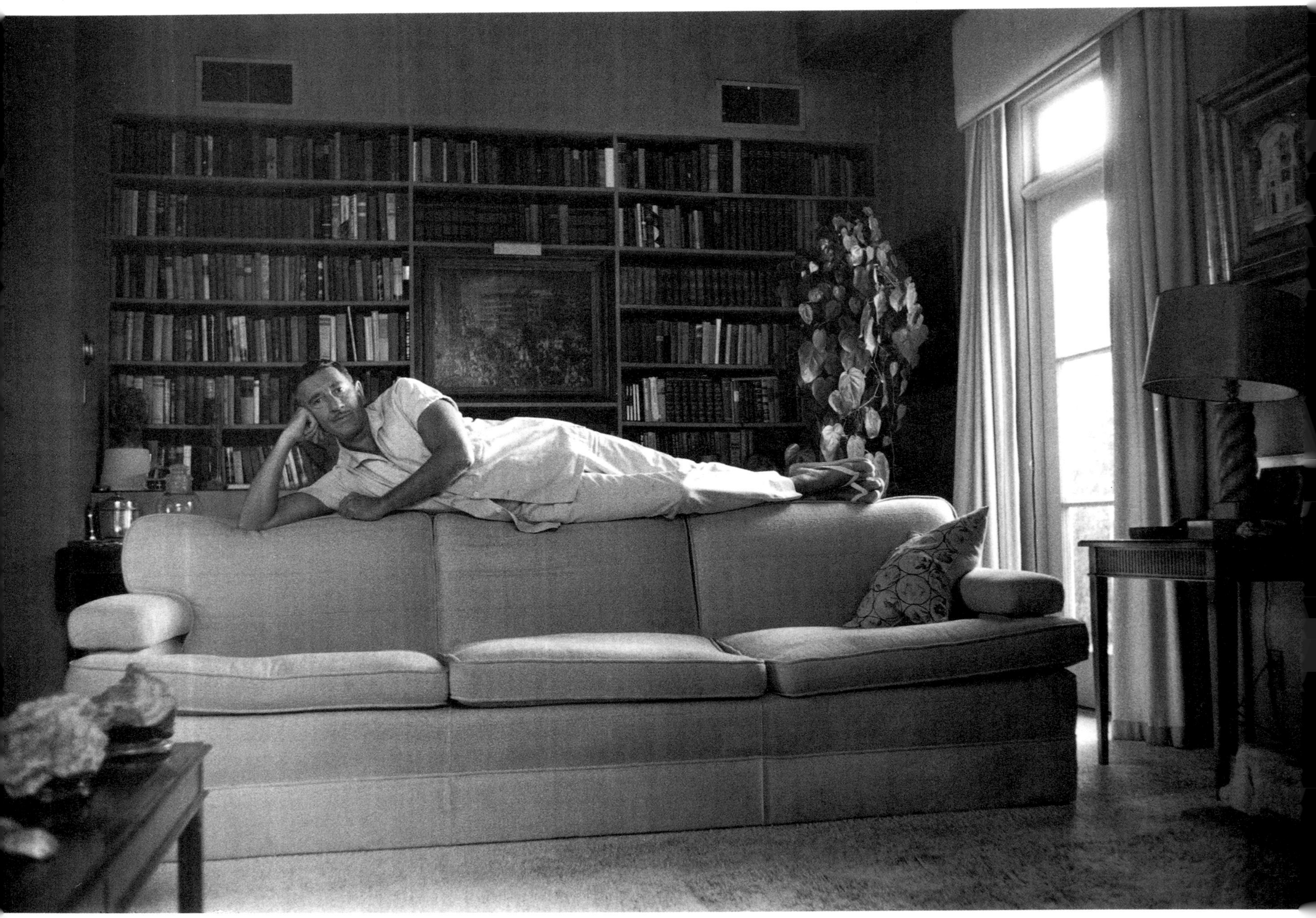

Richard Hadyn
BY
Wendy Hiller

Richard was a very private and reserved man, but to me he will always be hospitality—fry-ups and bubble and squeak in the kitchen; laughter—his sense of the ridiculous was a joy. So many things in common. We "wrote" sound tapes to each other, and talked of everything—from Thomas Hardy, who he knew when he (Richard) was about 20—to gardening; we sent each other vegetable seeds and reports of triumphs and failures. I was in the middle of a rambling gossipy tape when the news came that he would never hear it I do miss him.

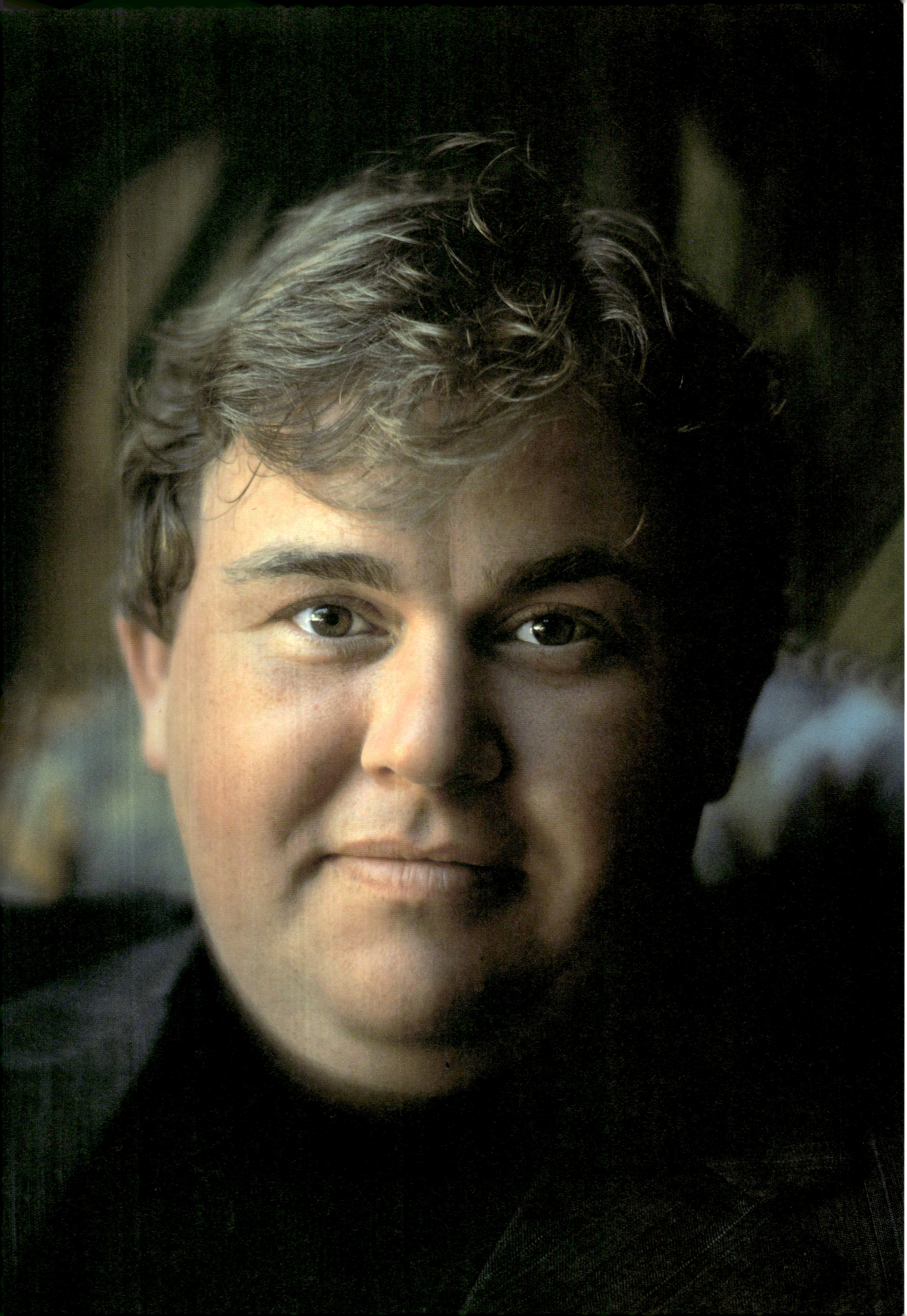

John Candy
BY
Tom Mankiewicz

Candy. A deliciously volatile confection. Blend in equal amounts of invention, whimsy, talent and humor, stir vigorously, then stand well back.

Commonly consumed red-hot at the box office or over ice at an L.A. Kings game, but most thoroughly enjoyed when experienced warm, as in a kind, loyal, caring human being.

Los Angeles 1990

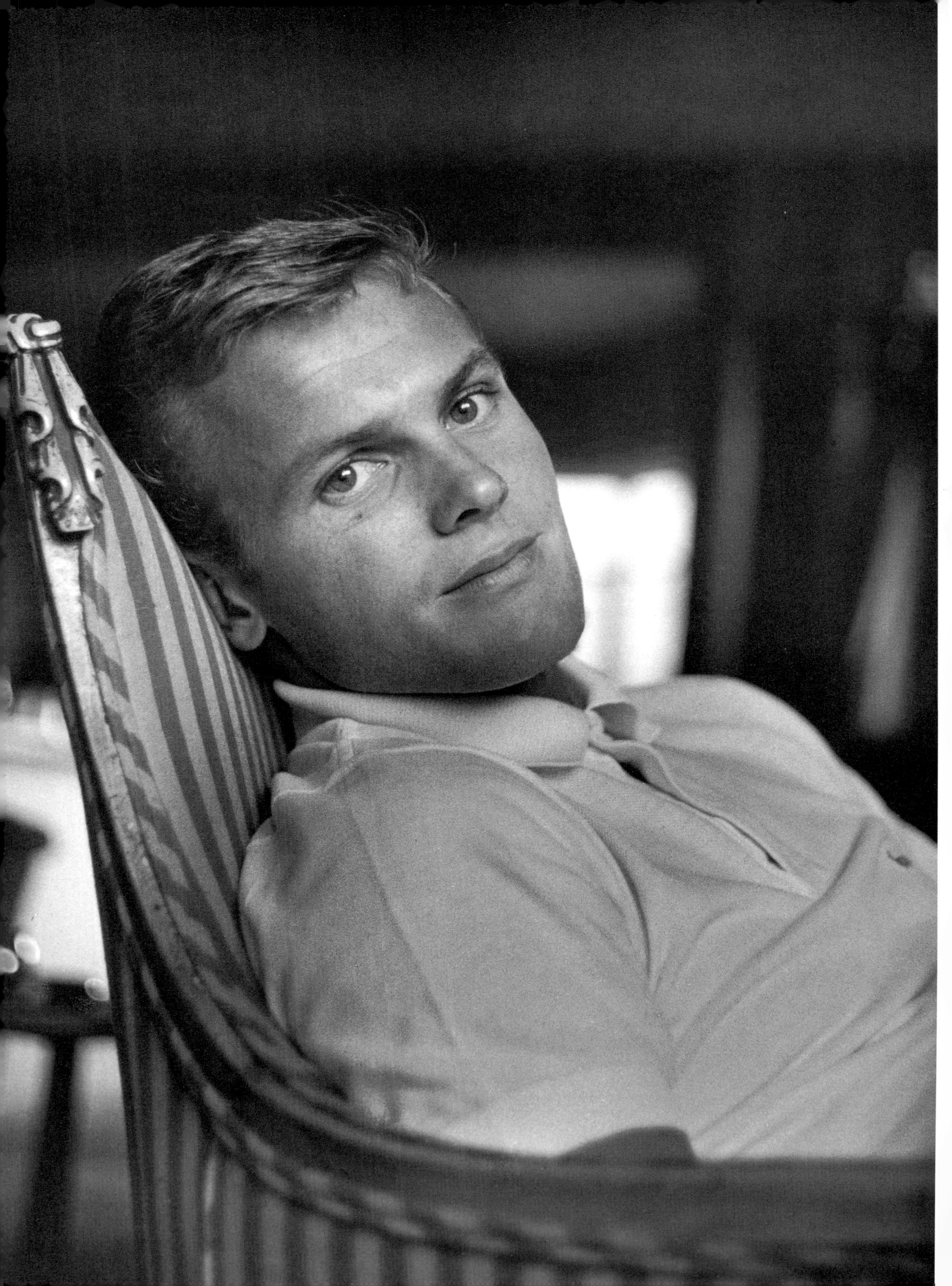

Tab Hunter
BY
Evelyn Keyes

Take my word, Tab Hunter is not just another pretty face, as one might be inclined to imagine when first setting eyes upon the gentleman.

"I'm Tab Hunter," this fellow said to me one night at one of those Hollywood galas honoring somebody or other as The Town is wont to do from time to time.

"You certainly are!" I responded emphatically. Because standing there before me, in the black tie outfit that so enhances the male good looks, was this . . . well, this veritable Apollo. Tall of stature, blue of eye, a smile that dazzled, properly proportioned features all exactly where features should be, the man possessed every little thing a movie star is bloody well *supposed* to possess.

Except surprise, surprise, what was on this handsome actor's mind had nothing whatsoever to do with being in front of a camera, but rather what happens on the other side of it.

It turned out that Tab had read a novel of mine, and was hoping I might turn it into a screenplay for him.

Which was how I found out that Tab Hunter had become a producer of movies. Learned that he knew quite a lot about screenplays, and what made them work. Found out that he hadn't spent all his sound stage hours just sitting there learning his actor's lines.

Besides that the guy skied when the snows came, rode his beloved horses all year round, could whip up some delicious dish at a moment's notice, his whippet dogs weaving in and about his legs as he basted and tasted and stirred. He knew furniture, too, and where to place it. He thought nothing of going out and laying the tiles on a new terrace he'd decided to add on, even muck out stalls if necessary, and he knew where to plant tall green growing things for enhancing purposes.

You see what I mean. Certainly anybody who loves dogs and horses and furniture and green growing things, who can also cook and ski downhill like a maniac, plus *turn a screenplay of mine into a movie,* is a lot more than just another pretty face!

New York City 1958

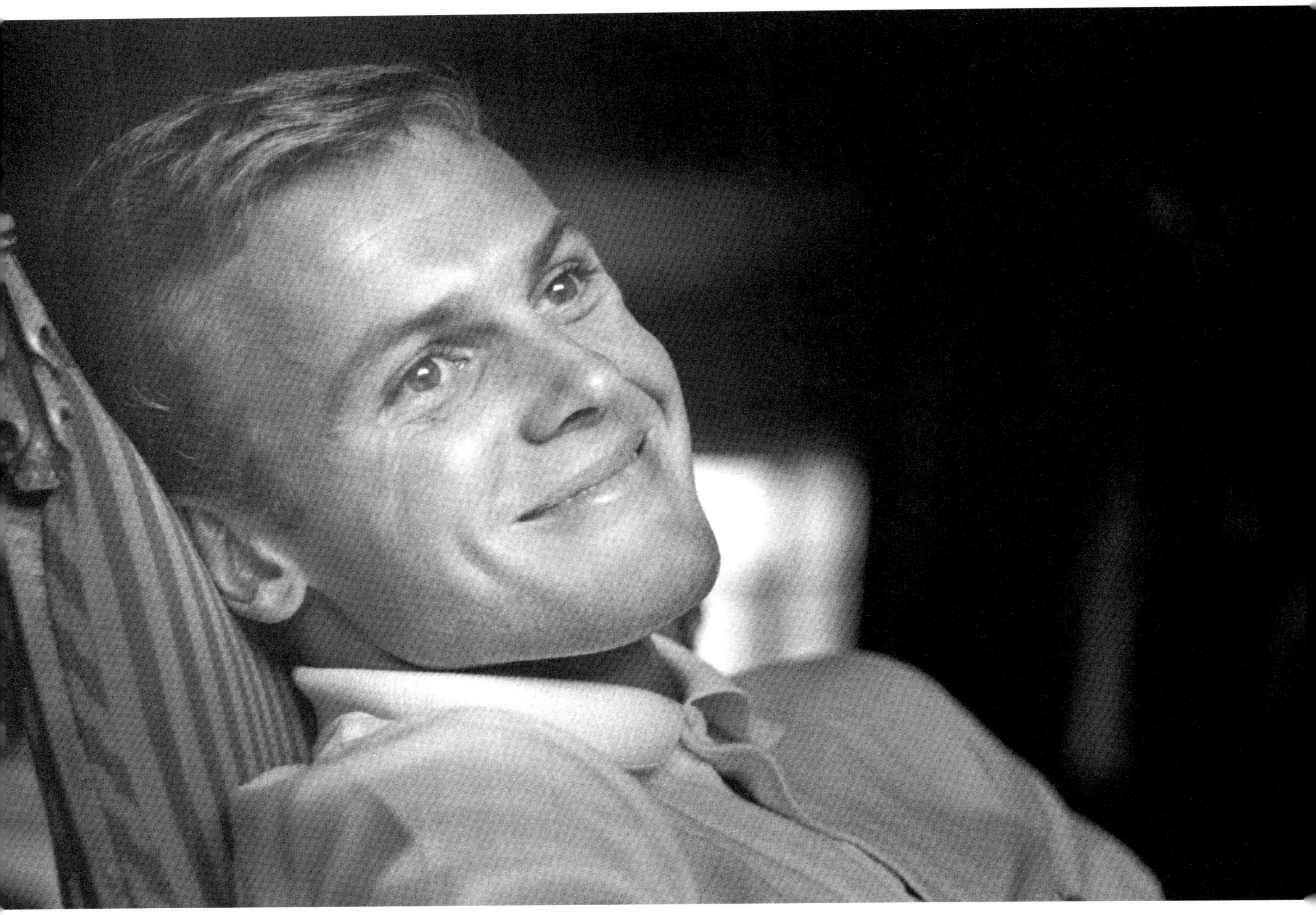

New York City *1958*

Sylvia Sidney
BY
Joanne Woodward

BLAKELY PICTURE SHOW—1935

My bare feet wriggle through the litter of Baby Ruth and Butterfinger papers stuck to the floor by the caramel remains. It is hot where I am. The theatre smells like the inside of my Orphan Annie Ovaltine Shaker, chocolate and sour together. I lean my head back as far as I can, following the stream of light from the screen across the ceiling of the theatre to its source, a small square high above me. Over the square is a window, figures moving hazily behind the glass. I look back at the screen. The light and dark becomes forms that are recognizable. I look far up into the enormous limpid eyes of the most beautiful face I have ever seen.

She smiles. Later I will know that the smile was for the very young Henry Fonda, but at this moment the smile of greeting, recognition, acceptance is for me and I return it with love.

The year was 1935, the movie was *Trail of the Lonesome Pine,* the face belonged to Sylvia Sidney.

Forty years later I met the lady. I acted with her, I directed her, and I interviewed her—that extraordinary talent permeated my creative life. I also giggled at her irreverent humor, exclaimed at the delicacy of her needlepoint, restrained my desire to choke one of her beloved pug dogs, marveled at her ability to fend off adversities that would fell most people.

I love the lady as she is now—crinkly, feisty, tough as a west Texas boot. But every now and again I gaze at her with half-closed eyes, am transported back to the Blakely Picture Show, Summer 1935, and I glimpse once more the limpid eyes of the most beautiful face I have ever seen.

Hollywood 1989

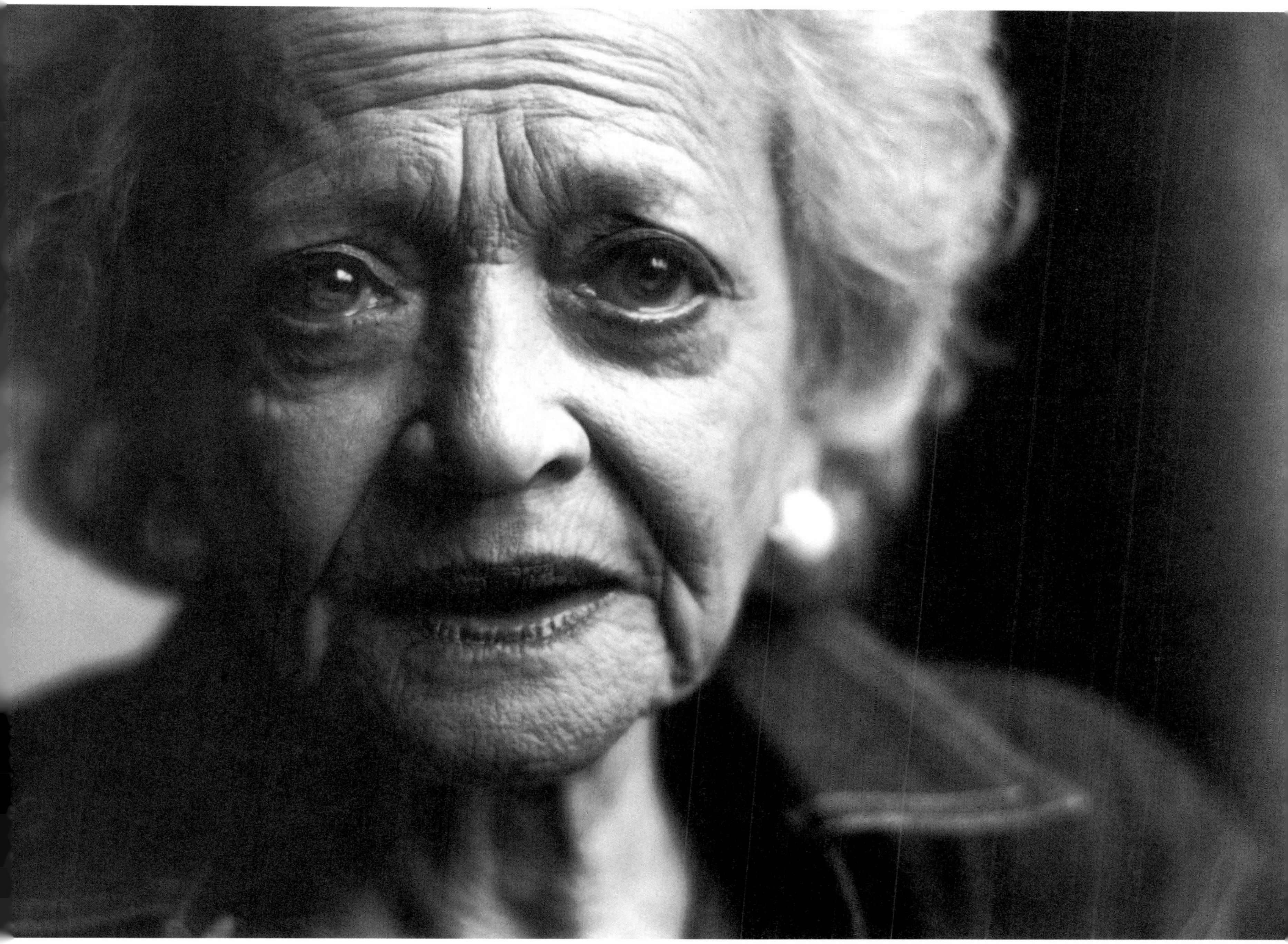

Warren Beatty
BY
Lee Grant

Complicated
boy
man

Relentless
pursuer &
conquerer
of
Romance
the Deal
the Idea

Formidable Warrior

apple pie & secrets
seductive
aphrodisiacal
un-haveable

Funny
Loyal
Friend

Bel Air, California *1965*

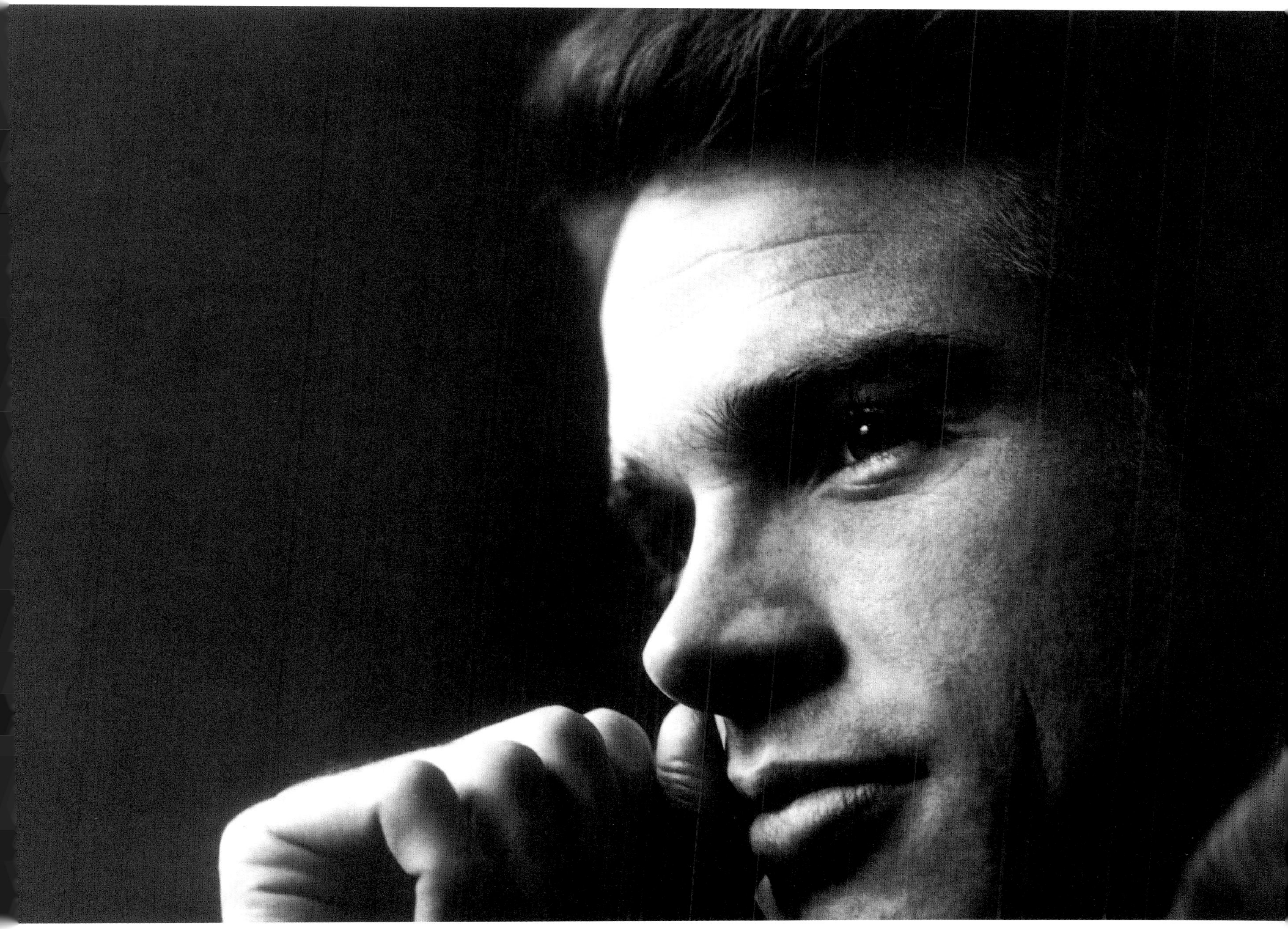

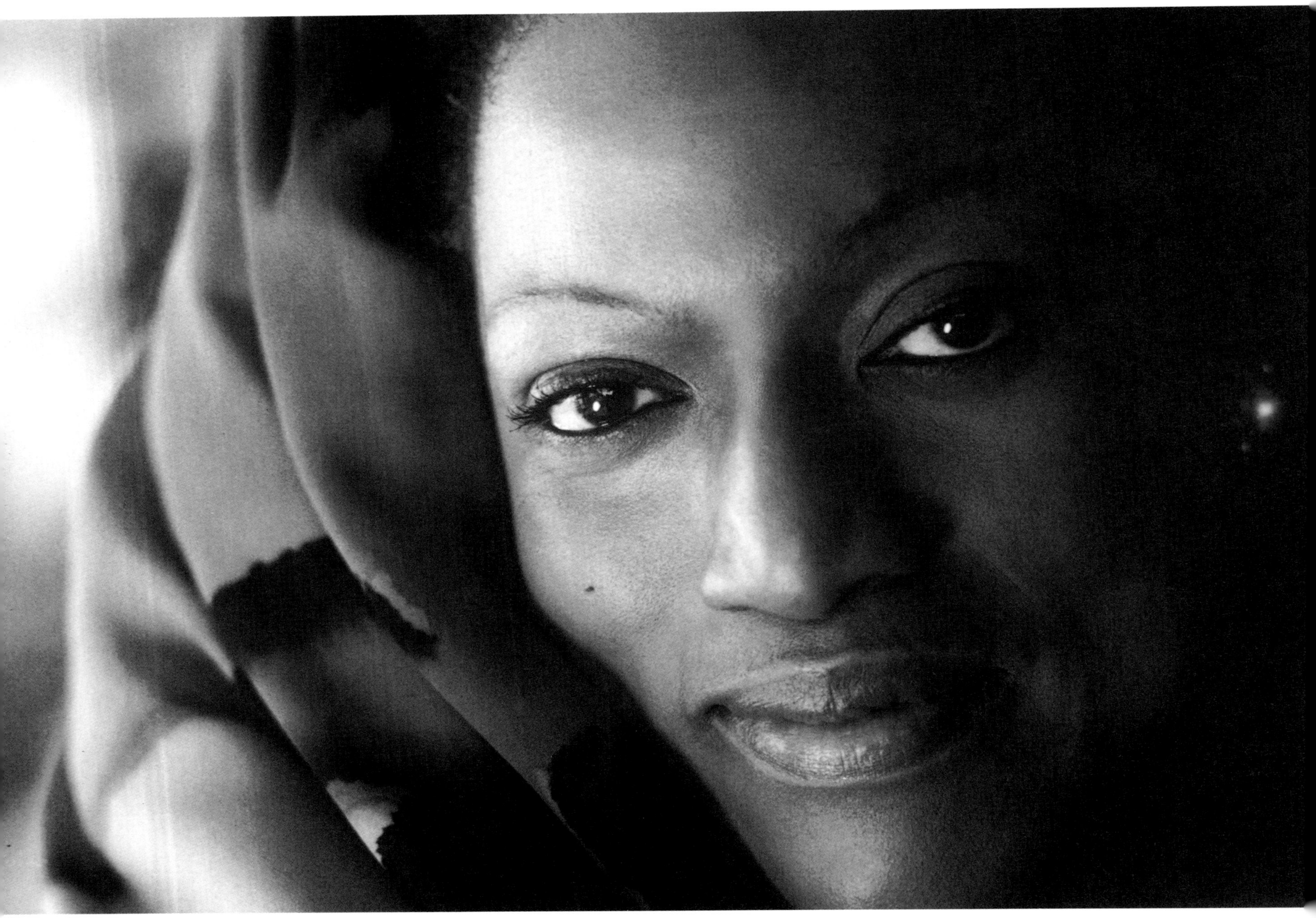

Jessye Norman
BY
Edward Albee

Who is this woman?—this pussycat who is also a tigress—this elemental force with the subtle mind—this thunderbolt with the sense of humor—this possessor of a voice equally at home with Wagner and Brahms, Mahler and Debussy—this alarming and exhilarating talent?

She is Jessye Norman, and she is here, and she is wonderful, and you are the less for not embracing her.

Chicago, Illinois *1990*

Michael Crawford
BY
Hal Prince

Michael Crawford is fearless. He is also a worrier. A perfectionist. Obsessively disciplined. (Yes, it's true he arrived at the theatre around noon each day to prepare for an 8:00 PM performance!) And he possesses a magnificent voice; few know he was a Benjamin Britten boy soprano.

Until *Phantom of the Opera* he was known primarily as a clown or a *farceur,* so it's not surprising to find him triumphing as one of the most poignant, singularly humorless figures in theatrical history. The gentlemen and ladies who make us laugh are often depressingly serious company. But back to "fearless" Michael Crawford.

The original script for *Phantom* called for twice as many illusions as survived in the production. I would inject stage directions. For example: "During the frenzy of the masked ball, the Phantom appears at the head of the grand staircase dressed as the 'Red Shadow,' masked (another mask covering his original mask, making it impossible to see!). He is standing on four-foot stilts, towering over the celebrants. Slowly he makes his way down the polished staircase, head held high, surefooted." I dictated it and never looked at it again.

We went into rehearsal, and after five weeks moved into the theatre. One morning I had an emergency call from Ruth Mitchell, my assistant. "Come to Her Majesty's quickly! Quickly! Crawford's going to kill himself!" And before I could hang up: ". . . and it will be your fault!" When I arrived there he was double-masked, managing a ton of red taffeta and brocade, and wearing four-foot stilts perched on tiny, polished, painted wooden shoes.

Michael apologized for being tentative coming down the stairs. It was only his third time. I stood at the bottom of the stairs and watched. Head held high, he took the first step—the *last* step, actually. "Stop! Not one more step! Take those damned things off!"

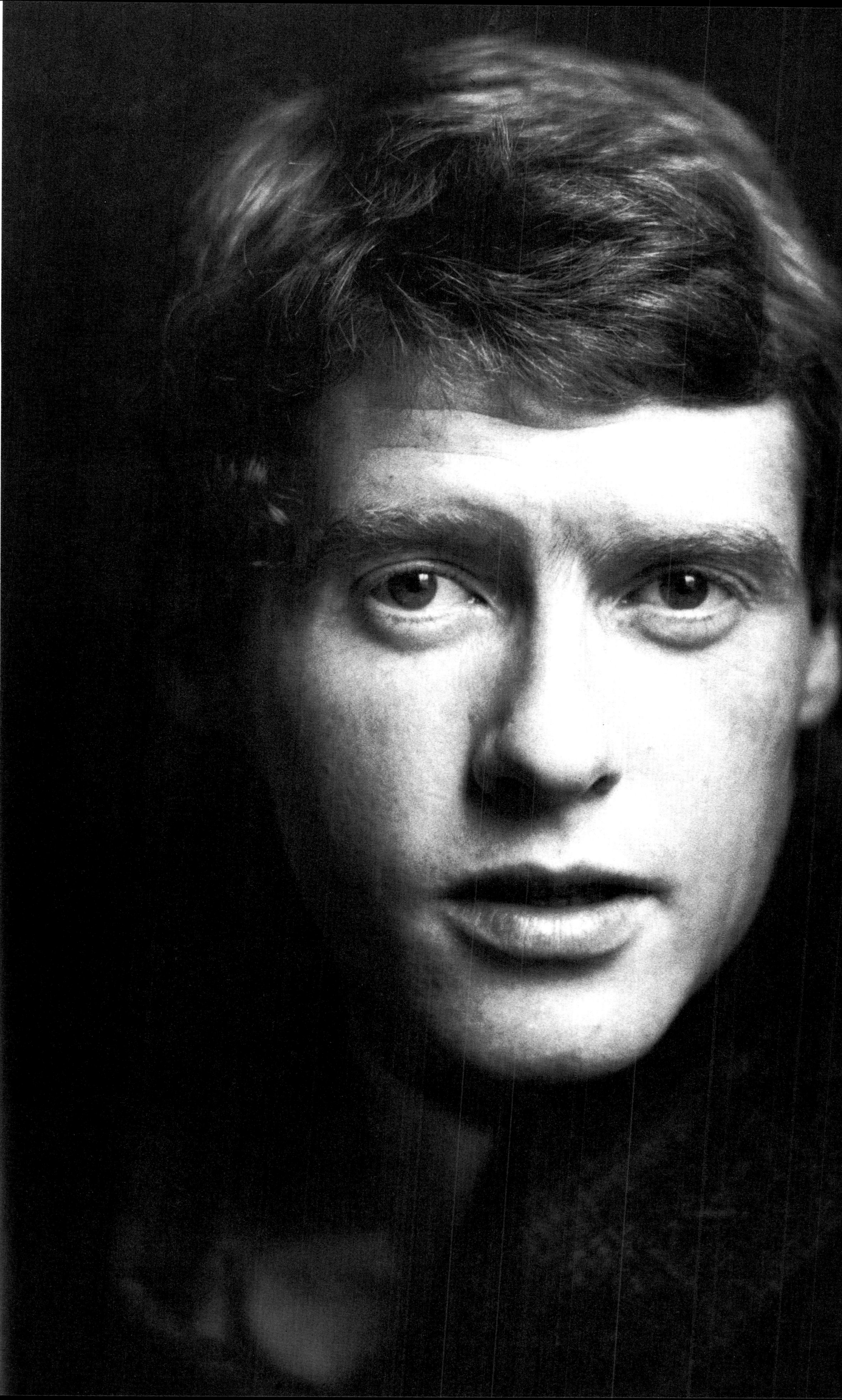

There followed the only argument we ever had. Michael took it personally. He thought I thought he was afraid to do it, or worse, that he couldn't do it. Well, I had seen him walk a tightrope below the proscenium arch of a London theatre in *Barnum,* and I had seen him take a header down a staircase in *Black Comedy.* I knew he could do it. I also knew *I* couldn't take it!

There's not much Michael Crawford cannot do. Add to that he is a gentle man. And he is a tortured soul. Up to now I suppose *Phantom* is the high point of his richly diverse career. But there will be more surprises.

❑

Kirk Douglas
BY
Suzanne Pleshette

Understand that I am an unabashed movie fan. My father ran one of the great movie houses of the world, and my earliest memories are of the magical figures that lived twenty times bigger than life, up there on my Daddy's screen.

In time, I went into the family business and found that very few ever measured up to the image of the dark.

Maybe it's the light that strips them of their shimmer, or the display of craft that steals some of the magic, or simply the nearness, which allows one to take a true measure. But, in all of the years that I have known him, KIRK DOUGLAS has always been twenty times bigger than life, and spelled in capital letters.

He *looks* like a movie star. The determined face which he moves first, as a way of steering his body. The chin with the definitive cleft, which seems less a genetic accident and more a chiseled exclamation mark.

The taut body serves as a testimonial to his discipline and respect for the requirements of his trade. Not vanity that keeps him loyal to his regimen, but rather the soldier's mentality which understands the need to be ready when the battle cry sounds.

He is a warrior, remembered vividly as a character fighting to survive. Both on and off the screen he has carried the moniker of "Champion" because his personal courage has measured up to that of the characters he has portrayed on the screen.

He's a bad boy, but a good man. Still astounded that his sons are older than he thinks himself, and, if his grandson did not so successfully match him chin for chin, I suspect he would want to stem the tide.

He, more than any other star of the generation when STARS were STARS, seems to have defied time. If he has feet of clay, he has shoved them into a pair of well made shoes and hidden that inconvenience with style. If his ethics have cost him fans, he has won others when he stood tall and spoke out on the side of humanity. He continues to think of himself as the son of immigrants who miraculously achieved the American dream, and he has tried to show his gratitude to a country that allowed him to succeed on such a grand scale.

He does not tempt the fates. He takes nothing for granted. He works like hell, every day, at something worthwhile, so that if God is taking measure, he will not be found either wanting or ungrateful.

If there is no movie to be made, he writes a book; and just in case that be perceived as simply facile, he writes another, as he turns his tenacity to another form of creative achievement.

No matter what he does, he is a STAR. He shines, he twinkles, he illuminates. He is that thing that goes flashing through the sky that we hang our wishes on. And in these times, as we grow more cynical, as one by one our heroes fail us and our leading men on the screen seem to be propagating the images of a world gone mad, KIRK DOUGLAS still makes me reach for my autograph book.

Rome, Italy *1961*
Two Weeks in Another Town

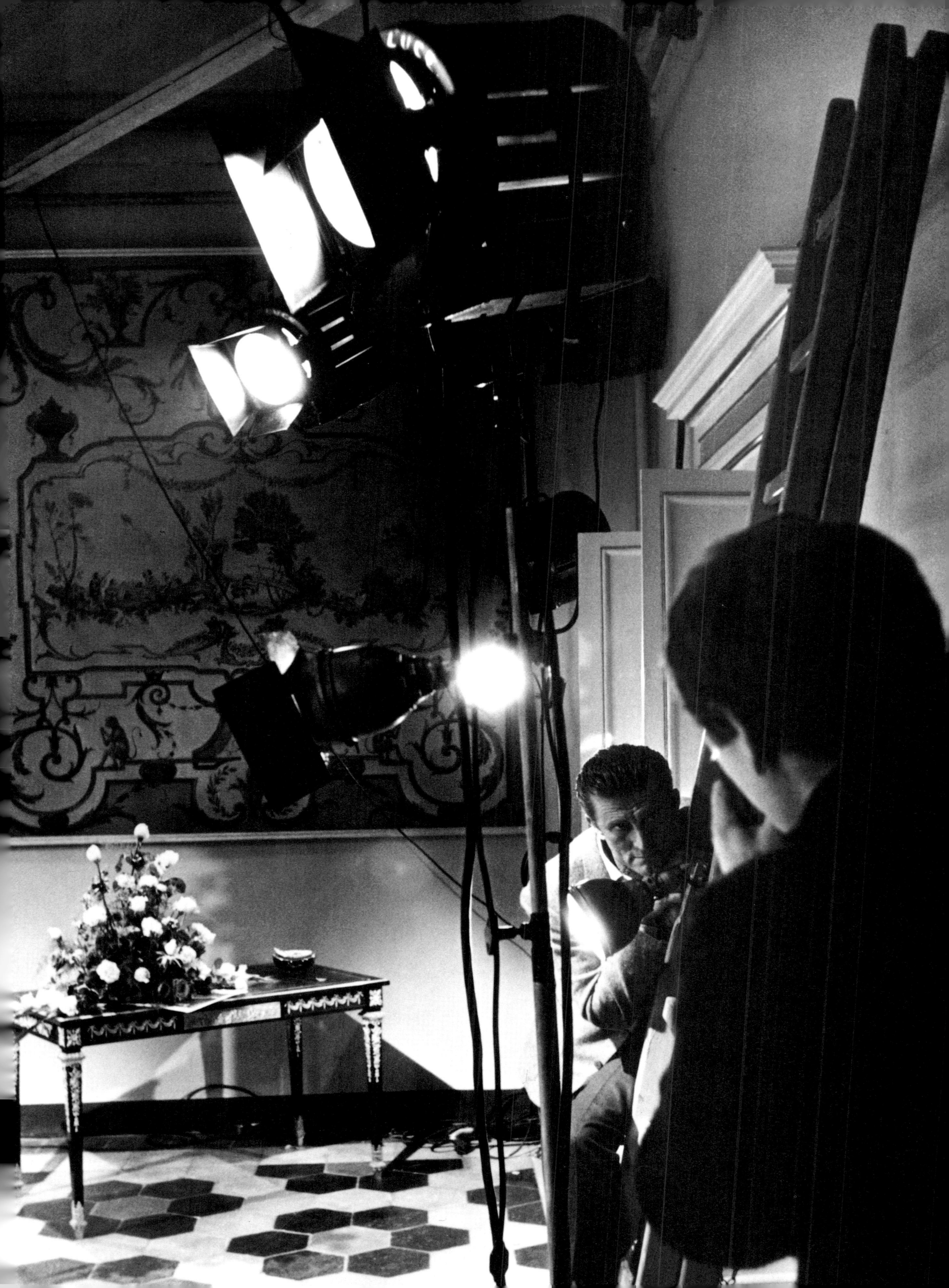

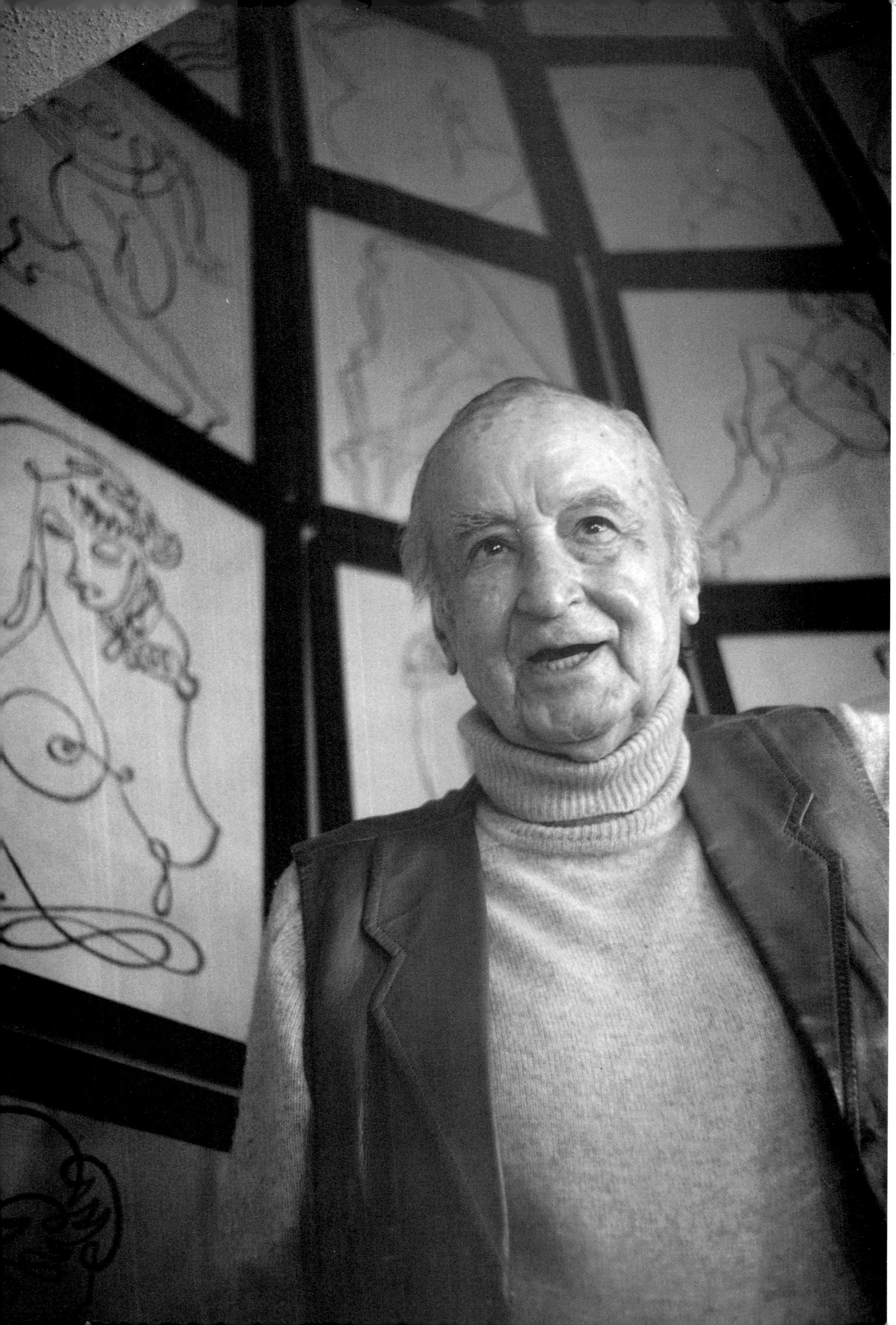

Jean Negulesco
BY
Jane Wyman

Dear Roddy,

I was thinking, you have done such a beautiful job of remembering so many of our friends in your books. Thought you might like to hear of one of my remembrances—Jean Negulesco. It takes me back to my *Johnny Belinda* days. I feel so fortunate to have had Jean as my director. This man is not only a very sensitive director but an accomplished artist in every sense of the word and a good friend and a loving husband to Dusty—an artist in her own right.

I was watching *Daddy Long Legs* not too long ago, and as I sat so comfortably watching and weeping—yes, weeping—unabated tears at the lovely performances of Astaire and Caron, I thought of *Belinda* and Jean and what a delicate job he did on that. We who know him *hope* that the new generations of artists will study his work and learn what an artist really is.

These are my thoughts for today. All good wishes for your continued success with your books.

Fondly,

Jane Wyman

Beverly Hills *1990*

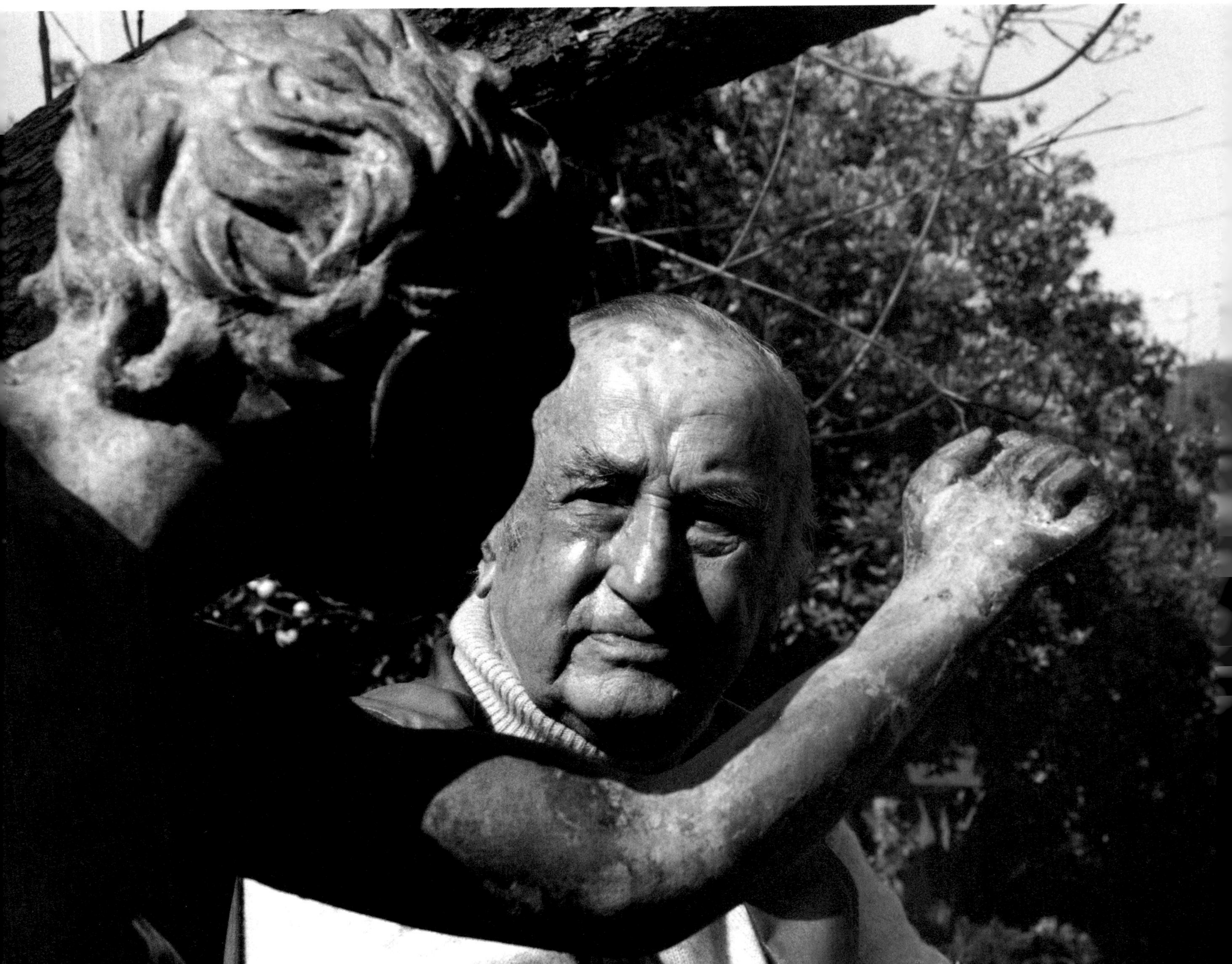

Beverly Hills   *1990*

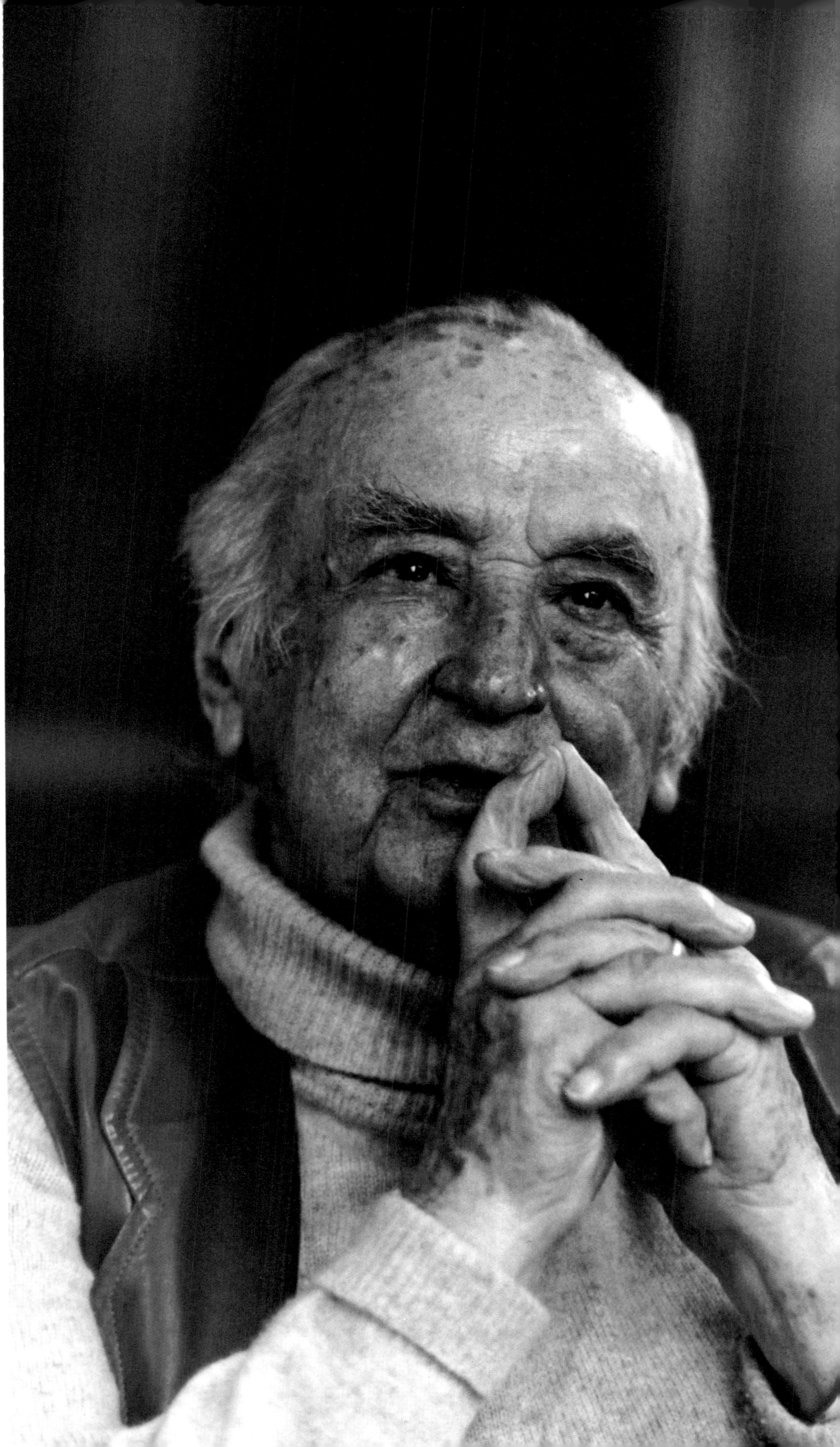

Jule Styne
BY
Jerome Robbins

Unfortunately, there isn't another man in the world like Jule Styne. Alas for that; we could do with more.

He is a jewel, a joy, a special friend and a hell of a composer. His is the music that always makes me want to dance. He is, at the age of eighty-something, still a kid, a joyous, infectious, mischievous elf who sees the fun and piquancy of everything in life and whose jokes and buoyant sense of humor melt all worries away.

Stories?—I could tell endless ones. Like once, in a Beverly Hills hotel's well-draped basement nightclub, Betty and Adolph and Jule and I were working midday on fixing *Peter Pan*—and some crazy argument blew up between us (I don't remember a detail of the when or why), but it ended up with Jule stomping off in a temper huff, leaving the rest of us crestfallen, downcast. We'd never had this kind of trouble before. We moped about for some terrible minutes—then suddenly we heard a loud "Ta Da!" and from behind a set of drapes on the bandstand, out bounced Jule presenting himself like a big star show girl, but stripped down to his underwear and looking, as he always does, like some delicious cupid—all rosy and full of laughter, primping down to the nightclub floor singing his own musical accompaniment. The only thing missing was another Jule Styne to play the piano for his show—as he sashayed around—broke us up—and healed any damage that might have been done before he left us.

As a collaborator, Jule's enthusiasms and single-mindedness on solving the problems of any show at hand are famous. He relentlessly comes up with new ideas, ways of fixing what's wrong, a new number or two—and gives out a great enveloping aura of comfort and ease—taking away all of one's anxieties. Often he gets carried away by his new idea of how to fix a problem . . . but his years of experience as a fine musician, movie composer, his nightclub and his vaudeville playing—have made his eye and ear as sharp as anyone's around, and usually puts him two steps ahead of the rest of us.

He is one of the rarest of people in show biz, a real love. He makes you so happy and glad you're a part of it—he, his joys, delights, and talents, are irresistible.

New York City 1990

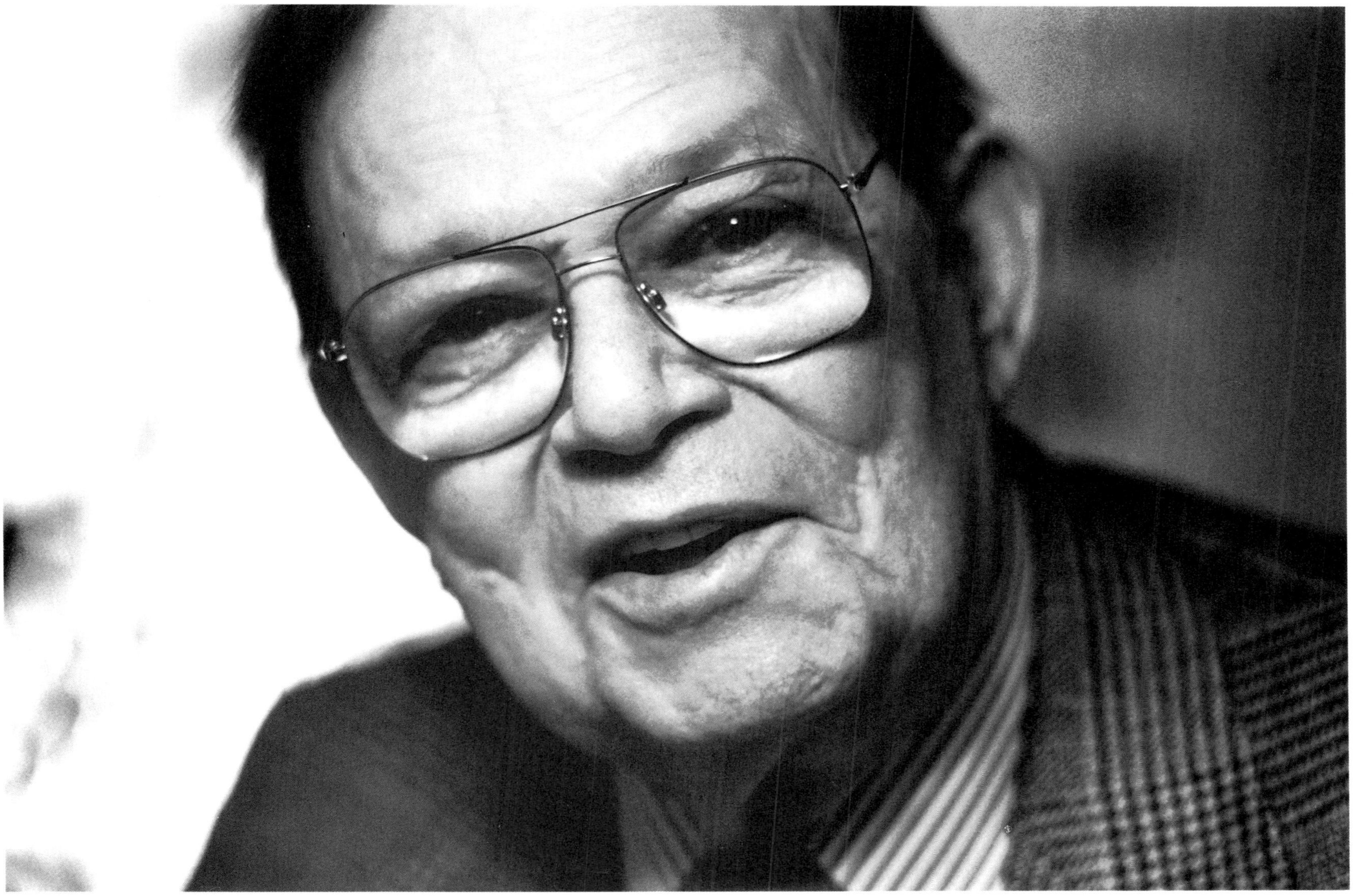

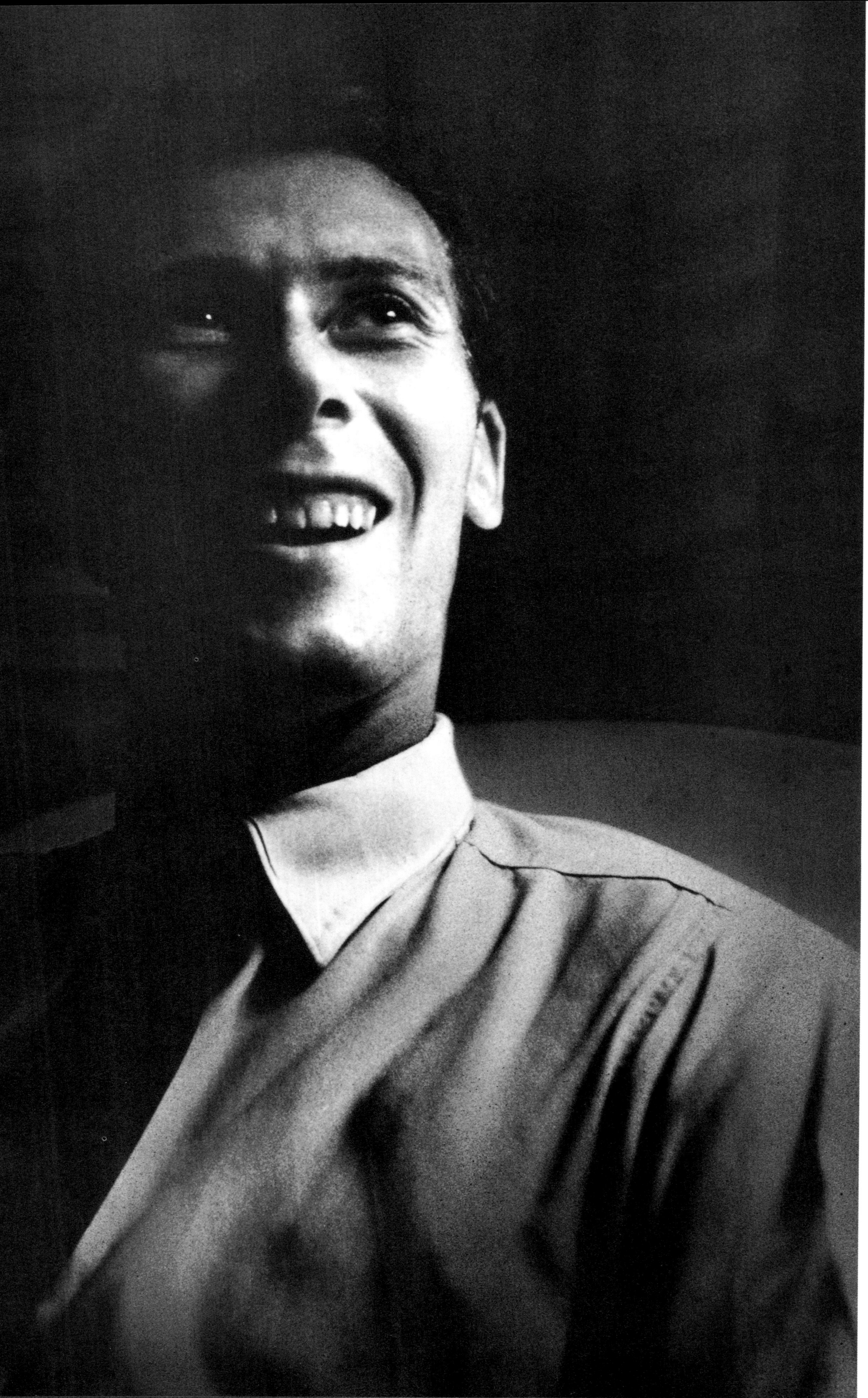

John Osborne/Mary Ure
BY
Jocelyn Rickards

In May, 1990, I spent a sybaritic week with Roddy McDowall while he was preparing this book. Surrounded by negatives, proofs, and blowups, he worked in his own intensely private and orderly manner from early morning until the light had faded. I prowled his equally private garden, entirely secluded with no other houses in sight. Occasionally he would come out of the house with two or three large prints in his hand and say, "Which of these do you think I should use?" One day he placed a large photograph of John Osborne on the table in front of me.

"Do you think I should print this?" he asked.

"When was it taken?"

"During the New York run of *Look Back in Anger.*"

"I've never seen a photograph of him laughing so spontaneously before—yes, I think you *should* use it—you must have taken it just before I met them, what were they like?"

Roddy produced a photograph of Mary Ure wearing a man's check shirt (a shirt I've always associated with Jimmy Porter) which he placed beside John. For seconds he was silent, then he said,

"New York was all freshly painted that year, John was full of laughter and wit and Mary was full of adventure. Oh what a lovely, lovely actress she was. John had freed the theatre as no one had since Ibsen, Strindberg or Noël Coward with *The Vortex*—without him there would have been no Pinter, no Wesker, no N. F. Simpson—he was an extraordinary phenomenon, so young and so unaware of the world impact he was about to have."

"What were you doing in New York then?"

"Dean Stockwell and I were playing Leopold and Loeb in *Compulsion*—I've not really seen John to speak to since those days."

We both looked at the photographs together, John and Mary, Roddy and I. He turned to me and said, "Will you write about them?"

Now I have to turn my memory back over thirty years, like winding a film backward to recapture my first vision of John and Mary as they walked into Harry Saltzman's house the

New York City 1958

evening of the day they returned from New York. It is no exaggeration to say they took my breath away, because they did. I was already involved with Loudon Sainthill and Tony Richardson over the visual aspect of the film of *Look Back in Anger* which Harry was to produce. Although their names were constantly mentioned, I had no preconceived ideas about them. Mary's hair was like corn silk, her skin matte and flawless, and although she was thin, her limbs were exquisitely rounded in an eighteenth-century fashion. All this was accentuated by a sleeveless empire dress made of violet suede; her neck and head rose out of the dark suede like a briar rose, and as she was excited she bubbled away a hint of Morningside Scottish in her usually controlled light voice. A briar rose because of its very nature describes her perfectly—natural, honest, and wild. Mary was no pampered overbred hybrid; although she could, and sometimes would, overlay her personality with an actor's tricks, she was by nature truthful and honest; the thorns on a briar rose make it more difficult than a nettle to grasp, and if she felt that she was being lied to, betrayed, or even overlooked, she could attack and defend herself with an inordinate number of spiky thrusts. Perhaps the thing I found most curious about her was that she never seemed to displace any air. Sitting on a chair, lying on a sofa or beside me in the back of a car, she was there, but there was never any indentation in the upholstery, on the cushions, or in the leather of the car—she appeared to be totally weightless as though she might blow away.

That same evening John was a physical Oberon to Mary's Titania, very lean and sunburned, his light hair streaked by the sun and his eyes a truly blazing blue, he wore pleatless khaki trousers with diagonal pockets on the hips, a shirt of bright pink cotton open at the neck and with the cuffs rolled back. I wondered where he'd found the shirt, I only knew one place to buy them, the Naples market—workmen's shirts, the top pocket embellished with a red embroidered buttonhole for placing the Bic or Biro in safety.

They were both so high with pleasure to be home, competing with each other in their Truman Capote impersonations and, for that evening, they were both full of laughter.

I was the only person there unknown to them, but nothing could have blighted their gaiety and pleasure and it left me free to gawk—observe—and wonder at their outrageous vitality and glamour.

Although over months and years I grew to know them well, it is that very first impression, strong and clear as rock crystal, that remains. The most potent image I have of them together.

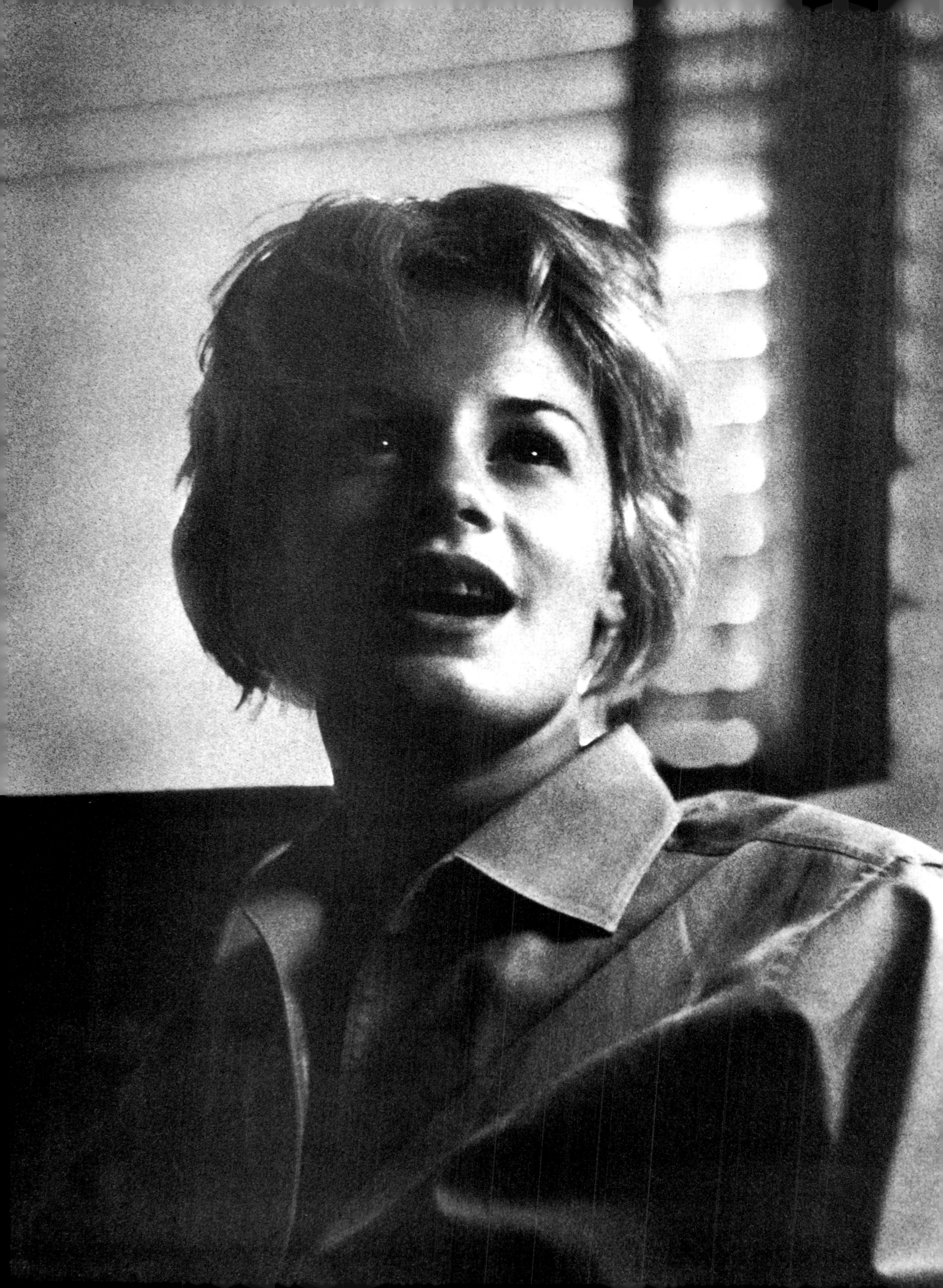

Cesar Romero
BY
Anne Jeffreys

Cesar Romero personifies the image of a true Hollywood star. His dignity reflects the heritage of his grandfather—José Martí—the great Cuban liberator and martyr. He is a gentleman of integrity and elegance—recognized everywhere by his many fans and admirers. He is a true humanitarian and a loyal friend. Hail Cesar!

Los Angeles 1990

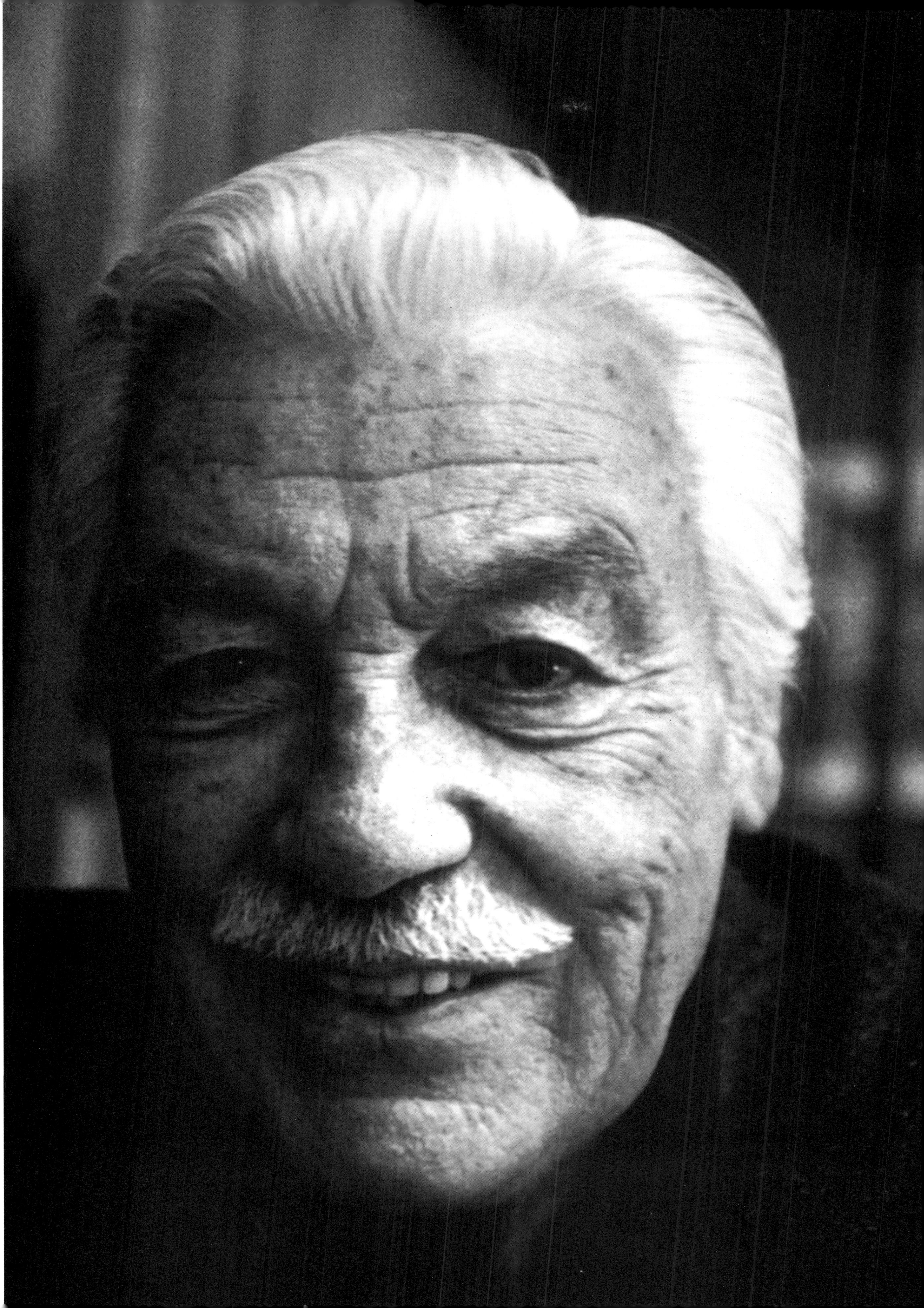

Raymond Massey
BY
Christopher Plummer

That face could have belonged to the Renaissance, to Bunyan's Pilgrim, to the Empire Loyalists. It had been carved from oak—it had seen ghosts and war, sorrow and death; and, it could terrify! I was 10 when I first saw it on the screen and it scared the hell out of me. Fifteen years later I was confronted by that same face again, this time in person, and to my relief there seemed not a trace of menace in it—in fact it fairly twinkled with an endearing expression of perpetual surprise which gave to its tall dignified owner the quite disarming if unexpected hint of a rather large overgrown schoolboy. I made a friend for life that day.

Born to privilege, Captain Raymond "Pappy" Massey, fresh from his native Canada, Balliol College, Oxford, and the First World War, walked with fiery determination through the nearest stage door he could find and became one of the Theatre's favorite sons. Now, push fast-forward and let the tape spin us on to his later years. For some time now he's been a star and a legend—this is our third production acting together—the curtain is down—we are in his dressing room enjoying drinks and jokes, as is our habit, far into the night. As I listen to his stories I can't help but wonder why this jovial, highly intelligent man, armed with an education and background that might have set him firmly along the "corridors of power," should have chosen to be, of all things, an actor. Then I remember, he once ran his very own theatre in London (The Apollo)—he once persuaded George Bernard Shaw to cut his royalties for him—he directed a young Charles Laughton and an even younger Laurence Olivier—and he staged the world premier of Sean O'Casey's *The Silver Tassie!* I'm sharing a scotch with Cardinal Richelieu, Hamlet, Ethan Frome, Abe Lincoln, Henry Higgins, Black Michael, Prospero, Brutus and a host of grand old war-horses to whom he has given such substance. No! He had to be an actor. He wouldn't have had it any other way! Now, the booming voice shatters my reverie and "Pappy" is announcing in sepulchral tones that I am to be a life member of a mysterious fellowship (founded by Ty Power, Greg Peck, and himself) known as "Iggumfoo" (IGMFU)—which venerable title when spelled out in full means—"I Got Mine—Fuck You!"

My father (who had known Massey at school) had fallen victim to an "old-fashioned" divorce which had separated him totally from me and my family the rest of his days. With great presumption I have often secretly thought of Ray, more than anyone else, as the most likely candidate in life to play the father I never knew. I didn't get the chance to tell him this—ever—but then—how could I? Anyway, even up to the very end he was far too damn young for the part. So I content myself by remembering him in waves of gentle irreverence and fierce devotion as a warm, talented, exceedingly lovable, slightly "naughty" bigger brother.

Stratford, Connecticut *1955*
The Tempest

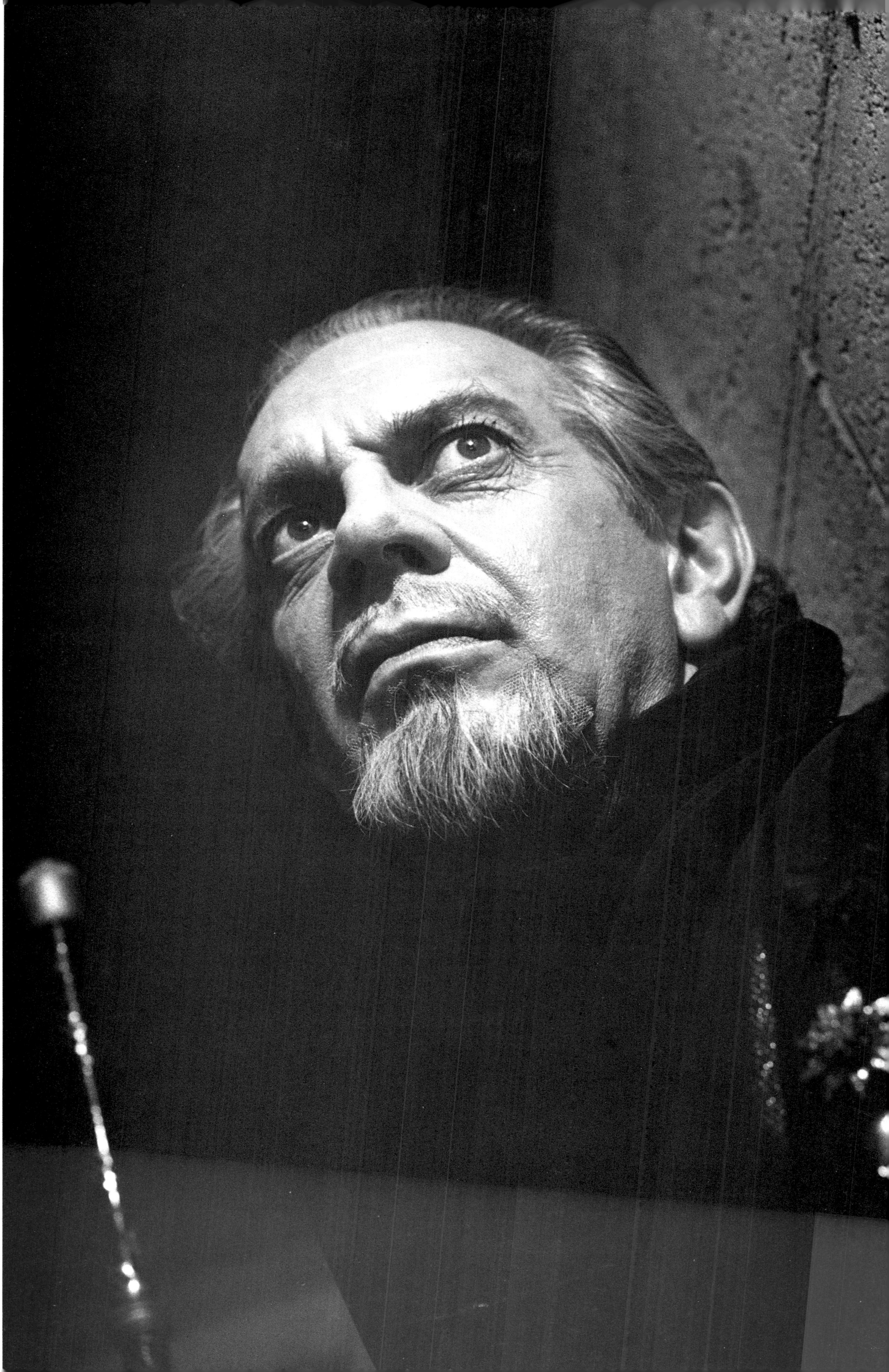

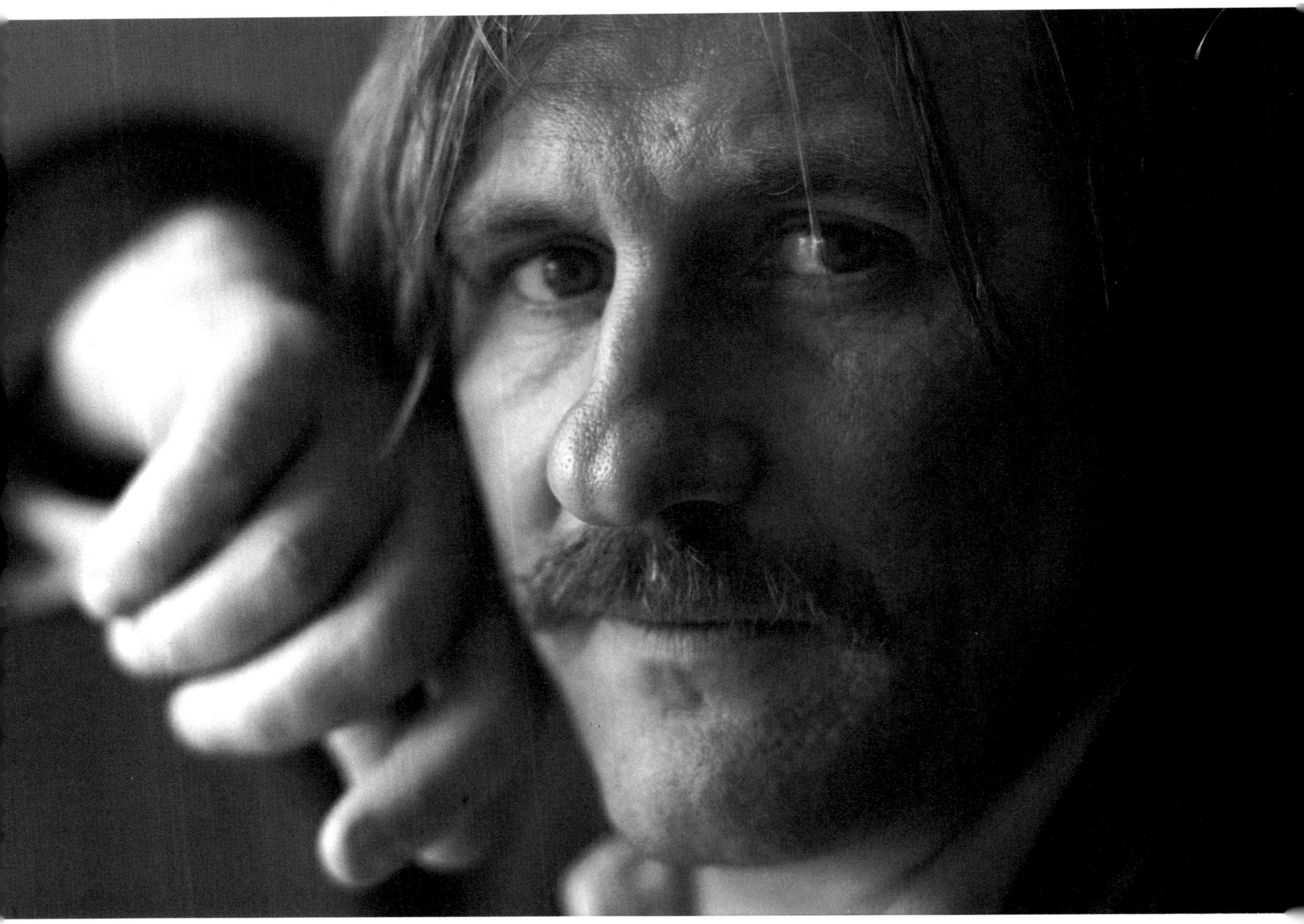

Gérard Depardieu
BY
Peter Weir

Working with Gérard

"I'm really not an actor," he told me back in 1988 when we met. At the time we had little enough language between us to ask exactly what he meant, so I took it that he was saying he wasn't the "actor type," that he wasn't difficult. That was true enough, but after making a film together I also know that wasn't what he meant at all.

Firstly, his unique approach to the craft works most effectively with an author/director, because he not only searches with you for the character but he also studies you, the author, at the same time. So he's kind of "co-writer," meshing parts of author, character, and himself into the final creation.

It's no surprise to discover his wife of twenty years is a psychologist (and actress) and that Gérard himself has read widely on the subject. That's not to say the process is entirely conscious—I'm sure for the most part it's intuitive—the instincts of a survivor, living in the streets and on his wits from a very early age. But then it hardly matters what he calls himself as he's destined to find his place in the pantheon of the screen's greatest stars in time to come.

Culver City, California *1990*

Jane Powell
BY
Ralph Bellamy

Jane Powell has the vitality of two "hyped-up" people.

We worked together in her first picture. She was quite young. Her mother and father were with her on the set. She cried a lot between scenes. It could have been because, even at that age, she was intelligent enough to be aware of the crime we were perpetrating—the Picture was *Delightfully Dangerous*.

We have been good friends during the years since then. And it has been wonderful to watch her achieve and sustain professional heights in the theater and pictures, in the United States and abroad, acting and singing with that same vitality.

Actually it prevails in her private life too: She arrived at her Los Angeles home only the day before New Year's Eve one year, and had invited thirty people for supper on New Year's Eve. She cooked the meal herself, including cookies and cake. I was there.

She is married to another old friend of mine, Dick Moore. He was "Dickie" Moore—age four years—when I worked with him in a picture called *Strictly Dishonorable.*

Janie and Dick are good old friends and she is a flourishing Star.

New York City *1956*

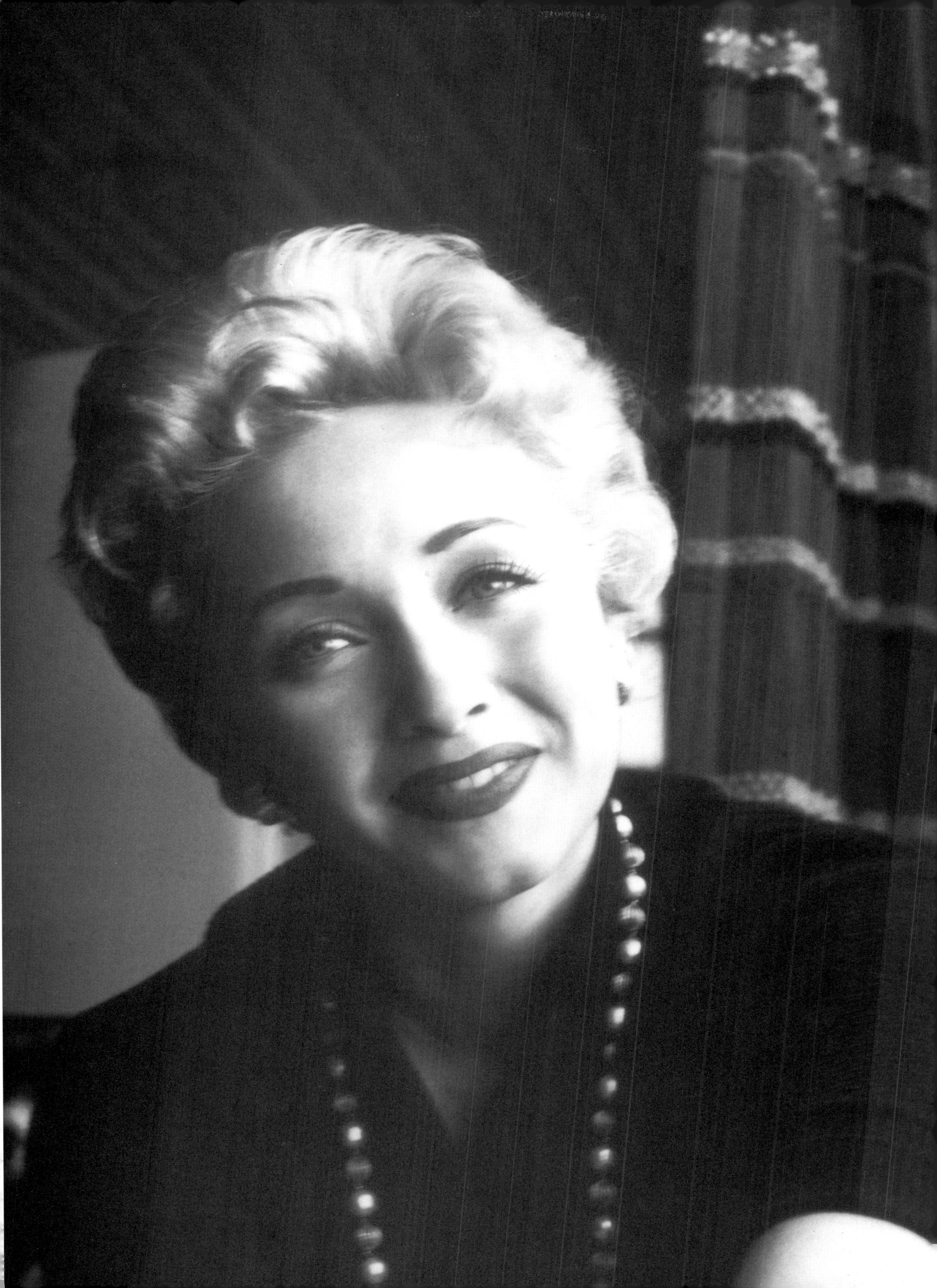

Steve Martin
BY
Martin Short

28 November 1990

Dear Roddy,

Being asked to write something about Steve was one of the most exhilarating moments of my life. To be able to worry for six months about what I was going to write about a guy who makes me laugh, not only once a year, but sometimes once a month, excited me endlessly. However, I put it off for six months and never once during that time did I escape from the gnawing ache that I hadn't done my homework. And, that one day you, Roddy, were going to show up at my door and punish me.

The worst part of it was that Steve knew I couldn't quite get it done and he enjoyed taunting me—which perfectly describes our relationship. We can talk on the phone for a long time and never get to the reason we're calling because we take off on a tangent of comic abuse that doesn't end 'til we hang up. A typical conversation might go like this:

STEVE
(bad New York accent)
Marty???

MARTY
(fake overblown excitement)
Steeeeeve!!!

STEVE
(fake overblown excitement copying my fake overblown excitement)
Marrrrrty!!!

MARTY
I love when you celebrate the people
that dwell within you.

Beverly Hills 1990

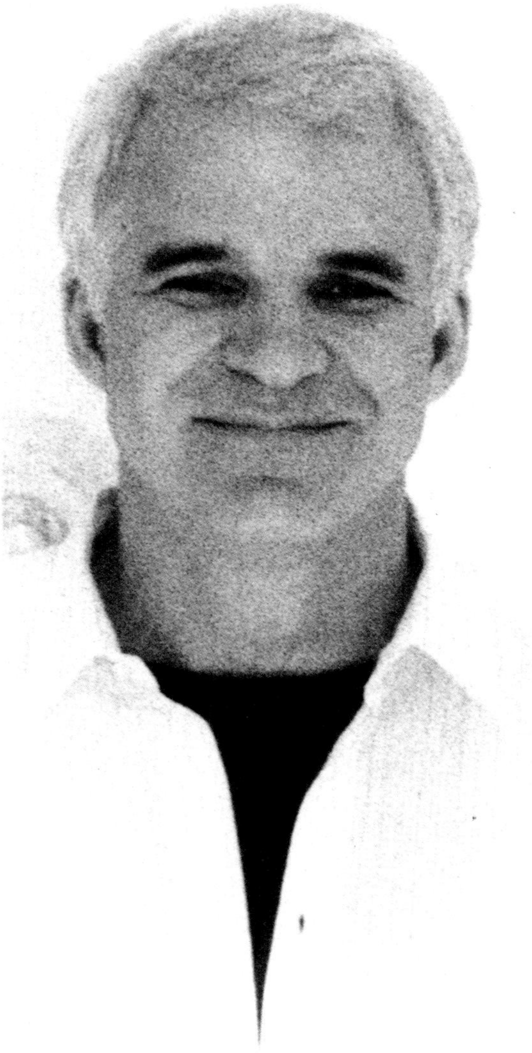

STEVE
And I love when you do what you do.

MARTY AND STEVE
(raucous laugh degenerating into lecherous laugh)
HAHAHAHAHAHAHAHAHAHAHA!

This may not sound funny to you, but to us it is ten seconds on Mars. And I think if a friendship can give you ten seconds on Mars, that's more than one can ask.

I first met Steve during the filming of *¡Three Amigos!* I found him to be funny, smart and surprisingly shy. He's one of my heroes, which is nice because he's also one of his. But enough about Steve. How are you, Roddy? Hope all is well. Regards to Lassie always.

Your Pal,

Martin Short

Dear Marty,

How's this? Call me

Steve

Hal Roach
BY
Spanky McFarland

Hal Roach, Sr.

Born in Elmira, N.Y. in 1892, he went through many occupational scenarios: drifter, prospector, mule skinner, cowboy, movie extra, and film producer.

Just prior to 1919, Hal Roach, Sr. had discovered and made a star of Harold Lloyd. Thanks to the popularity of Lloyd, his pictures were the highest-grossing money-makers of that time. This enabled and led Hal Roach to expand his "stable of stars" to include Snub Pollard, Ernie "Sunshine Sammy" Morrison, Stan Laurel, Oliver Hardy, Charlie Chase, Theda Bara, Thelma Todd, Zasu Pitts, Will Rogers, and the *Our Gang* kids. Along the way, he managed to find time to build the HAL ROACH STUDIOS.

Volumes would be required to list the names of stars, directors, and production people who passed through the turnstile of Hal Roach Studios to populate the film industry through the golden years of 1930s, 1940s and the early 1950s. John Ford, Buster Keaton, John Wayne ad finitum. Hal Roach, Sr. was a pioneer in early 1950s television, producing some of the biggest and best known TV series in America! *The Life of Riley, My Little Margie, Amos 'n' Andy, Fireside Theatre, Blondie,* and *Beulah* to name just a few.

As a member of the *Our Gang* (now known as *Little Rascals* on TV) circa 1931–1938, I was constantly around Mr. Roach. Although my memory of him is dim at best and filtered through a child's eyes, I do remember him to have been an affable "bear" of a man. He was not afraid to give a kid a big hug, tousle his hair, and remember him/her generously at Christmas and birthday.

To the *Our Gang*sters, he was Mr. Roach; to everyone else he was "the Boss." A term of endearment used by all the people who made up what was then known as "the family" at Hal Roach Studios.

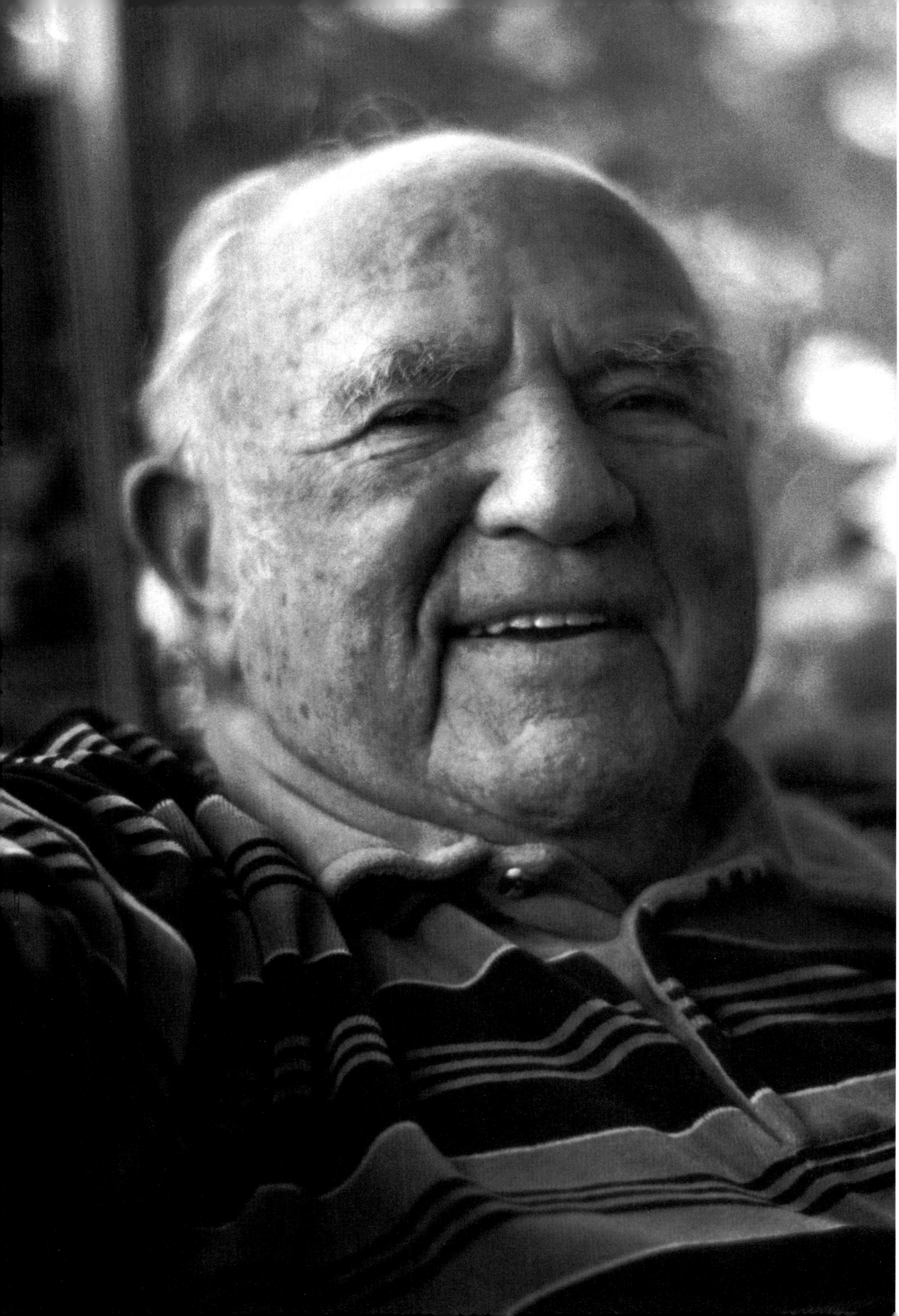

I have a more personal reason to remember and love Hal Roach. I had the high honor and distinct privilege to present Hal Roach, Sr., with an Honorary Oscar in 1984 for his outstanding contributions to the film industry.

At this writing, I am 62 years old and I have been gainfully employed for 59 years! I could not make this statement if Hal Roach had not film-tested a little fat kid from Dallas, Texas, in 1931 and cast him in the *Our Gang* comedies.

My name is Spanky McFarland and "the Boss" gave me my first job at the age of three!

Bel Air, California *1988*

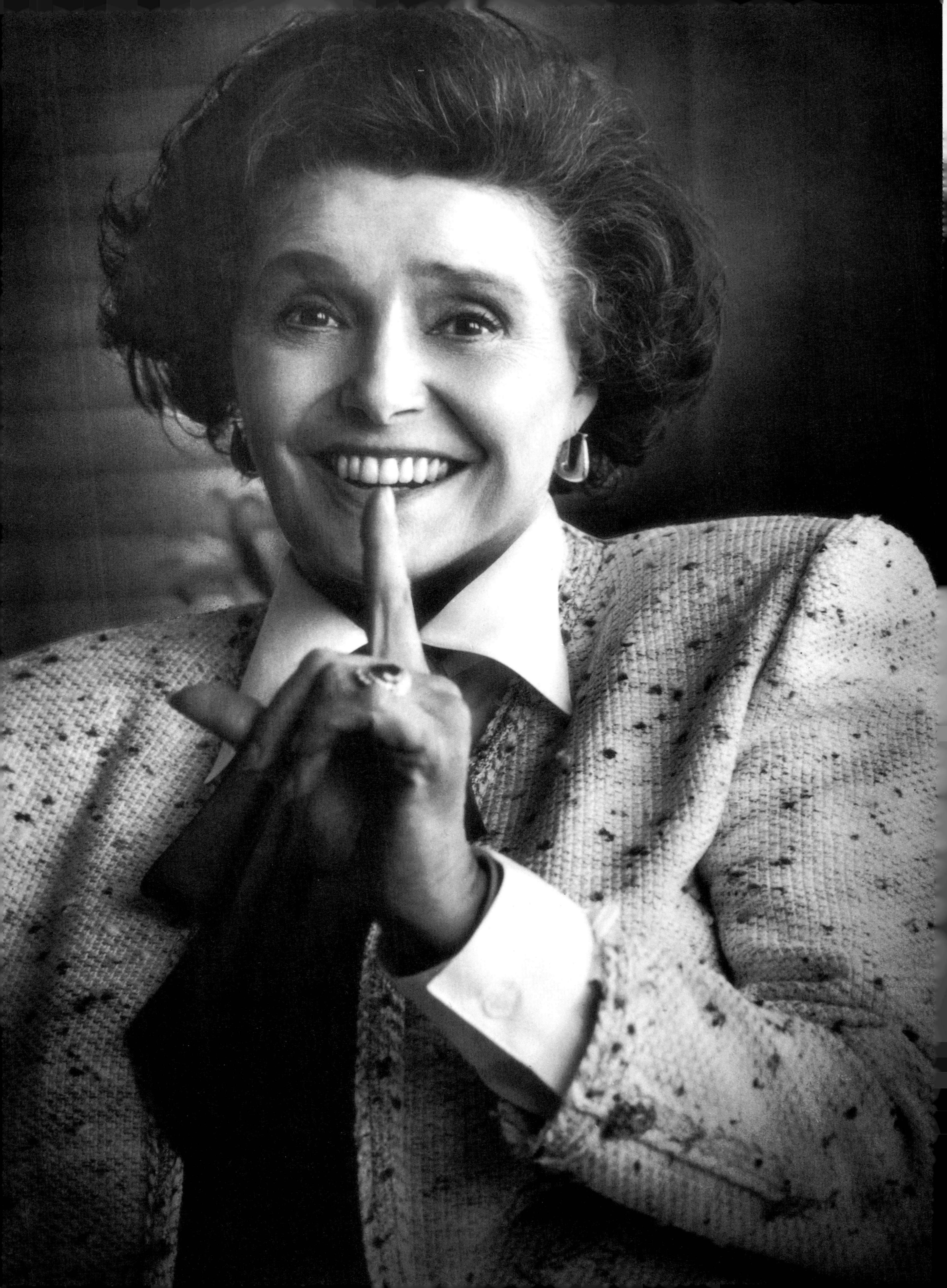

Patricia Neal
BY
Anne Bancroft

A TRUE GENTLEWOMAN

KIND

UNMASKED

VULNERABLE ALWAYS TO FRIENDS

HONEST, IN SPITE OF THE FACT THAT IT'S MAKING HER BLUSH,

INTELLIGENT . . . SHE KNOWS SHE'S REVEALED HERSELF.
SOME MOMENTS IN HER FILM WORK ARE SO REVELATORY, I GASP.

INTUITIVE

SPONTANEOUS

HER HUMOR IS SO PERCEPTIVE SHE MAKES ME LAUGH OUT LOUD.

SHE IS FROM THE EARTH

REAL

HUMAN . . . SHE IS THE MOST HUMAN, HUMAN BEING I KNOW.
HER HUMANNESS MOVES ME TO TEARS.

Los Angeles 1989

Maximilian Schell
BY
Stanley Kramer

The dynamism of Maximilian Schell is almost unbelievable. The secret is his controlled power which suddenly explodes into total domination. As the defense attorney in *Judgment at Nuremberg*, this control is unleashed into a tirade which remains unforgettable for me.

It was Schell's responsibility to make a defense of the Nazi war criminals against insurmountable odds. He assessed the responsibility of the Vatican, the pacts with the Nazis by the Soviet Union, Winston Churchill's abatements, and the support for Hitler from American industrialists. If the defendants were found guilty—then so was the rest of the world. His impact in performance was unbelievable.

One day Spencer Tracy told Schell: "The Oscar is yours—not a doubt!" It happened that way. More than that, Schell is a successful director because he always evidenced patience, creativity, and an open mind for a new concept or idea. When the Maximilian blow is needed—when the drama called for catharsis—when the performance becomes the character—these were all the marks of Max Schell.

My hat is off to him as an example of the lengths to which the human spirit can be extended in search of truth. He made a difference.

New York City *1959*

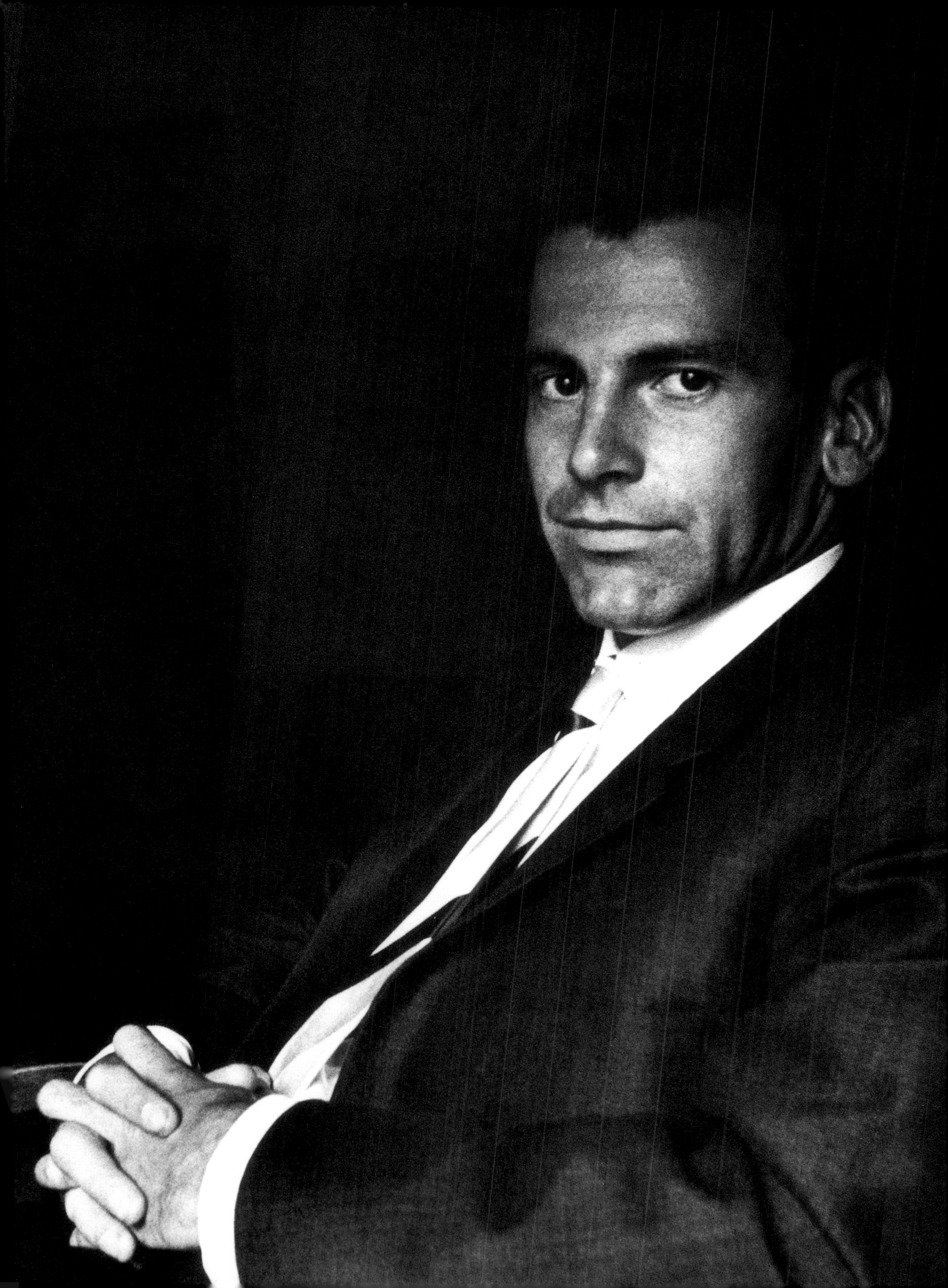

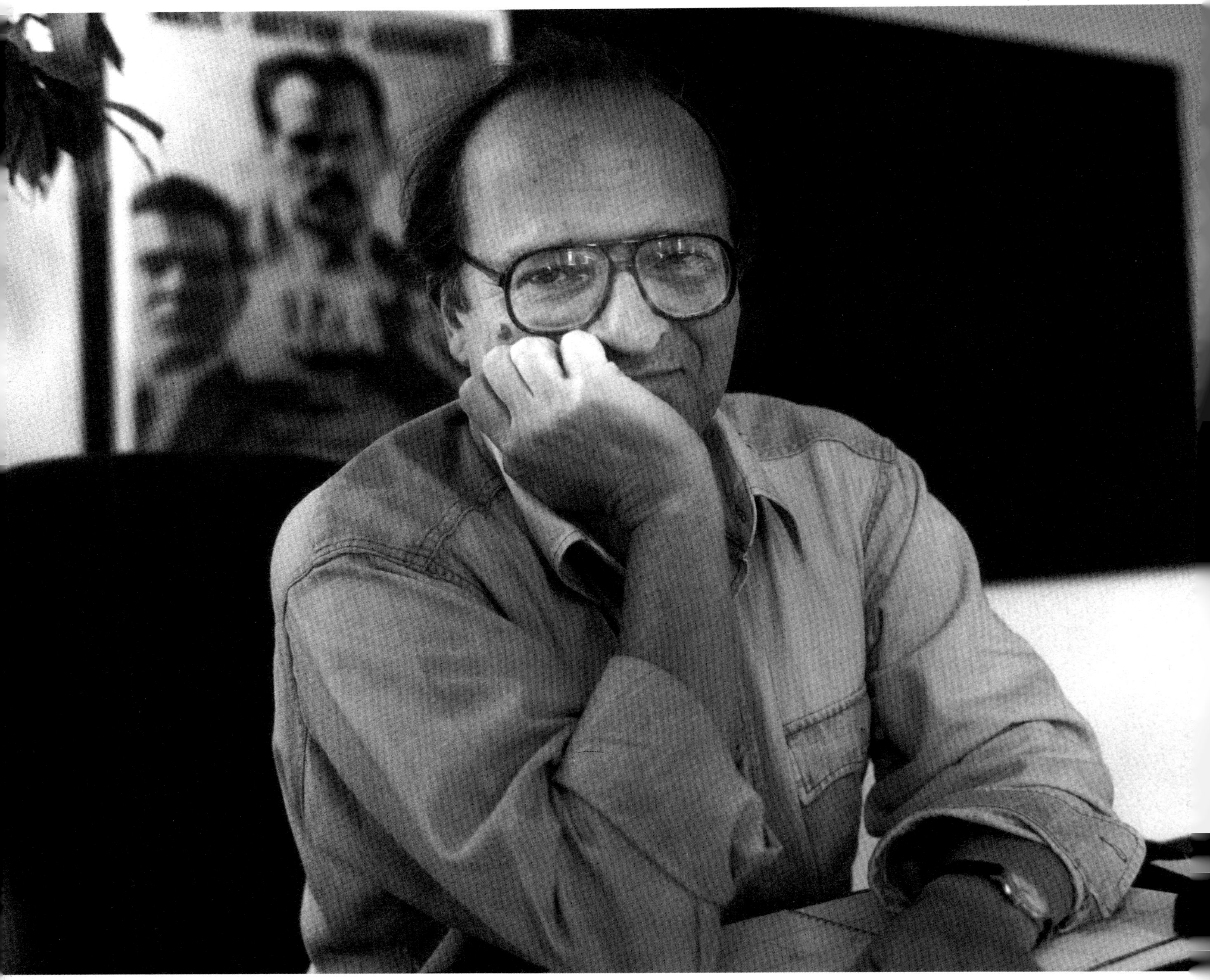

Sidney Lumet
BY
Herb Gardner

When I first met Sidney Lumet I was thirteen and he was twenty-three. Now I am fifty-five and he is thirteen. I wish him the very best at whatever he plans to do when he grows up.

New York City *1990*

Bob Hope
BY
Ronald Reagan

What more can you ask of someone than his friendship when that someone is a truly great entertainer who used his time and talent to bring a touch of home to literally millions of young Americans who were willing to give their lives for this blessed land?

Bob is truly a master showman, one of the greatest. He literally spent more time entertaining our military during three wars than he spent on entertaining audiences here at home. I'm more than proud to have him as a friend.

Toluca Lake, California *1990*

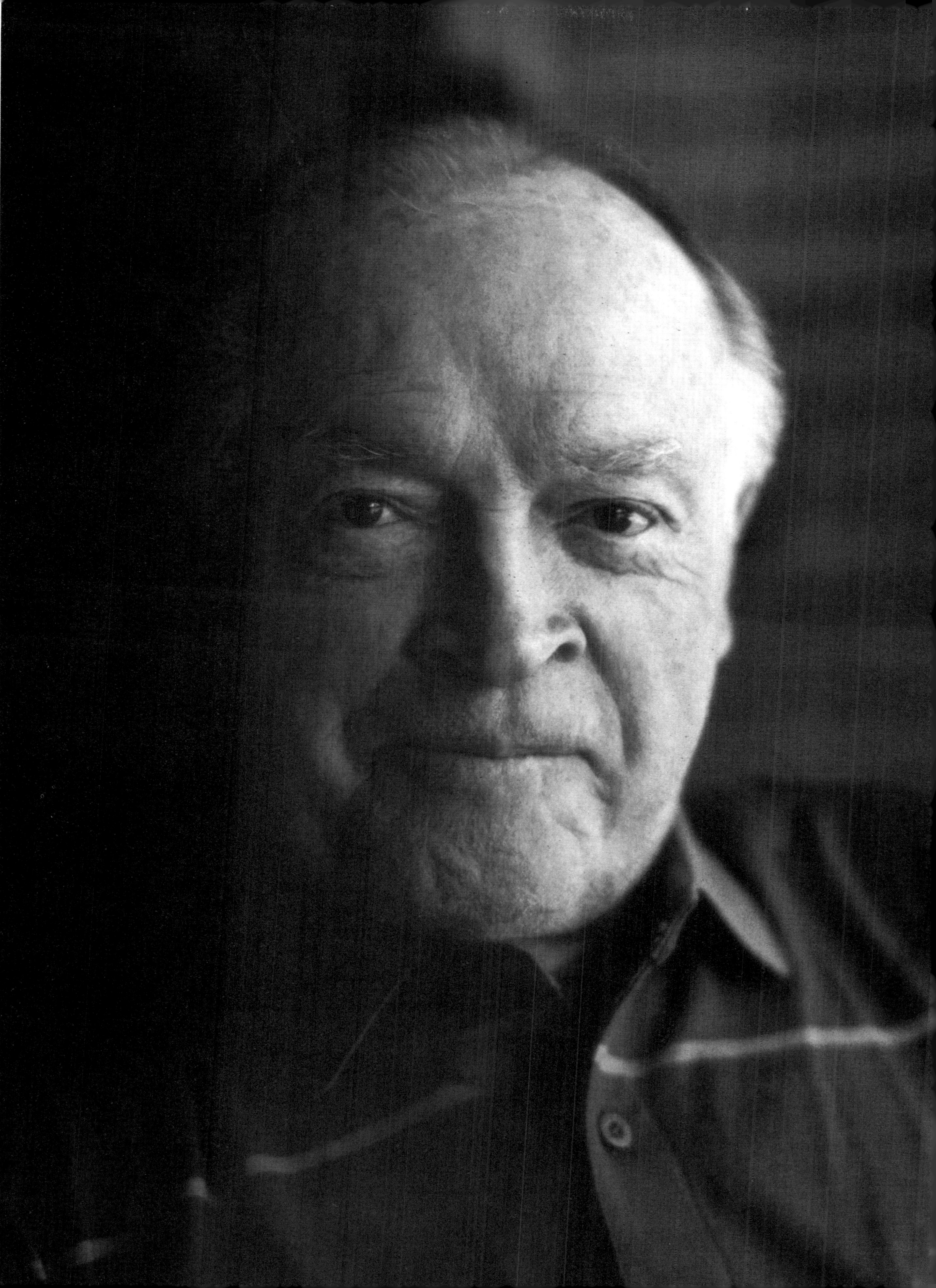

Dizzy Gillespie
BY
André Previn

Jazz is the supreme American art form, and Dizzy is one of the very few unarguable, bona fide, genuine, 24-karat giants in that field.

He is also one of an even smaller handful of innovators, a player who changed the face of jazz improvisation forever.

Unlike some other innovators in the arts, his life has not been ruled by deprivation, lack of recognition, or personal visions of hell. He has certainly been colourful during his career, but melodramatic—no.

He loves clowning, but it all cloaks an enormous intellect, a razor wit, and a deeply impressive knowledge of music.

At the first Newport Jazz Festival, one of the hostesses, floating on clouds of tulle, came up to Dizzy, who was on the sidelines listening to the Basie band. "Look, Mr. Gillespie," she trilled, indicating the society audience, swathed in white evening dress and sitting on little gilt chairs, "what do you think of all this?"

Dizzy took in the view. "I think it's the end of tennis," he said.

In other countries more given to bestowing public honours, he would have done very well by now. In France he would have been nominated for the *Légion d'honneur,* in England he could have made the Queen's Honours list, and in Germany they might have dubbed him Dizzy von Gillespie. Here, all we can do is give him a great deal of respect, a great deal of gratitude, and tons of admiration.

He's something else.

Hollywood 1990

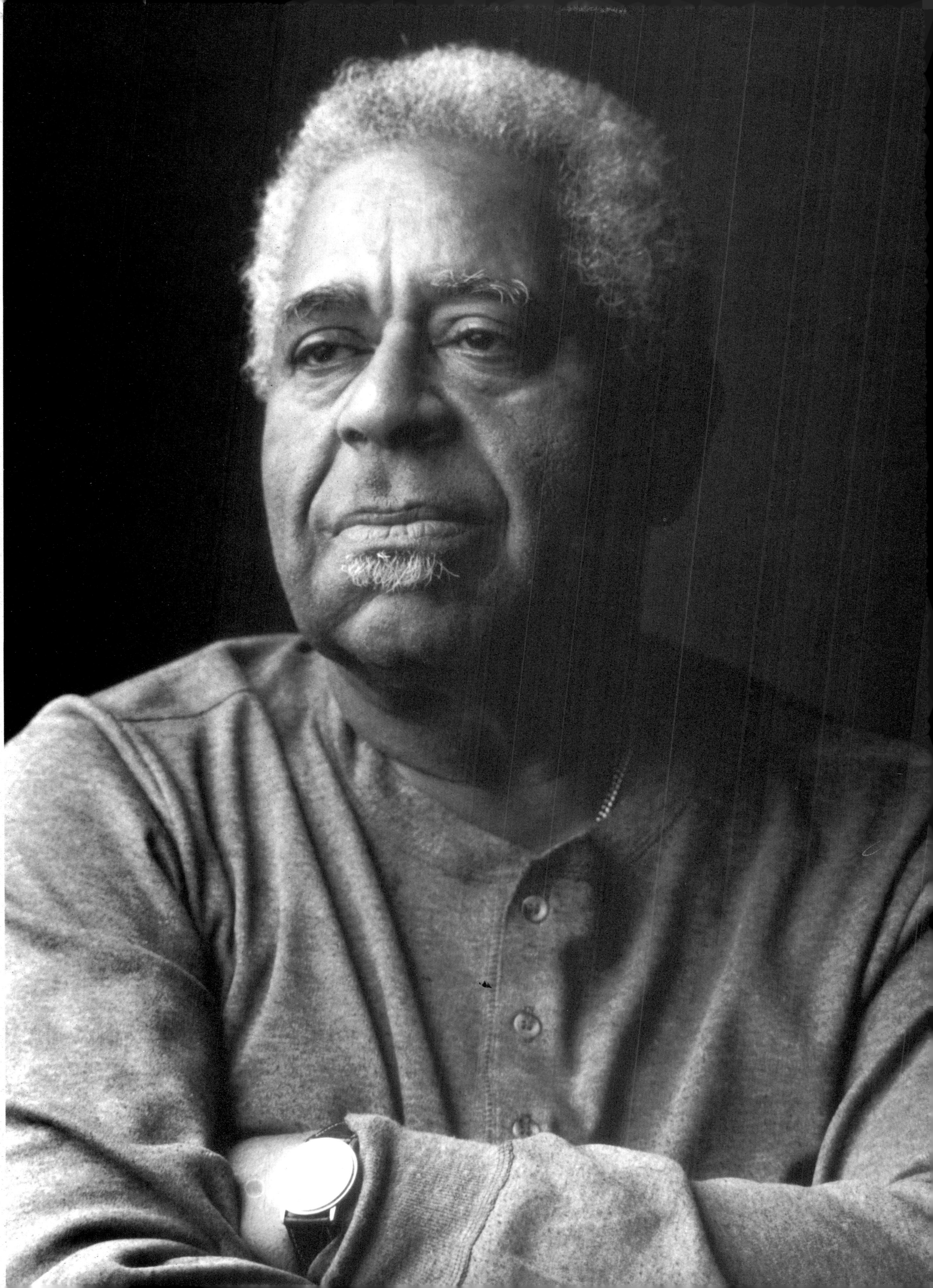

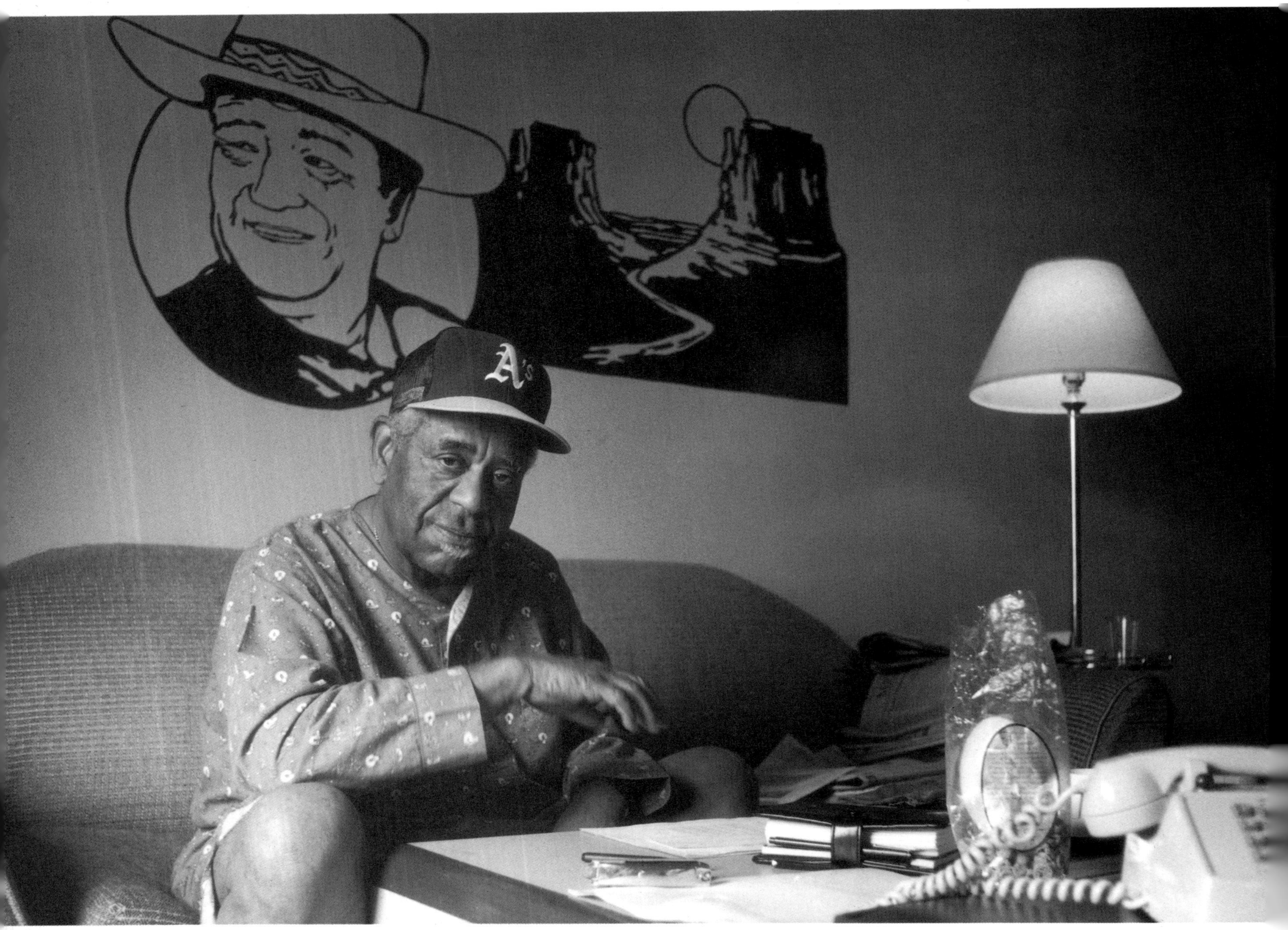

Hollywood · *1990*

Anne Jackson
BY
Eli Wallach

One picture is worth a thousand words—so it is said . . . my knowledge of the lady in question is made up of a thousand pictures which I'll try to put into words.

She cries aloud in theatres, talks back to the movie screen, loses ten pairs of eyeglasses annually, mentally tears down ugly office buildings in New York, dreams of directing traffic, issuing summonses and parking tickets. I give her watches but she is never on time. She always surprises me. She never went to college, but has a Doctor's degree; can't carry a tune, but she's musical. Her timing on stage is as perfect as a Movado watch.

I love her.

Eli Wallach
BY
Anne Jackson

I don't know what to say about Eli Wallach as an actor. I feel self-conscious . . . my admiration for him may seem suspect or self-serving, coming as it does from a teammate as well as a devoted wife.

I tried, believe me, to search out his faults so that by indirection I could list his frailties and thereby endear him to you—but the truth will out.

He is, in fact, the least difficult actor I've ever worked with. Acting with him is an eventful, joyous experience. His enthusiasm for a project is infectious. His pride in his work and in that of his co-workers knows no bounds. If pride is a fault, then, yes, he is guilty of it.

It is because of this fault or virtue that he has never known failure. He's been in plays that get rapped by the critics, that have not been box office hits, but he is always convinced that whatever he does is an unequivocal success. His loyalty to everyone concerned is fierce. He never gives in to the tyranny of critics.

Hard work is his criterion for success and his philosophy has rubbed off on me and his children.

If it appears that I am smothering him with praise, well then, in my defense, I'll plead that it's a crime of passion.

New York City 1961

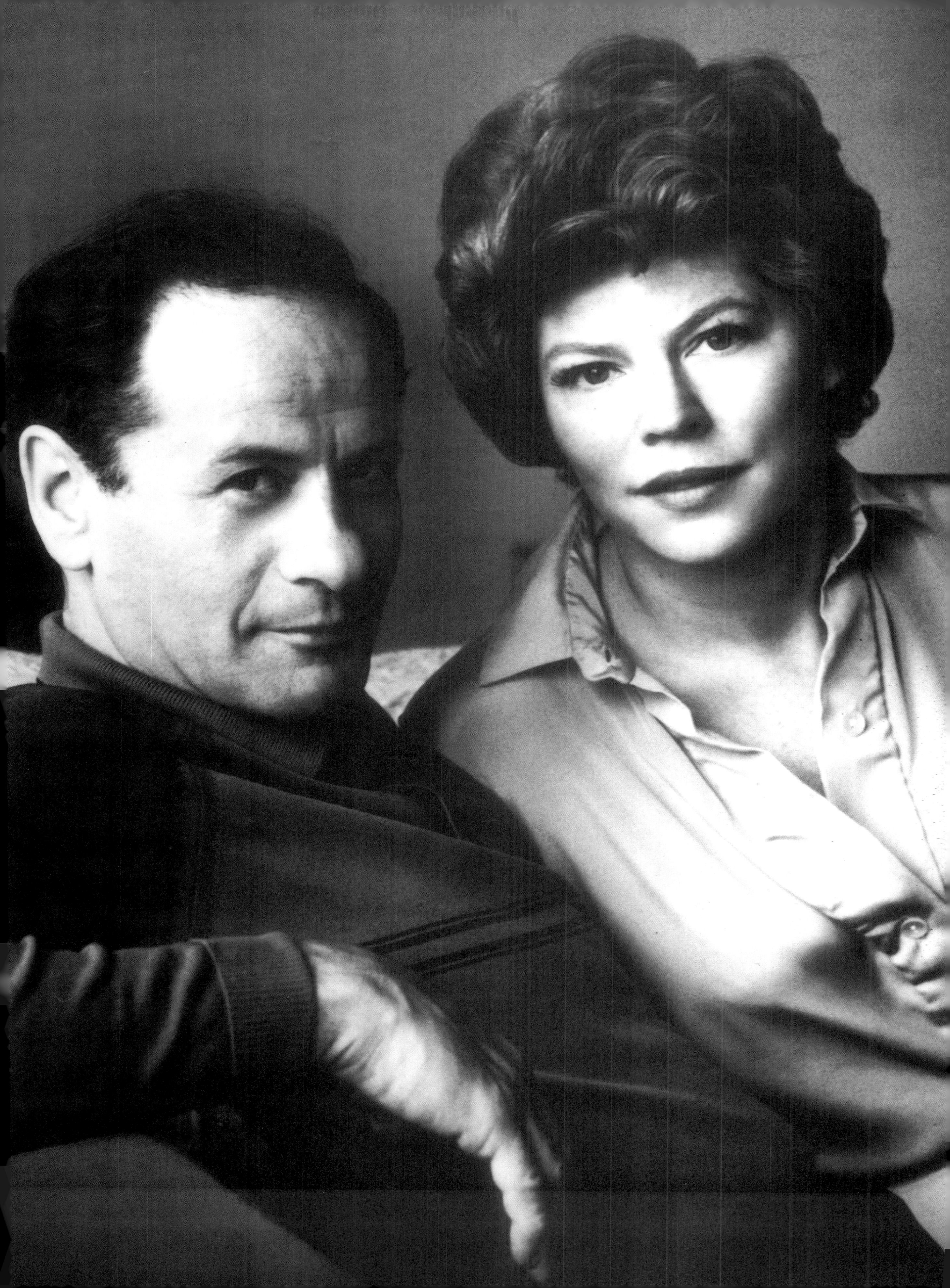

Stephen Collins
BY
Christopher Guest

He likes talking about baseball and rock 'n roll. Sometimes the subject of show business comes up. Sometimes.

Studio City, California *1983*

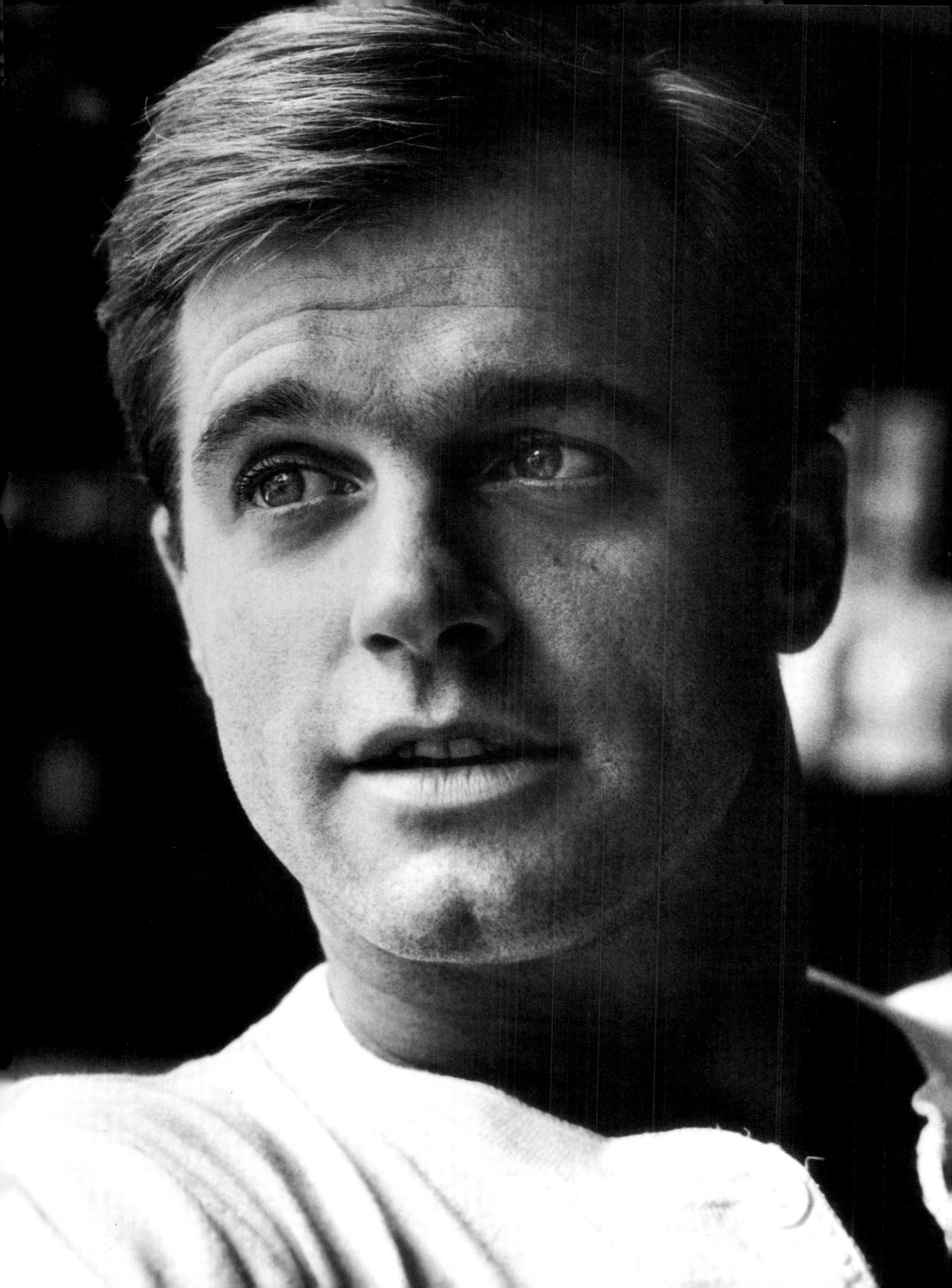

Luise Rainer
BY
Sam Wanamaker

An actress by birth.
An actress in life.
An actress in every pore of her being.
To act—on the stage or screen—anywhere—
    anytime—is a compulsion.
The quality: radiance. Or is it passion? or
    vibrance?
Or an undiminished current of
    high voltage energy?
The flame of her need to act burns
    as fiercely today—
More than half a century later, as when, a
    16-year-old, she first played Juliet under
    Max Reinhardt's direction in Berlin.
Given the right opportunity, she yearns to
    and will—for the third time—
    win the coveted
    Oscar for best actress.
She's impossible—she's delightful—she's
    beautiful.
She's slightly mad—she's extraordinarily
    talented.
Maybe that's why I love her.

Studio City, California *1982*

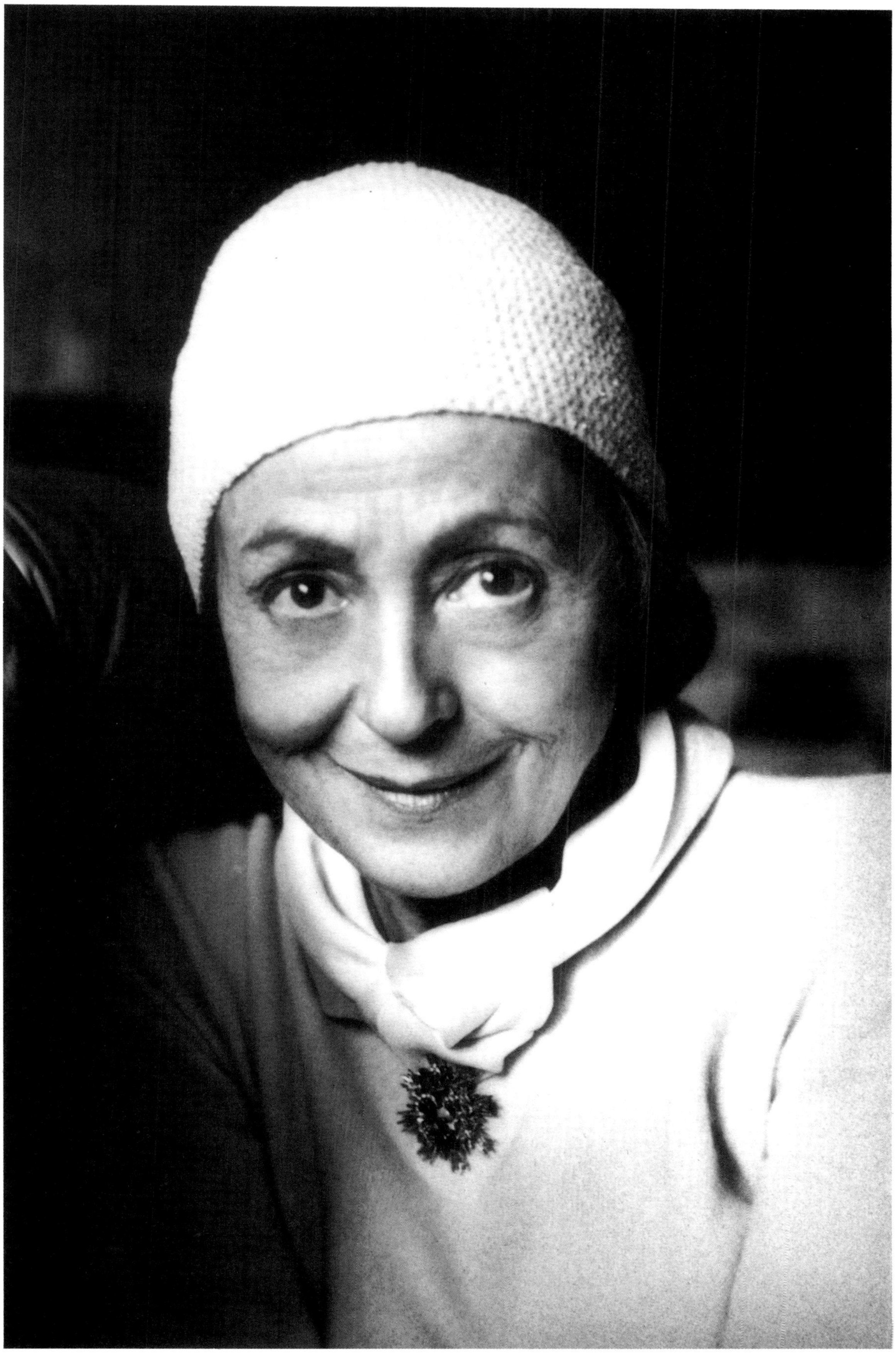

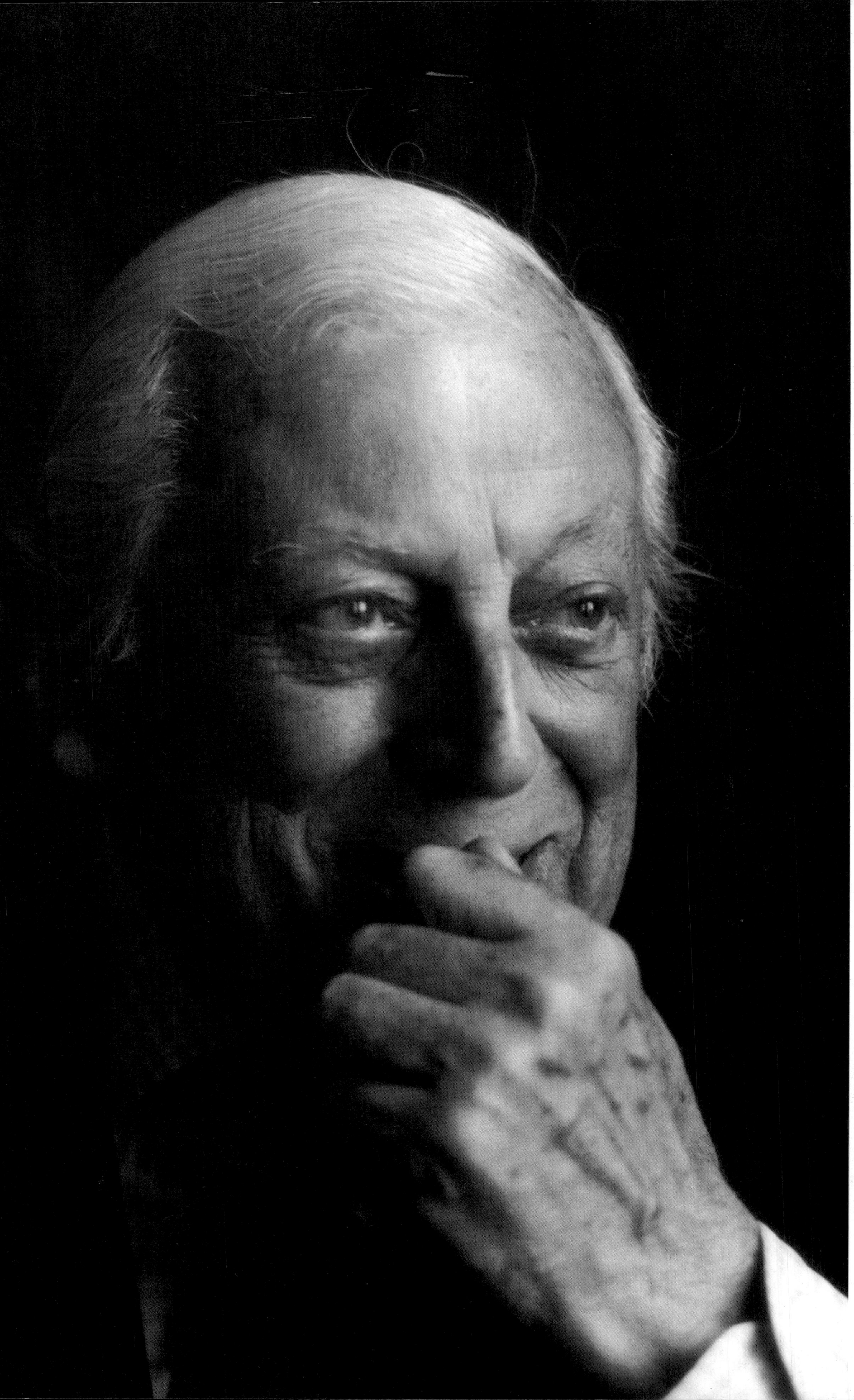

Alistair Cooke
BY
Lauren Bacall

He made my Sundays from 1952 to 1961 with *Omnibus*—He taught me about parts of America that were only names to me. He is my lifeline when I live in London with his Sunday morning BBC talks from America.

He knows more than almost anyone I have ever known—certainly more about America than most Americans.

He has the most astounding—awe-inspiring—jaw-dropping mind—be it history—*anything* to do with current events—anything to do with books—both fiction and non.

A man of words whose thirst for knowledge is unquenchable.

An extraordinary man—great wit—incredible charm—quite dazzling good looks—impeccable manners—an amazing capacity for friendship—plus, and you can't believe it—a mean jazz piano player.

Unhappily for the distaff side there is only one of him and he is taken by an almost equally fabulous Jane.

New York City *1990*

Carol Kane
BY
Diane Keaton

I don't know when I first started to call Carol "Whitey." People say Jack Nicholson coined the term on the set of *The Last Detail.* It fit her. Her shoulders, tiny bird things, were burdened with the weight of her long blonde hair. Her pale face enclosed her, like fog, her huge pastel blue eyes, even the air reflected her whiteness. The name stuck.

Before we became friends, I used to invision "Whitey" drifting off in a diamond-and-gold encrusted boat navigated by a handsome young Italian gondolier. As they slid through dark Venetian canals, I could dimly make out a porcelain "Whitey" reclining in a lace gown, her face masking a world of sorrow, her diaphanous hair flowing into a sea of tears, with only a jagged sliver of light to guide her through the dark clouds of her journey. I pictured a perfect marble "Whitey" drifting on a dream, floating into the amber light, armed with her brilliance.

Like Cattaneo's *Fortuna* with flying hair, her delicate feet stood on top of a bronze globe in a glorious stance of truth unveiled. But things changed. As I got to know "Whitey" the perfectly formed statue of my making began to crumble. Her polished marble arm got chipped near the elbow; in its place appeared skin, touchable stuff that left an indented pink mark when pressed. With her movable arm of flesh, she stopped looking like the virtuous Lady of the Lake drifting off in an allegorical hymn to feminine humility. She began to act like someone I might want to get to know, someone I could actually like, someone I could talk to. She stopped floating through walls, and dancing in the air. She started to open doors, and walk into rooms. Her other elbow shattered into little pieces leaving two arms that bent back and forth. One day I saw her pour me a cup of coffee out of a thermos at 5:30 in the morning. I saw her walk and talk for real. I saw her mouth slowly pull up into a smile. I saw her blush. I saw her have opinions. I saw her wait in line. I saw her sign her name on a petition against the war. I saw her stand against a winter sky, I saw her melt in the Florida heat. I saw closed doors whispering her song from under their cracks. I saw her cry in a little house outside Wilmington. I saw her when I was sad. I saw her sit with me in the dark. I saw her hold my hand. I saw that she was not going to Aspen for the winter.

Hollywood *1991*

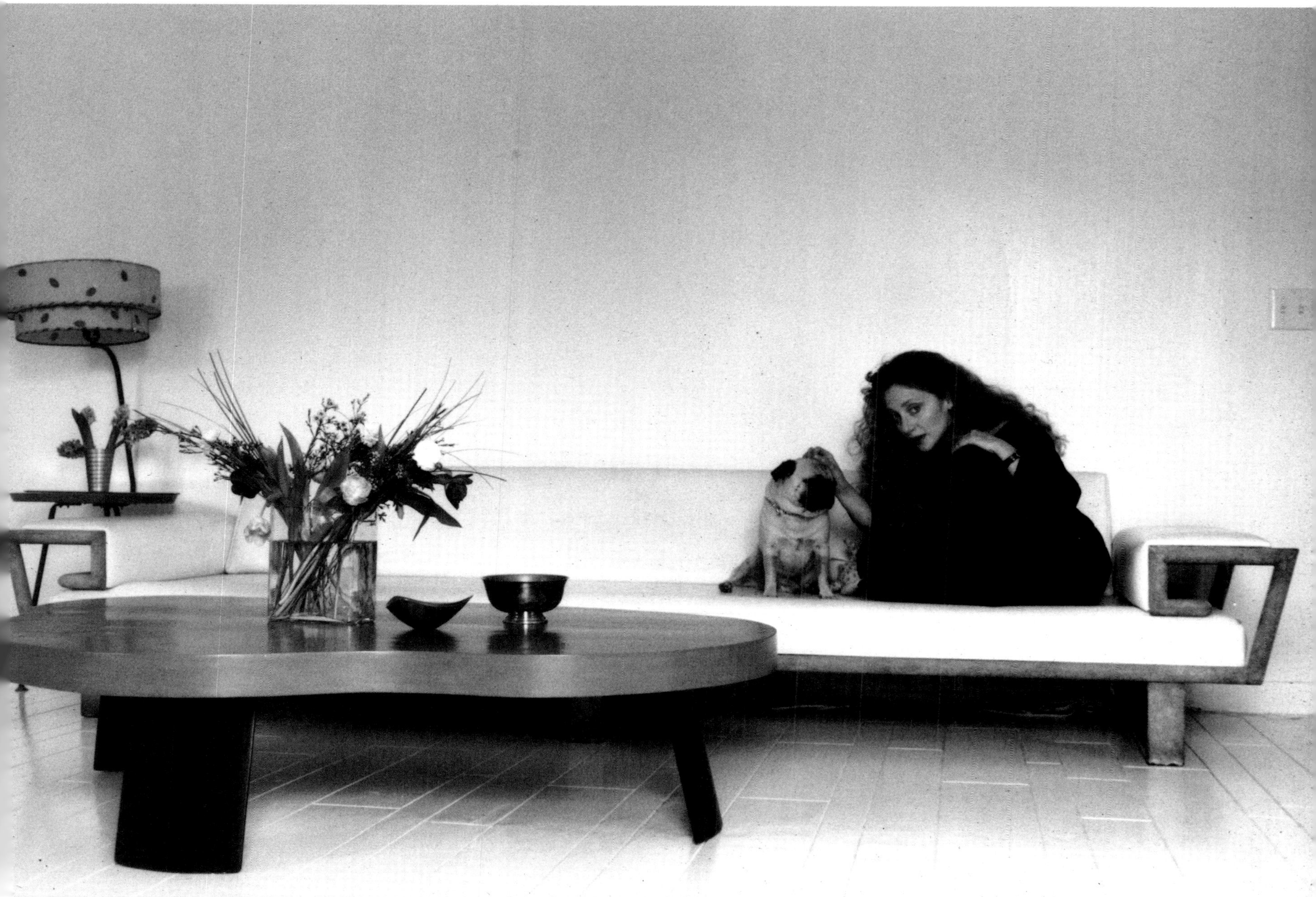

She was no longer a princess from a Maxfield Parrish illustration. Her skin lost the hard lustre of rock. She filled out, and opened up with the responsibilities of a long close friendship. No longer a superimposed myth, she became a unique, fully developed, beautiful woman, "Whitey" disappeared, and Carol was left standing in her place.

I still call Carol "Whitey" sometimes, but it's a holdover from the old days, when dazzling castles in the sky promised me and my friends shelter from past mistakes, and failures, and disappointments. It's a holdover from the old days when pretty took precedence over the less secure, less solid, but greatly loved flesh and blood vulnerability of a human being. I call her "Whitey" out of nostalgia, and memories of the past, sweet memories, but I don't regret Carol's imposed coat of stone peeling off layer by layer transforming her into the hand-clapping, foot-stomping, head-shaking, Carol of this world, this earth, this strange mix of uncertainty called life. I love Carol as a person, not as a look drifting off in the hush of a white cloud.

Hollywood 1991

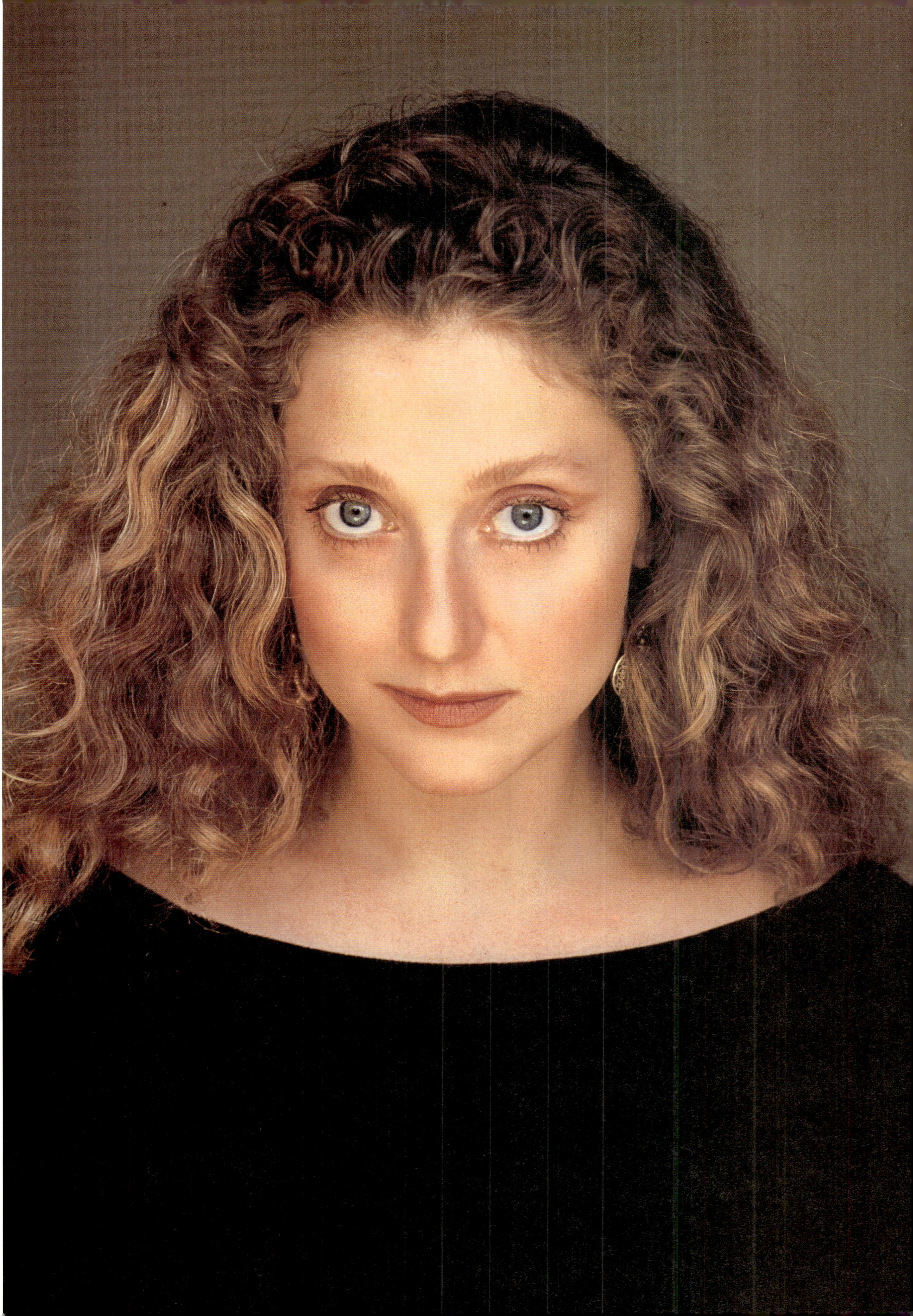

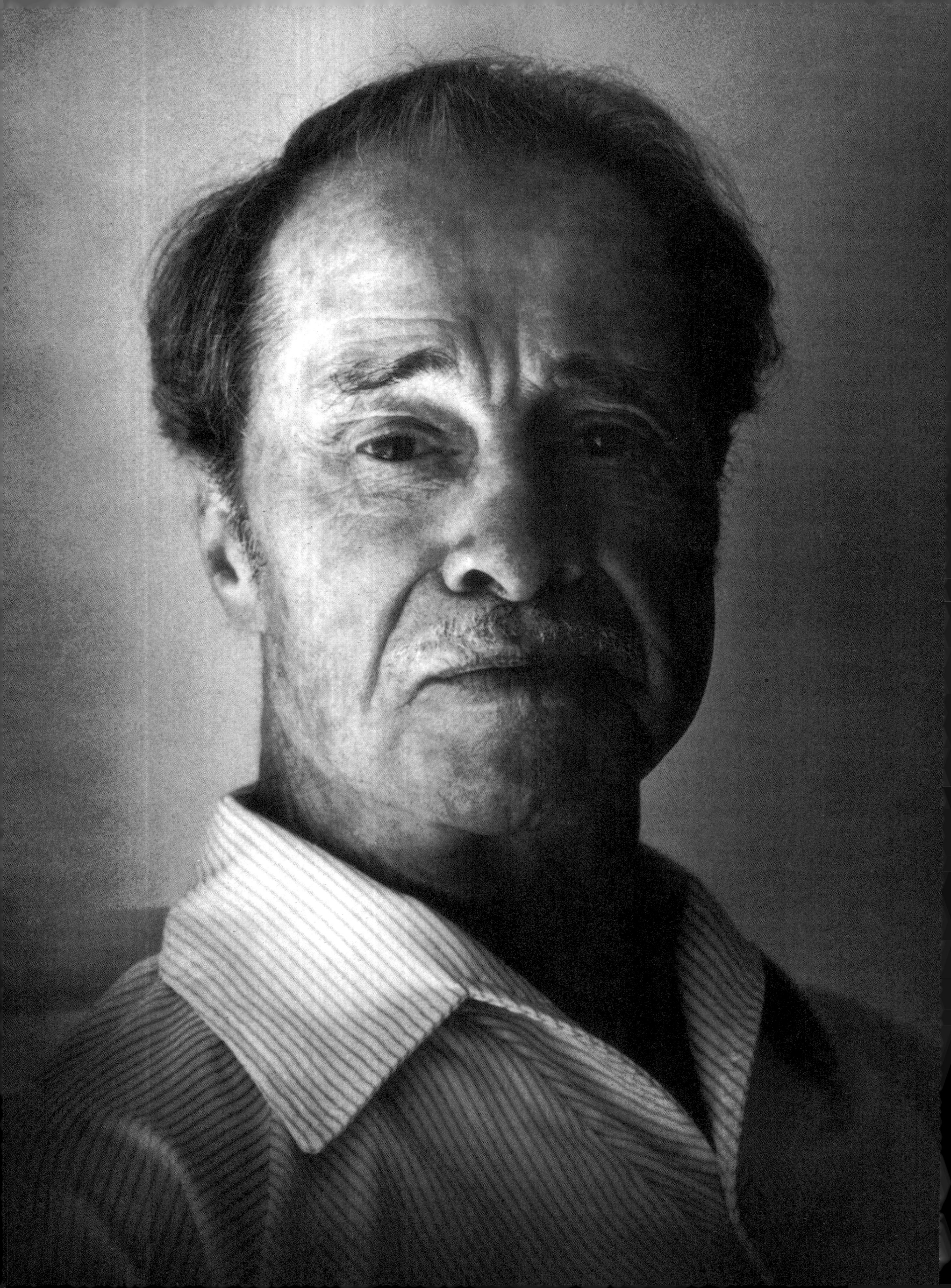

Don Ameche
BY
Alice Faye

I was so happy when Don won the Academy Award for *Cocoon*. You see, he is so versatile—so full of spirit—so full of joy—he is *so* good an actor—and all these years he has made it all look so easy. That's how good he is. Unfortunately, there is a tendency to take such excellence for granted because he makes it seem as if anyone can do it when, in fact, it demands a real artist to make it all appear so simple.

We shared six movies together in the 30s and 40s at 20th Century Fox—we also toured together in *Good News* in the 70s—and, while a very private guy, he was so professional, so expert, so full of fun.

You see, besides being so good at what he does, he is a dear. He is a grand old shoe!

Santa Monica, California *1990*

Kyle MacLachlan
BY
Isabella Rossellini

I met Kyle at a dinner with David Lynch in New York. I guess they asked me to dinner to find out a bit more about me and to see if I could be Dorothy Vallens in *Blue Velvet.* After dinner we went to David's hotel and rehearsed and improvised scenes from the script. David sat in a corner looking at our performances—once in a while he would interrupt and give us direction. Kyle extended a great gentleness and the scenes, quite brutal and shocking, weren't difficult to play with him.

I was hired for the part and a few weeks later I joined David, Kyle, Laura Dern, Dennis Hopper, Dean Stockwell, Jack Nance and Brad Dourif just to mention a few of the marvelous people I met and worked with.

Some people say *Blue Velvet* is a devilish film. To me it was like paradise to work with all of these talented, fun, sensitive and great originals. Kyle distinguished himself with his graciousness—it is not an adjective I use often, yet it seems to fit Kyle perfectly. He is a very gracious man.

Studio City, California 1990

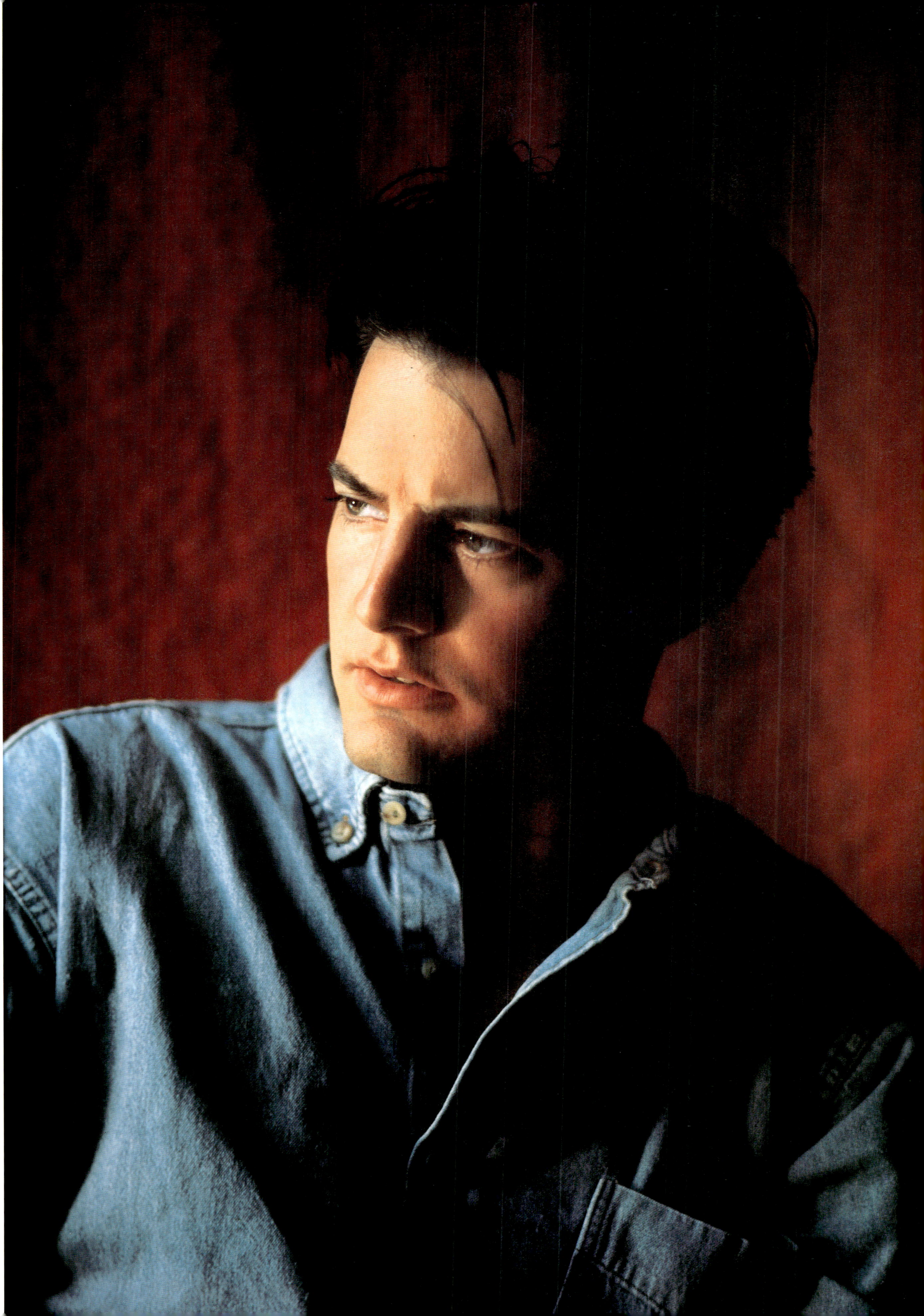

Elizabeth Taylor
BY
Arthur B. Krim

Elizabeth Taylor is a woman of extraordinary beauty, talent and commitment; her entire life is an example of how to use fame to bring compassion and aid to those less fortunate than she.

Elizabeth Taylor
BY
Mathilde Krim

To most, Elizabeth Taylor is the quintessential distant star whose flawless beauty and talent, but little else, are altogether familiar. Few have known her well enough to have discerned in her the down-to-earth, no-nonsense woman whose healthy instincts and sense of humor make her an astute judge of people and endow her with a healthy business and political sense. Still fewer people know personally of her loyalty as a friend or her capacity for tenderness.

Her extraordinary empathy for the unfortunate led her to assume the National Chairmanship of the American Foundation for AIDS Research (AmFAR) at a time when the cause of AIDS was profoundly unpopular and dangerously evaded. People with AIDS the world over have no better friend; nor I, who have the privilege of working with her on their behalf.

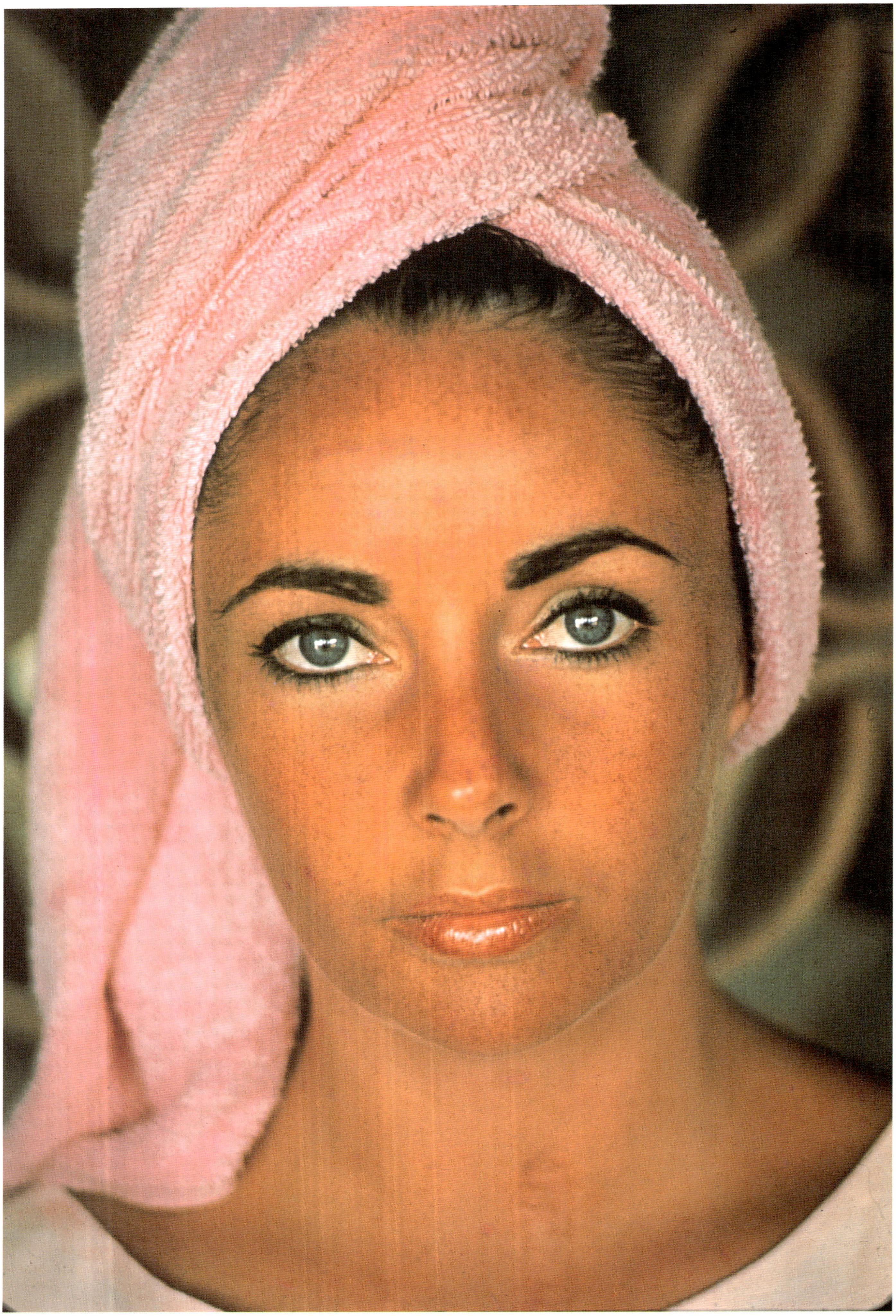

Puerto Vallarta, Mexico 1964

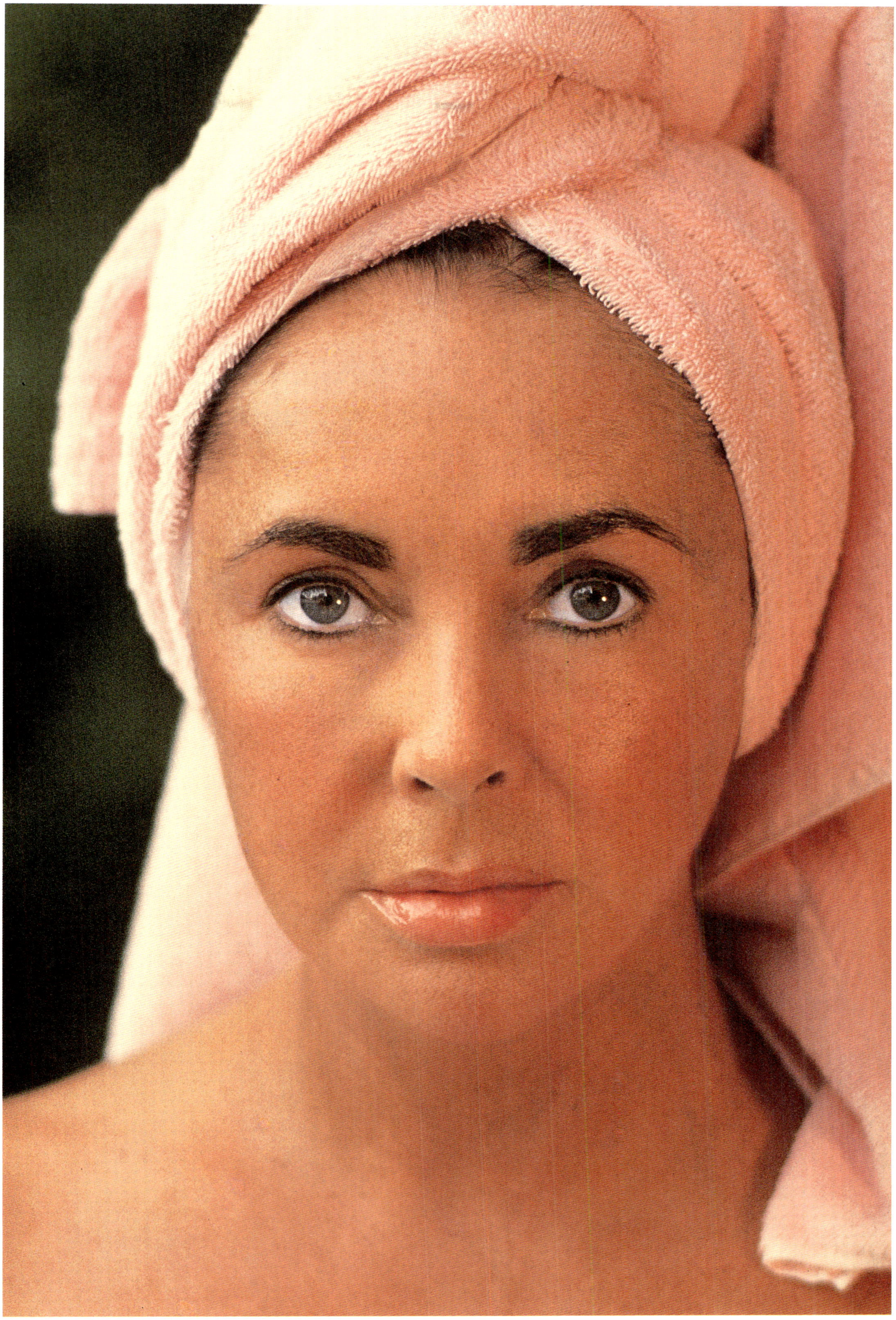

Bel Air, California *1991*

Howard Dietz
BY
Barbara Cook

The plot can be hot
Simply teeming with sex
A gay divorcée who is after her ex
It can be Oedipus Rex
Where a chap kills his father
And causes a lot of bother

Howard Dietz was one of the most famous wits of his time. Many people with that kind of wit use it to wound people, but Howard used his humor to gentle me, to charm me and to ease many a painful situation.

He had heart.

And he wasn't afraid to show it. We just have to be ready to hear it.

Dancing in the dark
Till the tune ends
We're dancing in the dark
And it soon ends
We're waltzing in the wonder
Of why we're here
Time hurries by
We're here
And gone.

Sands Point, Long Island *1958*

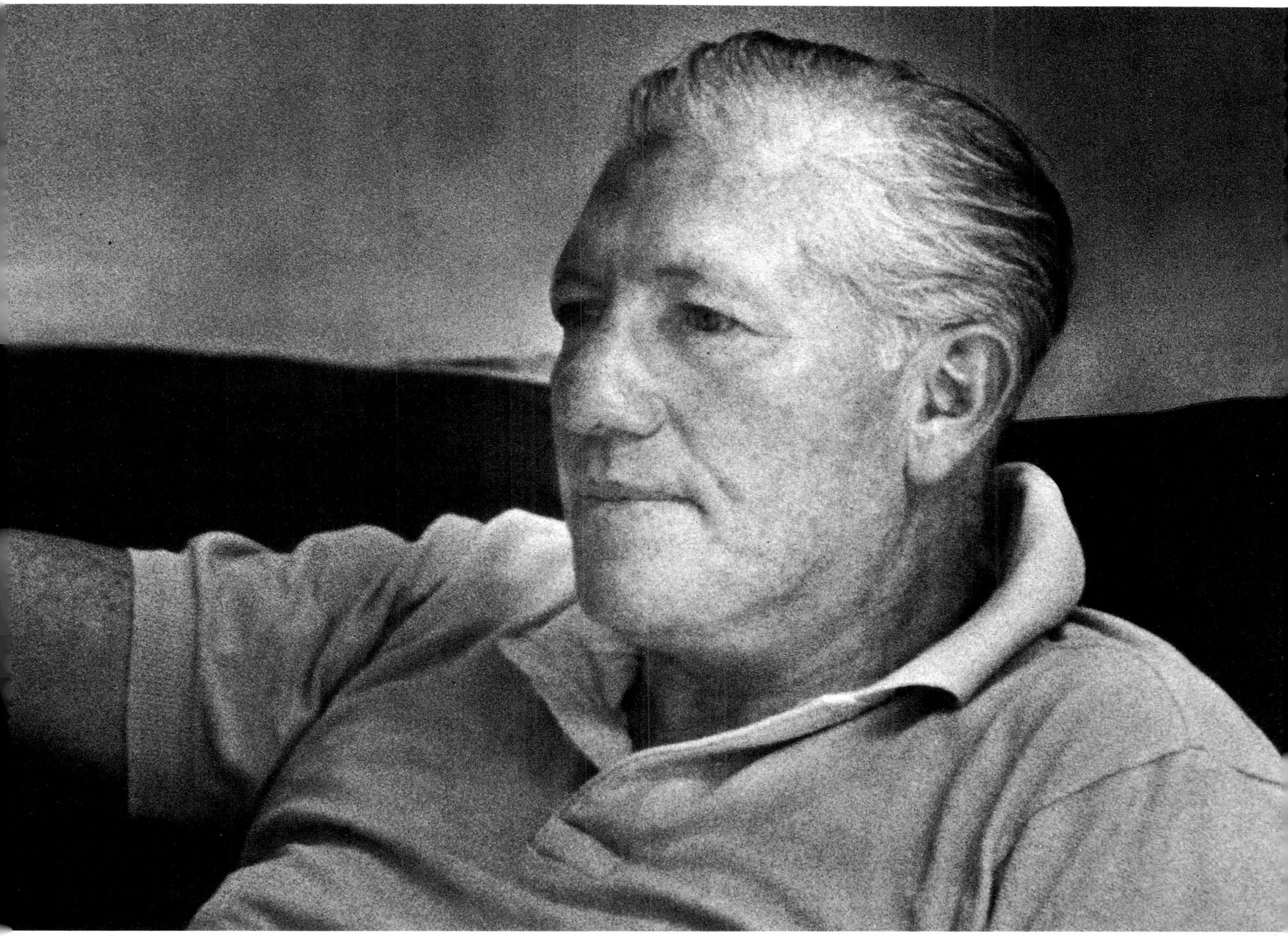

Greer Garson
BY
Gregory Peck

I called her Big Red. Not to her face, although I'm sure she would have been amused. But at the time, 1946, Greer was the Queen of MGM, Academy Award winner for *Mrs. Miniver,* and Hollywood's Grande Dame, serene atop the pedestal L. B. Mayer had created for her.

Greer was also a mischievous clown, a delicious comedienne, and a smashing beauty. With her English (or Northern Irish) rose petal pink complexion, her startling red hair, and a figure that, although never flaunted, was unquestionably a 10, Greer was a lot of woman.

I, on the other hand, was a new boy in town. Leland Hayward, my killer agent, had left town to become a Broadway producer. One of his last capers was to sign me up for pictures with Jennifer Jones, Ingrid Bergman, and Greer Garson on the theory that they already had worldwide followings, and that I would thus ride to fame on their petticoats, so to speak.

Greer was, along with all of her other attributes, a great actress. I was impressed, a little intimidated at first, but soon I learned that she was, off the pedestal, a wonderfully warm and lovable woman. She was aware that the crew on the sound stage were a bit awestruck in Mrs. Miniver's presence. She had a way of cracking the ice with her quick sense of humor, straight from English Music Halls. We all felt we were in on a well-kept secret: The Queen of MGM was a redheaded clown.

Naturally I fell a little bit in love with her then. How not? She was entrancing. I love her still, and still think of her as the incomparable Big Red.

Indian Wells, California 1990

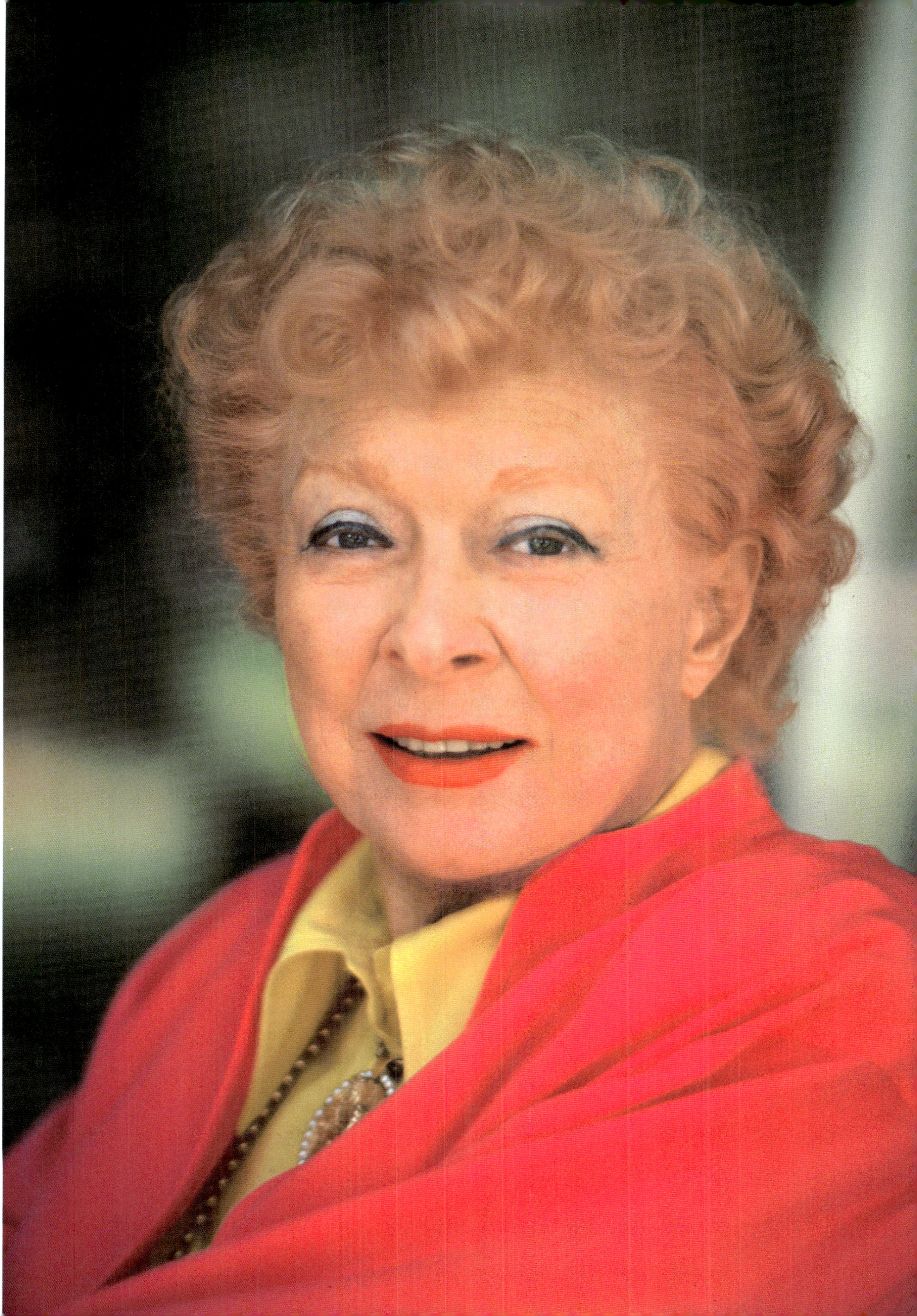

Anthony Perkins
BY
Sophia Loren

Meeting for the first time Tony—
it's like facing a difficult puzzle:
when you solve it, it's a treasure.

Los Angeles *1957*

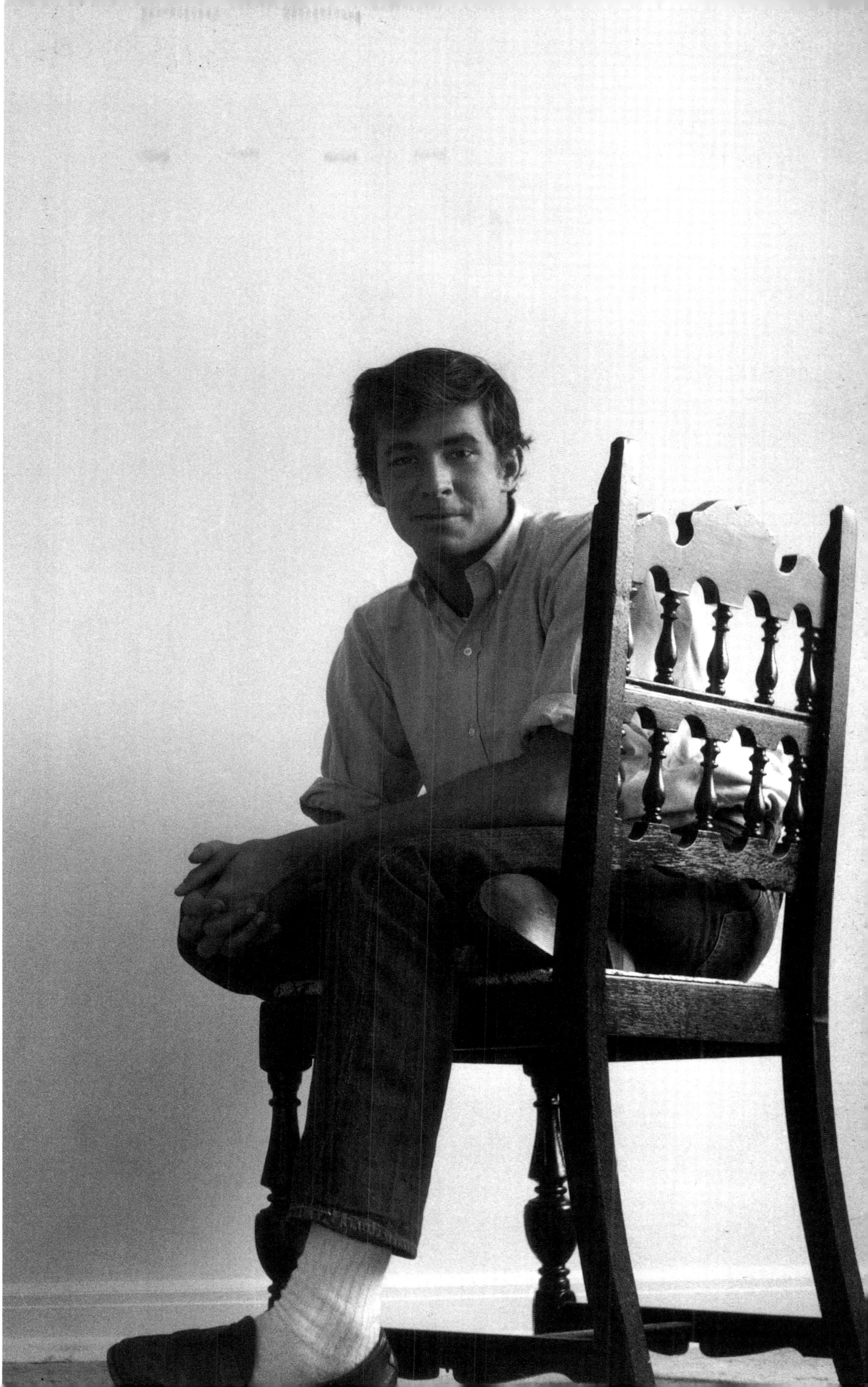

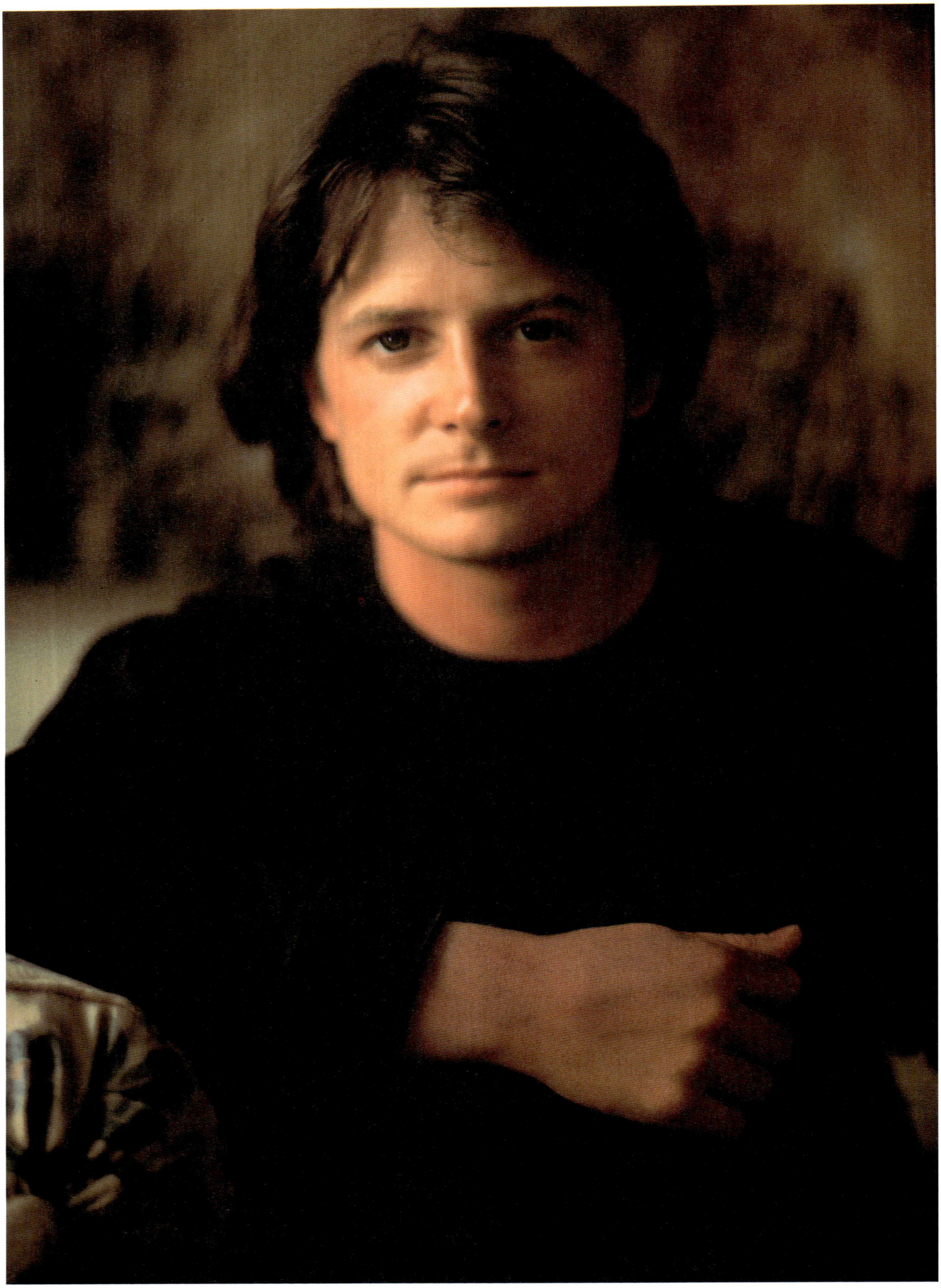

Michael J. Fox
BY
James Woods

So we're standing in the middle of Times Square, both covered in blood, both sneaking a smoke, though he quit last year, and it's about four o'clock in the morning. I said to him, "How do we do this, after what, four straight months of it? You've got a sore throat and swollen glands, I've got a broken finger and an injured shoulder, we haven't really slept too much, and we're here at four in the morning, in the rain, and we're, what, doing a *comedy*?!!?"

And he turns to me with that Cheshire grin that sold almost a billion dollars' worth of tickets over the past four years and says, "Hey, Babe—May I call you 'Babe'?—we're professionals!"

I love Michael J. Fox. He is a professional. And he's bright (yes, he reads and when he reads, it's Neil Sheehan and not Jackie Collins, thank you very much), he's warm and, oh yes, he's funny.

Some people are genuinely funny and some people are professional comedians. Michael just happens to be both. He makes people laugh and they laugh because they admire him, they identify with him and, just a little bit, they envy him.

And envy him they should. As he himself is the first to admit, this guy won the lottery. He has a great career, a great wife and kid, his folks are simple down-home people, he's a good friend, and he owns, by latest reckoning, a couple of states by now. He has so many houses, they don't make a key ring big enough (rim shot, "Thank you, thank you").

Just a little over a decade ago, he was a street kid in Vancouver, with the second biggest hubcap collection in British Columbia. Just kidding. Maybe in the top ten, though. At any rate, folks, he came, in the relative nepotistic atmosphere of Hollywood, from nothing, and is now one of our leading young actors and one of our biggest box office stars of any age, any time. And just when you think you've got him figured out, he runs off to Thailand to do a great piece of acting in a Vietnam story with another fine young actor, Sean Penn.

Yeah, the kid has it all. And in the humble opinion of his friend here, he deserves it.

New York City 1990

Chuck Jones
BY
Ray Bradbury

There was a time a few years ago when the phone rang and a voice would say, "This is Chuck Jones. Did you know . . . ?"

And I would say, "No, Chuck, I *didn't* know. *Tell* me."

And Chuck would tell.

Sometimes I would say, "Have you been reading the *Encyclopedia Britannica* again?"

The answer was always yes.

Chuck Jones was and is just about the world's greatest encyclopedist. Which is why his animated films are richer and funnier than almost all of the others in recent history.

Friends brought us together in the early summer of 1966. It was instant love. By the autumn, we were busy at work on a full-length animated feature. It all came about over a plenteous supply of martinis one afternoon when Chuck suggested there were enough brains between the two of us to make at least one picture. "On *what*?" I asked.

"How about Halloween?" Chuck said. "That's *your* holiday, right? Your favorite month, October? There never has been a good film on the history of All Hallows. Kids nowadays don't know anything about the root system of the holiday. Last year, some kids knocked on my door and cried, 'Trick or Treat.' I replied: 'Trick!' Which confounded them. One boy turned, ran out on the lawn, and stood on his head."

That did it.

I wrote the screenplay of *The Halloween Tree* for Chuck. At which point, MGM collapsed all of its animation tents and crept away in the night. Unemployed, I wrote the screenplay into a novella. Someday, Chuck and I hope, we will get on with making the film.

Newport, California 1990

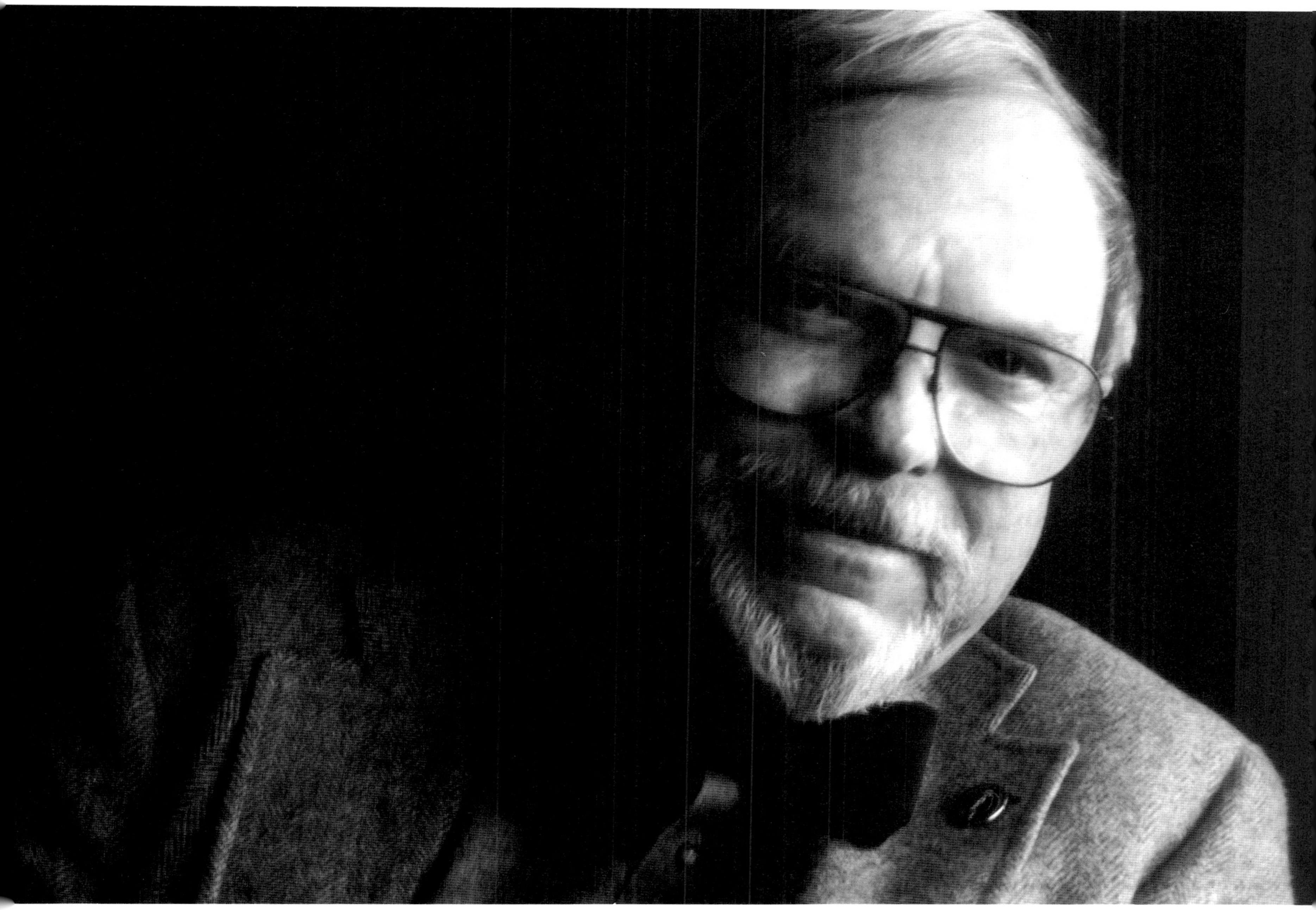

Meanwhile, along the way, I introduced Chuck to Steven Spielberg. "Listen to Chuck," I told Steven, "He has the uncanniest sense of timing in the entire animation field." "I'll *listen*!" Spielberg cried. "I'm making a comedy, *1941*. I'll need him. I'll call him."

Well, Spielberg never did.

If you saw *1941*, you know that what was missing was Chuck Jones.

There are many similar film disasters out there, which could have been saved by him. He knows exactly how to run off a cliff, hesitate, look down, realize he stands on empty space, show terrible surprise, and fall. That talent can't be taught. It is genetic. If his acolytes learn it at all, it is slowly.

Not as often as in the old days, but Chuck still calls me just before sunset, or at high noon.

Did I know that a plague was spread in an East Coast harbor because Egyptian linen mummy wrappings were used on imports from overseas? I didn't know that. Did I know that when Verrazano, the Italian explorer, visited the American continent in the sixteenth century, on behalf of Francis the First, he made landfall at Kitty Hawk? I didn't know that either.

How about grave robbers? Had I counted how many times they kidnapped Lincoln's body from his tomb? I hadn't. Three times. "I'll be damned," I said.

And so it still goes, twenty-six years later.

I remain the student, waiting for my teacher to phone.

What will he teach me next? Is he up to the *X*'s or *Y*'s in the *Encyclopedia*? And when he finishes *Z*, will he start over? God, I hope so.

With *your* telephone, you should be so lucky.

But don't call him. You can be sure as dammit, Chuck Jones will call you.

❏

David Mamet
BY
Joseph Mantegna

ACT ONE

Scene One

Roddy and Joe are talking on the phone.

Roddy: . . . so I was wondering if you might consider writing some comments to accompany a photo I've done of David Mamet.

Joe: I . . .

Roddy: It's for my new book.

Joe: Uh . . . I . . . uh . . .

Roddy: Say whatever you like. A couple of sentences, an essay.

Joe: Yes, I . . . (Pause)

Roddy: Excuse me?

Joe: I . . . uh . . . yes, of course, I uh, I'm flattered . . . I'll, uh . . . of course, thank you.

Scene Two

A few nights later. Joe is at his desk.

Joe: (Writing) "What can one say about a seventeen-year-old friend?" (Tears up page) Fuck! (Writing) "What can one say about a friend of seventeen *years*?" (Pause; tears up page) Obviously not much. (Writing) "There are probably a lot of writers who quote Jung as well as they shoot out candles with a .44 magnum pistol, I just don't know them." (Tears up page; pause) (Writing) "David Mamet writes like Shake and Bake makes chicken, 'no muss, no fuss'." (Tears up page) (*Sotto*) O God.

Scene Three

Roddy and Joe on phone.

Joe: Roddy . . . I, uh . . . I . . . well, they say a picture is worth a thousand words so maybe, well . . . you know . . . (Pause; silence) Roddy . . . Roddy . . .

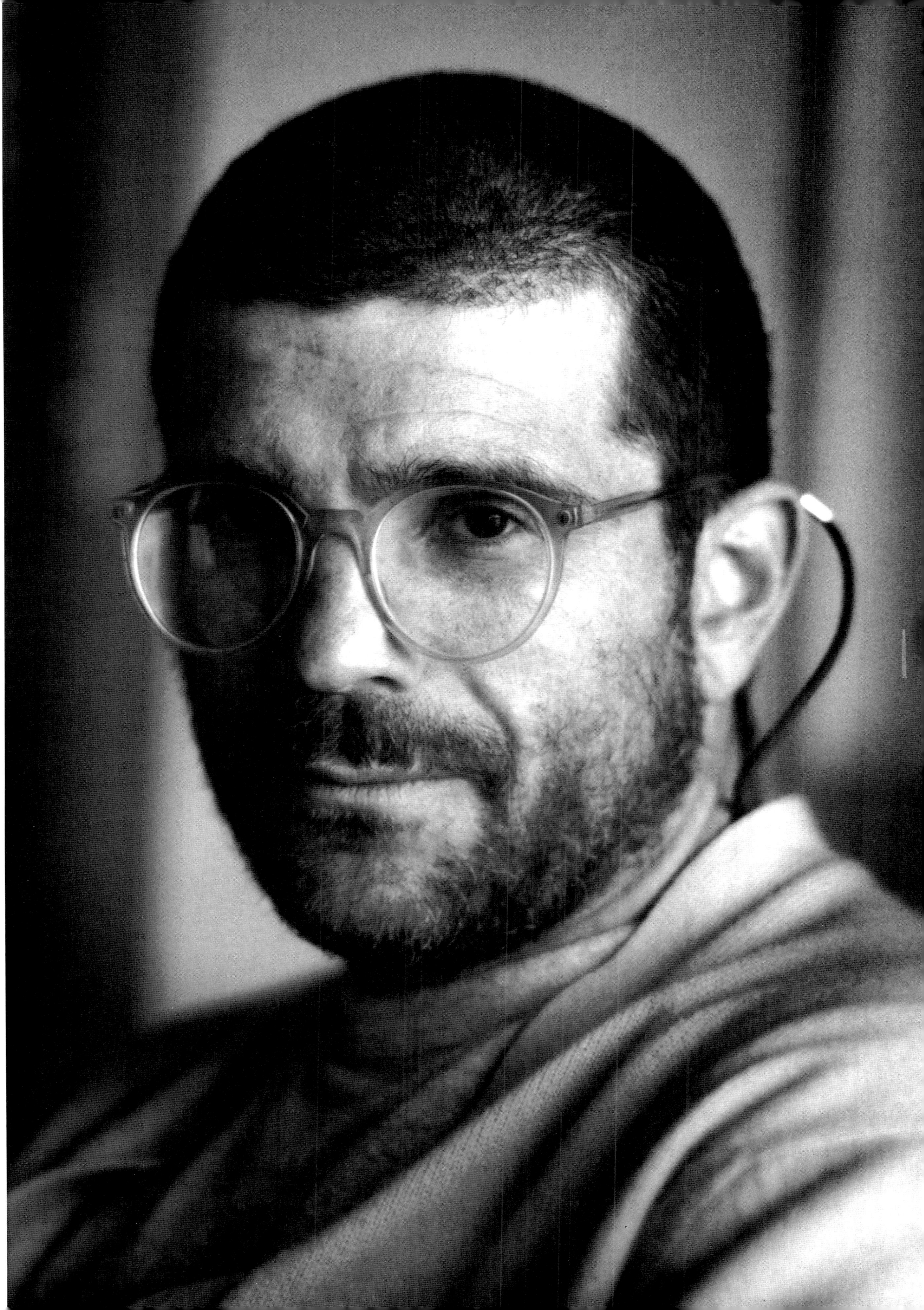

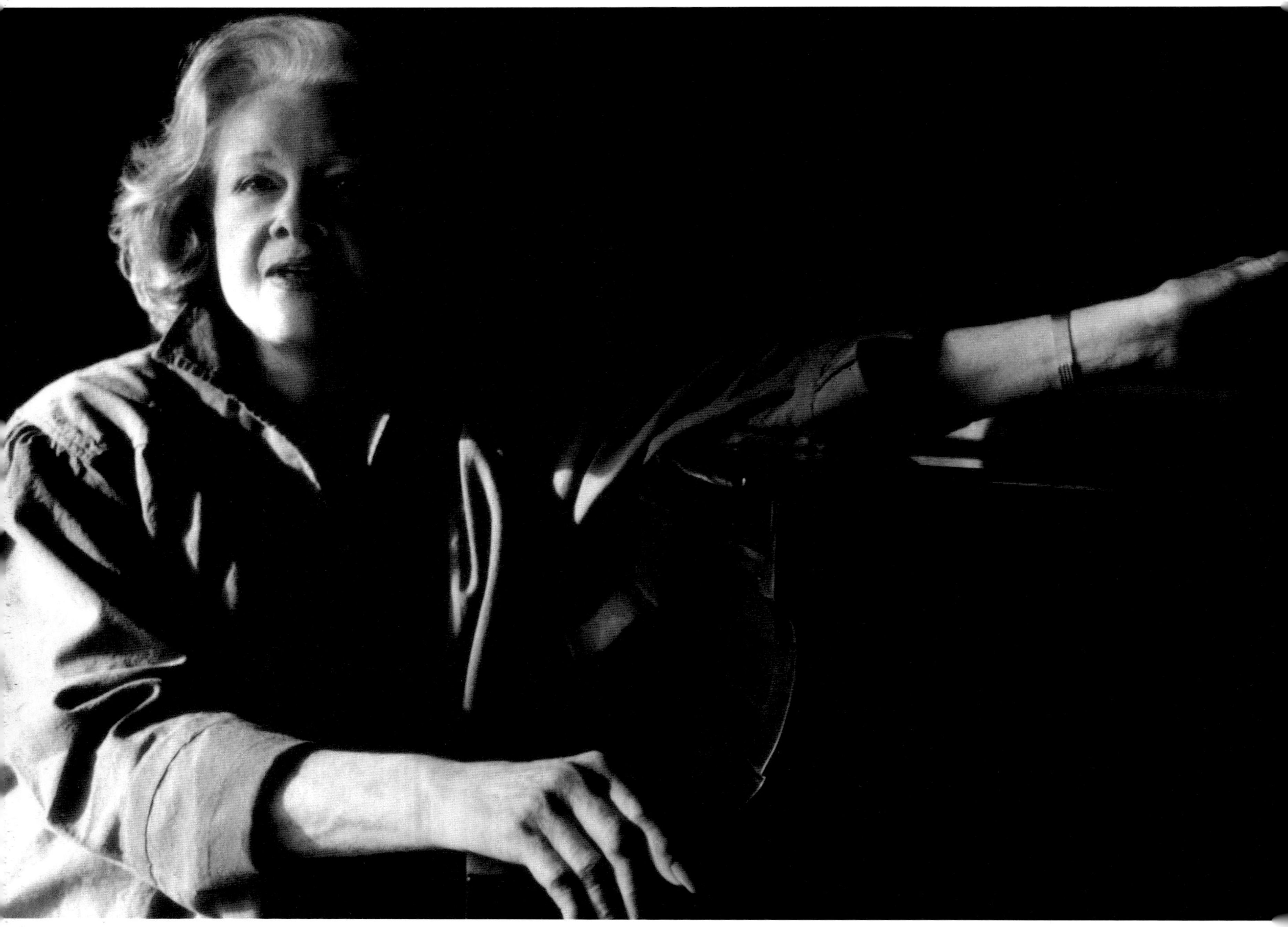

Jo Stafford

BY

Rosemary Clooney

The Voice says it all:
Beautiful—Pure—Straightforward—No Artifice—
Matchless Intonation. Instantly Recognizable.
Those things describe the woman too.
You think you really know her
But then she becomes Darlene Edwards.

Century City, California *1991*

Merle Oberon
BY
Burgess Meredith

Merle Oberon lived many lives in many places and although she had her share of ups and downs she lived gracefully and bravely.

I was not a close friend of the lady, but over the years events brought us together from time to time.

I remember we met for the first time on a movie set. The picture was called *That Uncertain Feeling*. Our director was the great Ernst Lubitsch. Ernst was a wonderfully gifted man . . . Viennese. Between scenes—instead of giving us direction—he played the piano and told relevant stories. By some magic, the music and the stories gave us the clue of how to act each scene.

Returning from Europe, while I was still a soldier, I briefly married a friend of Merle's—Paulette Goddard. We saw Merle often during those hectic post-war years. Merle had a faintly British accent. One day I asked her about her childhood—where did she come from? She shook her head and put a finger on my lips and said "I never think about that, Burgess . . . and neither should you."

Curiously, I got a similar answer from Paulette. Those star-lit girls kept their past separate from their present. You might say they were historically selective.

In the late forties Merle suffered some sort of skin-poisoning on her lovely face. She told us the doctors declared it was "make-up poisoning."

During her recovery, Merle married a cameraman named Lucien Ballard. They lived for a while in a sheltered house high above the Trancas cliffs in California.

She told Paulette: "I want to stay out of focus until I'm presentable."

Before and after that healing time, Merle married various men. I don't remember in what order they came, but the wise and worldly Sir Alexander Korda of England was one of her husbands. The rich and generous Bruno Pagliai of Acapulco was another. There may have been others.

Malibu, California *1965*

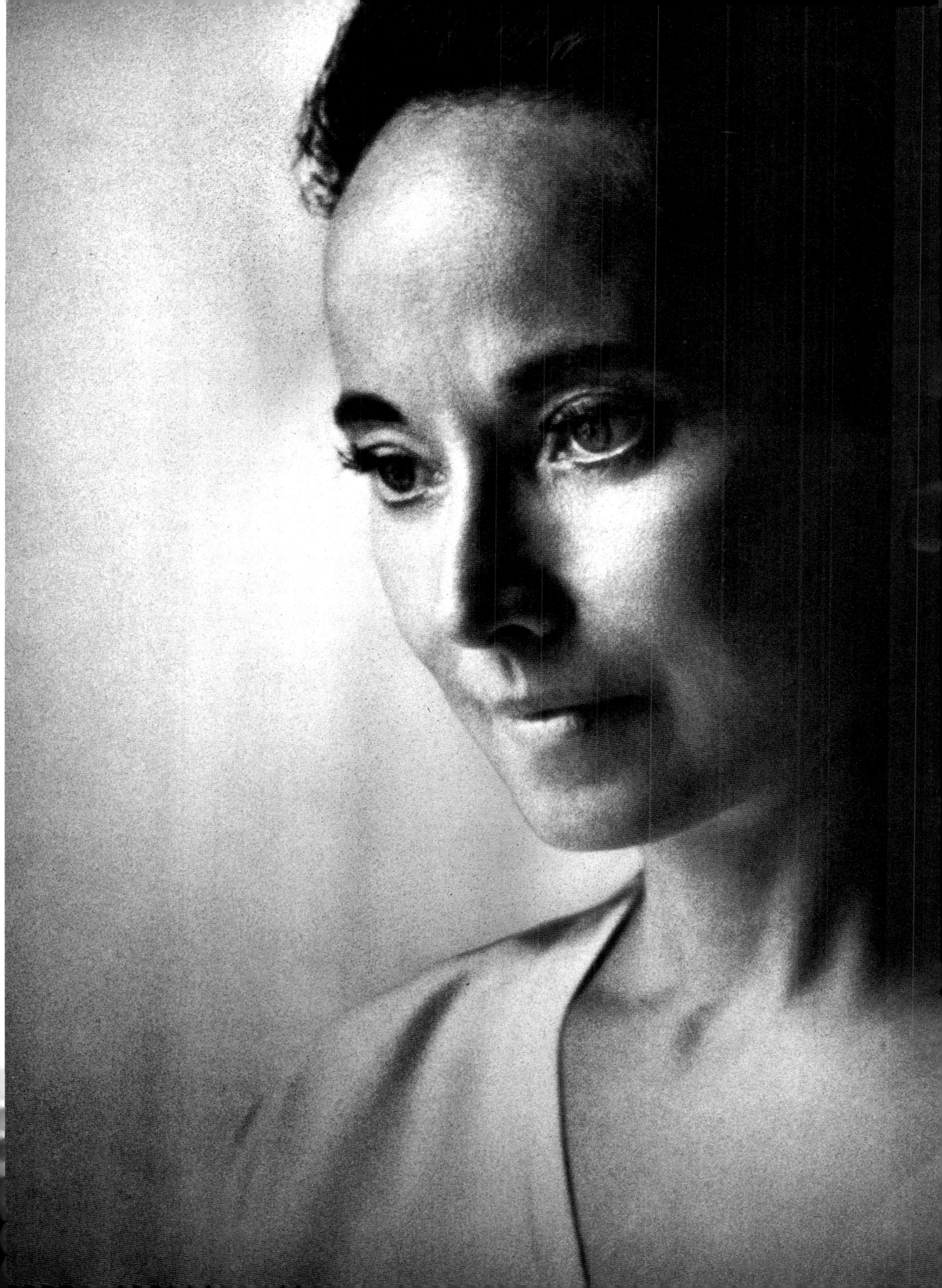

Finally, however, in a happy ending, Merle bought a modest beach house a few hundred feet from where I lived (and still do) on Old Malibu Colony Road. She married a gentle, handsome young man from Holland named Rob Wolders.

That Malibu Colony house was the last home she lived in, and Rob was the last man she married. The last man she loved. As I say—it was a happy ending. Rob was thoughtful and protective. If I look out the window where I'm writing this, I can still see the two of them—Rob and Merle—walking hand-in-hand down the beach, quietly talking, quietly smiling.

During that time they made a film together—the two of them. She said to me, "The movie isn't great, but I like it better than all the others." The movie was never released.

In Malibu she occasionally "entertained" as we say in Hollywood. But mostly her life became quiet, uneventful . . . finally peaceful.

The day she died, Rob asked a few of us over and we sat on the patio talking now and then, but mostly listening to what the ocean waves had to say. We stayed many hours.

So, as I told you, I was not close to the lady, but from time to time I happened to be around when important events happened.

Maybe one day, in the starry future, she'll finally answer my question to her: "What country did you come from? What blood ran through your veins?"

Or maybe she won't. It's none of my business, after all. But whatever her heritage, it served her well.

As I was writing these paragraphs, word came through that Merle's good friend, Paulette Goddard, died. (April 1990)

They were both unforgettable. And to me, at least, they were both touched by mystery.

❑

Charlton Heston
BY
Whoopi Goldberg

"Why," some folks asked me, "would you, of all people, want to write about Charlton Heston? He's so . . ."

And I'd stop them and say there are two Charlton Hestons that I know of, but only one I plan to write about. And it isn't the political one.

Will Penny, A Touch of Evil, The Omega Man, Soylent Green, and *The Ten Commandments* are five of my favorite films. I truly love watching him work because he's always so present. He's such a pro, an artist, and in many respects for me, an ideal.

The other Charlton Heston kind of makes me wonder what else happened on the way up to get those commandments—hummmmm! What a piece of work is man.

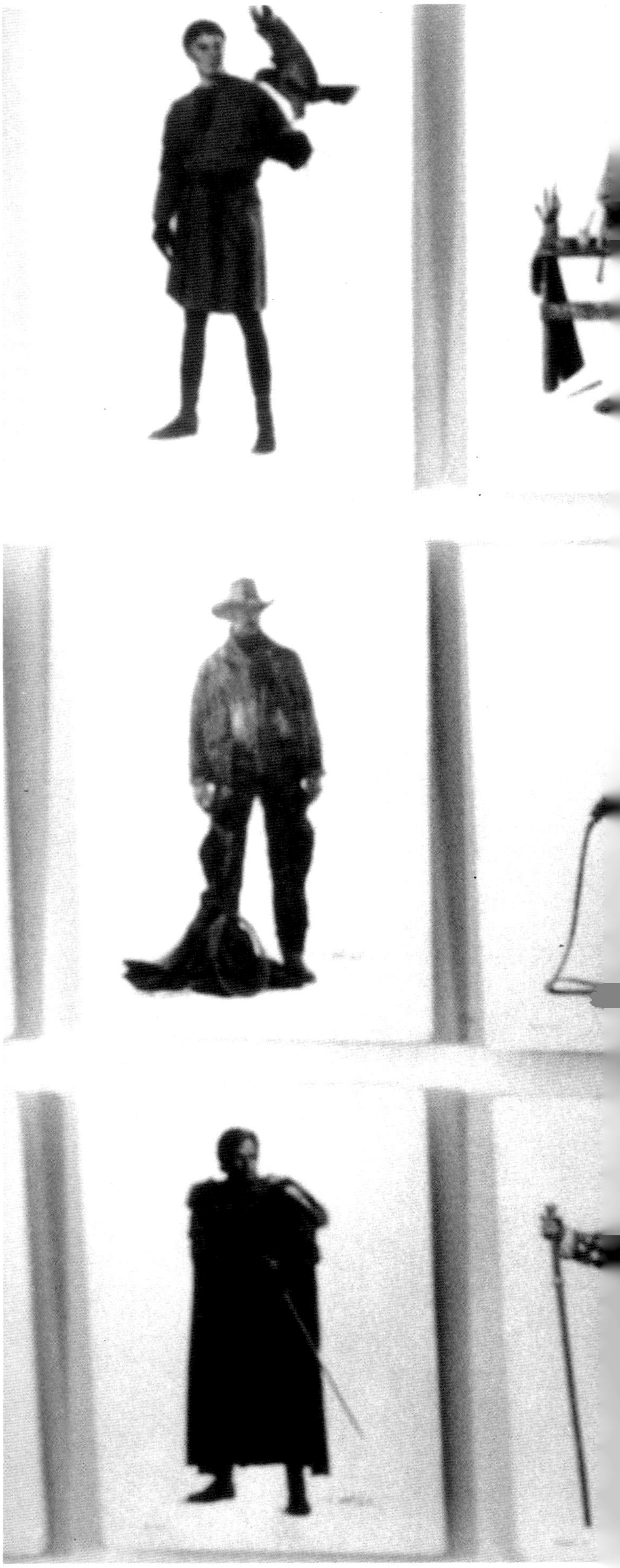

Beverly Hills *1990*

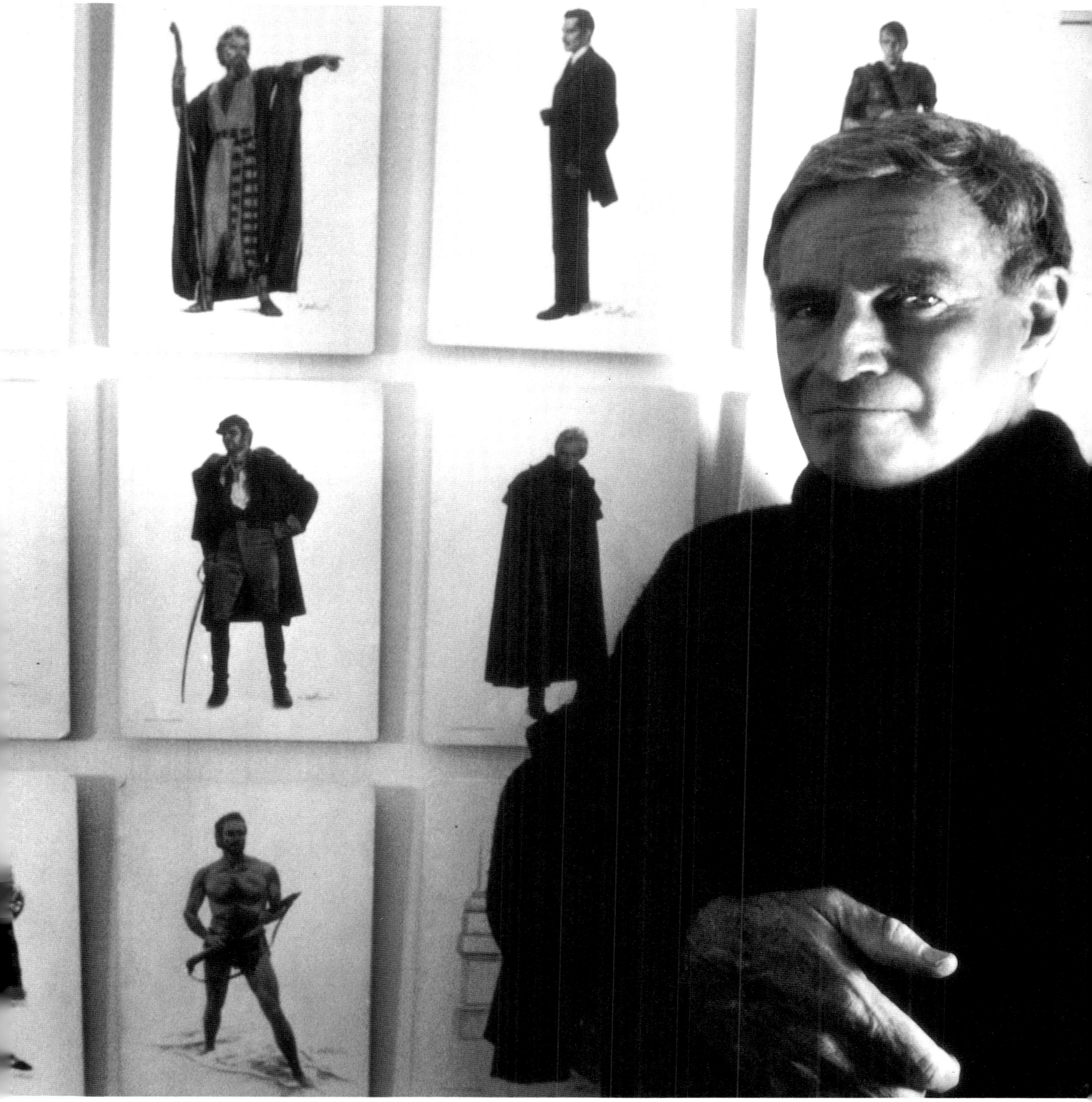

Arthur Miller
BY
Alan Ayckbourn

Arthur Miller is the complete playwright. He plots with his head and writes with his heart. He is also tall, charming and, according to a lot of women I know, extremely attractive sexually. Nonetheless, I still admire him greatly.

New York City 1990

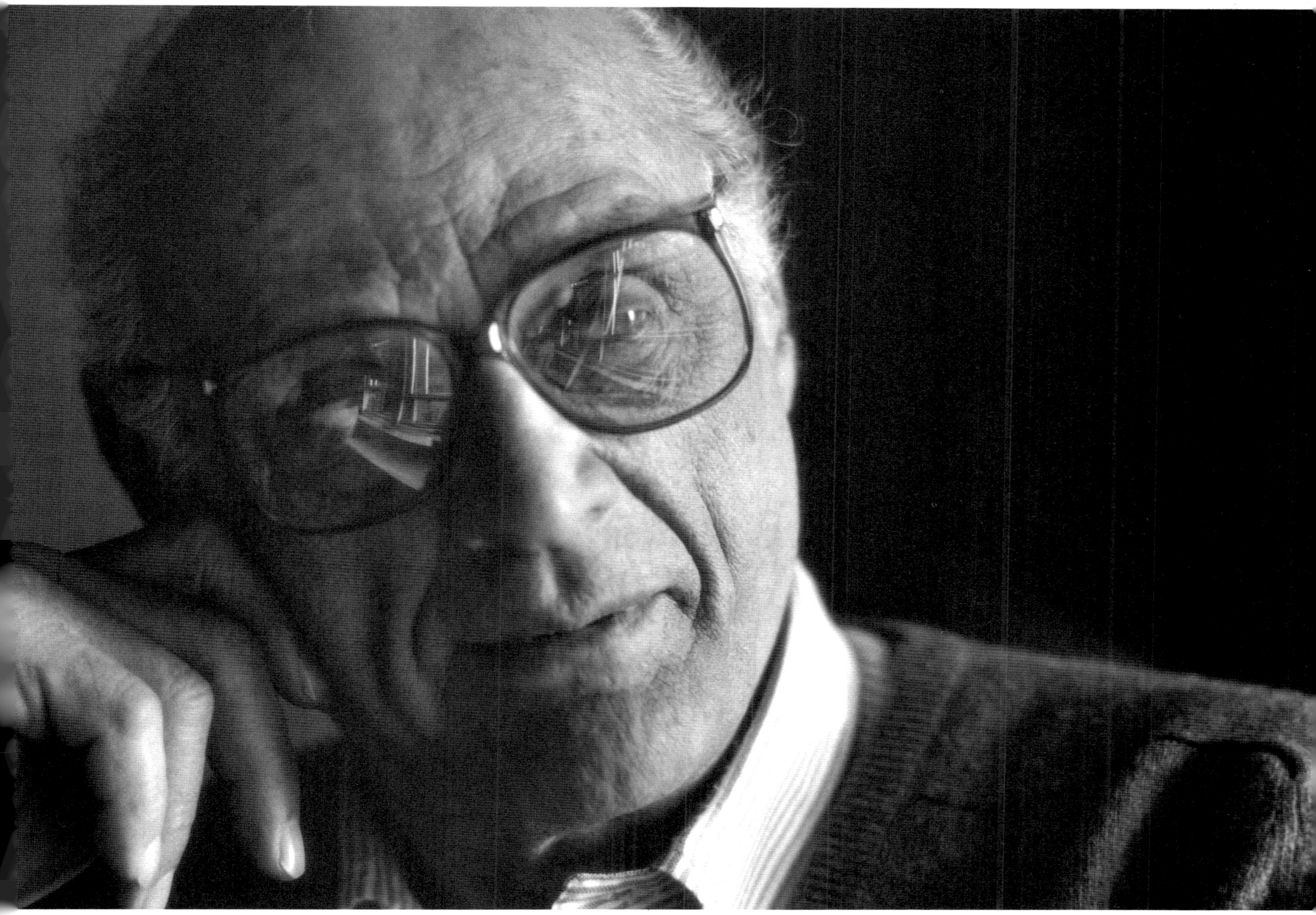

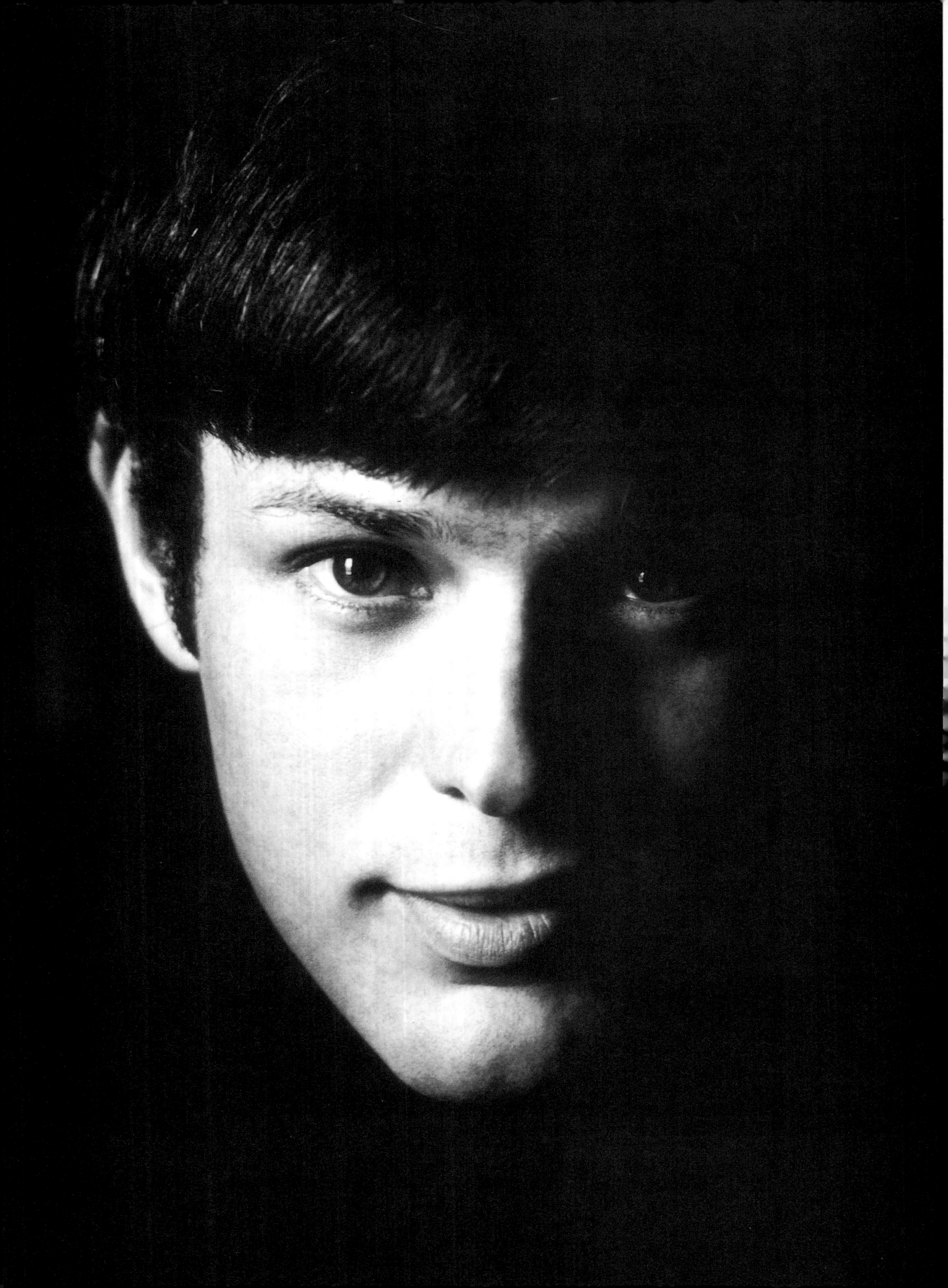

Bruce Weber
BY
Jeff Bridges

One of my most creative and pleasurable photo shoots was with Bruce on *Nadine*. He did something I had never done before with a still photographer. Bruce filmed what he called a "mock" movie. Caterers and catering were set up. Bruce asked Kim Basinger, my *Nadine* co-star, and me, "What kind of movie do you want to make?" I paint and play the guitar, so he took pictures of me painting him taking my picture. He created a great atmosphere very much like a fine film director would.

New York City *1967*

Robert Mitchum
BY
David Mamet

A line of dialogue is a little bit like a duck decoy. It's not supposed to look like a duck, it's supposed to look like a duck to a duck. The written dialogue isn't meant to sound like human conversation—it is meant to be a sketch of human behavior which, when said by the actor, will awaken some sort of recognition both in him and in his audience.

As such, there is not much that can be done to aid the dialogue. If the play is bad, "helping the lines" is only going to make it worse. If the play is good, the lines don't need any help. The mediocre actor treats his lines with taste, and respect, and approaches them in a spirit of invention. The great actor does none of these things. He invents nothing, he denies nothing; he says the lines as simply as possible, and he means them.

This gives him the quality which used to be called "dangerousness." When we see it, we can't stop watching.

And when we see it, it's not the lines we respond to, and not "the way they are said," but the spectacle of someone *meaning* them. "I love you. I hate you. I need you. Don't take another step. I have some bad news."

We respond to the show of courage on the screen, because it makes us feel the possibility of our own courage.

"Yes," we say, "that's how *I'd* act, there. Yes. It is."

And it seems so obvious to us, and so simple. We never call it Great Acting. But it certainly is. We don't recollect Robert Mitchum's performances as "something that he felt"—we remember something that he *did,* and something that *we* felt.

Studio City, California *1990*

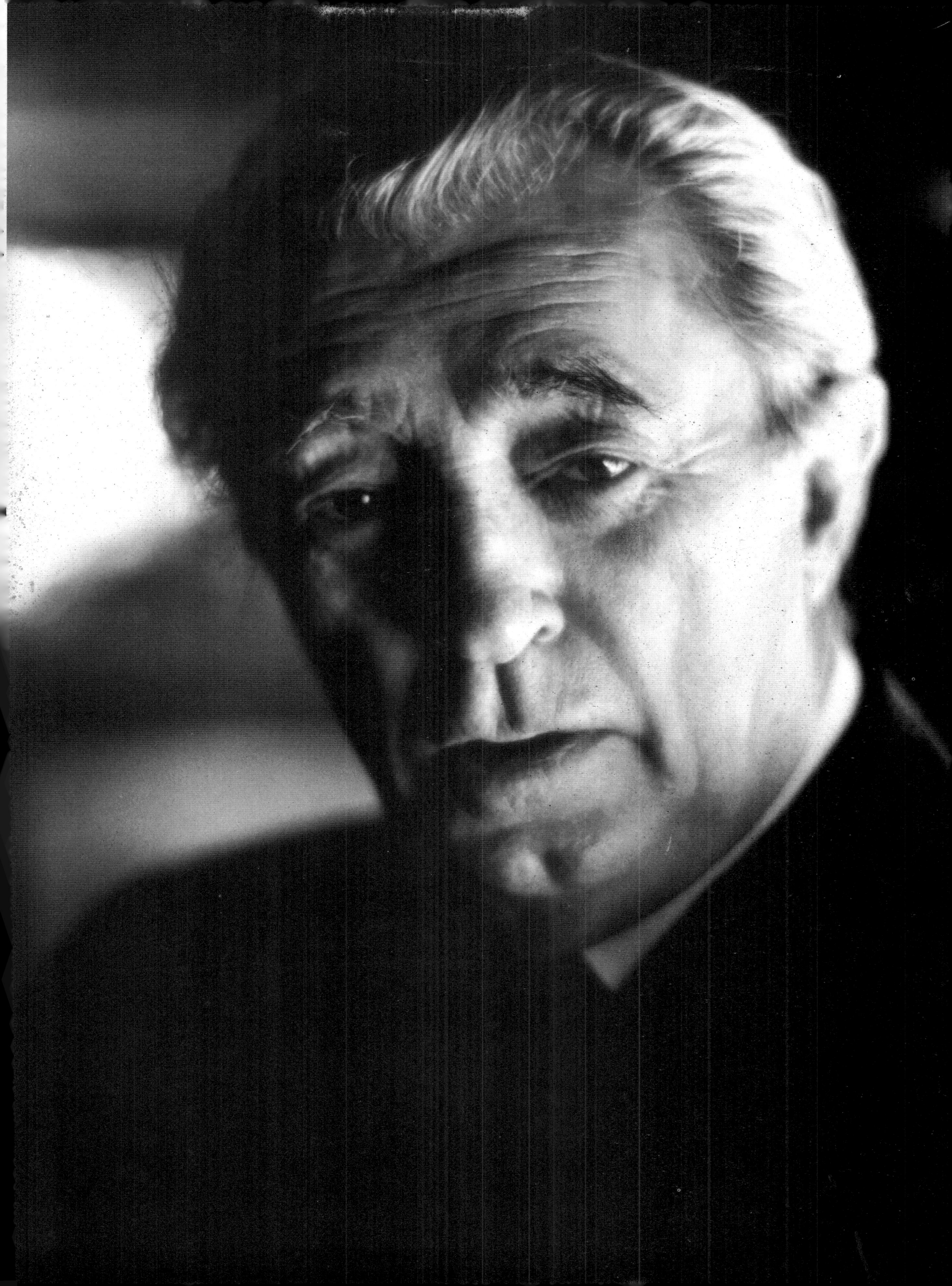

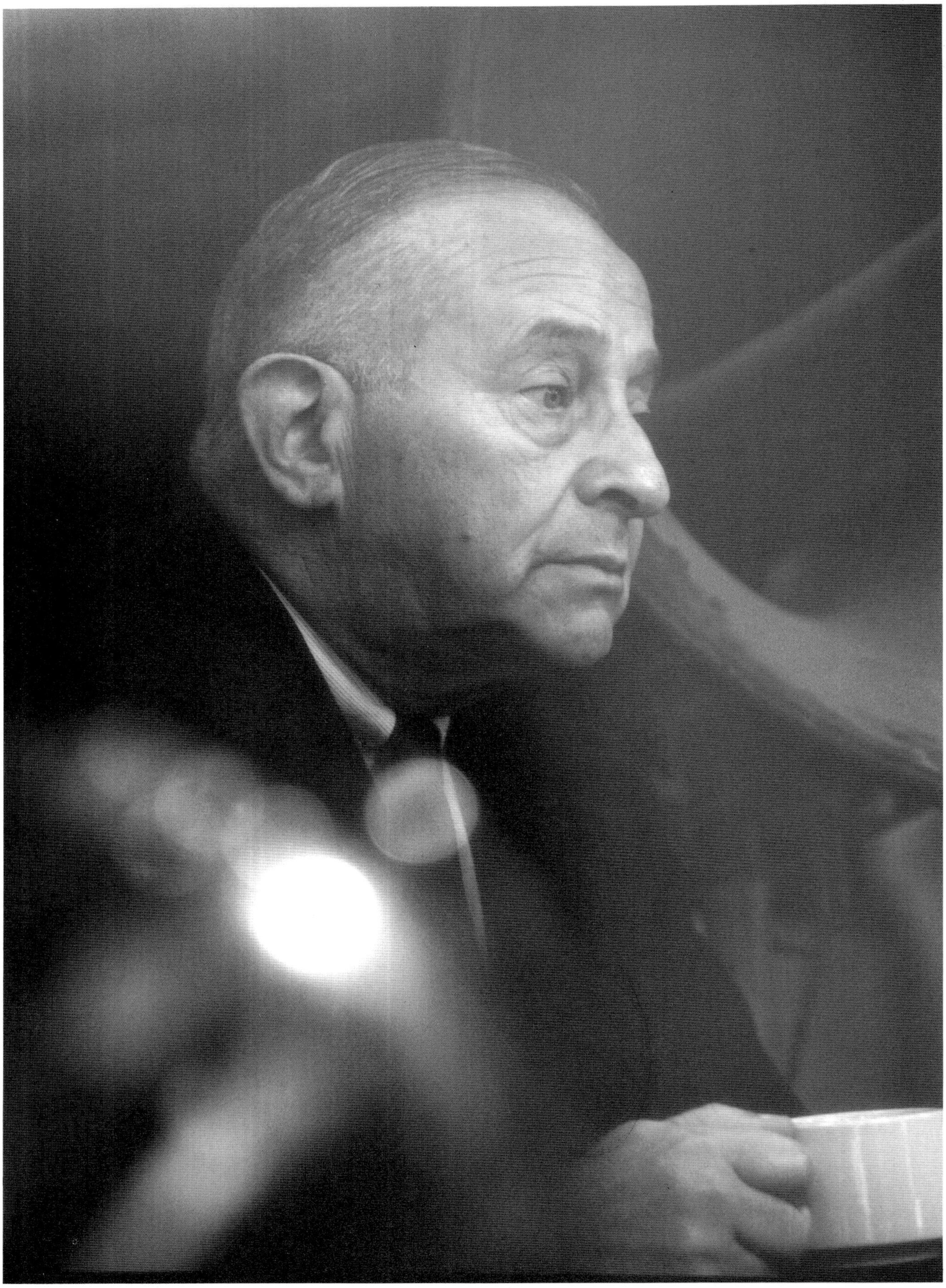

Arthur Freed
BY
Gene Kelly

I knew Arthur Freed . . . I knew him well.

I knew him as a gentle man, whose hobbies were raising orchids and collecting fine paintings. And though some people called him "tough" and "brusque," I never found him to be that way. He loved talent and he loved professionalism. He never went through a production looking over the creator's shoulders. He was a joy to work with. And even more important, he was my friend.

I knew Arthur . . . I knew him well.

Culver City, California *1959*

Jamie Lee Curtis
BY
John Cleese

Vivacious, complex, perceptive, imaginative, articulate, talented, humorous, and insightful are all words Jamie uses quite a lot. However, most of the words she uses a lot cannot be printed in a nice book like this.

At the moment, Jamie, as well as being a mother and actress, is studying for a degree in "Not Dashing Around All the Time Like A Benzedrined Road Runner."

When she graduates (in 2012), she'll be the most sublime creature in the solar system. At the moment she's merely the most lovable.

Studio City, California *1990*

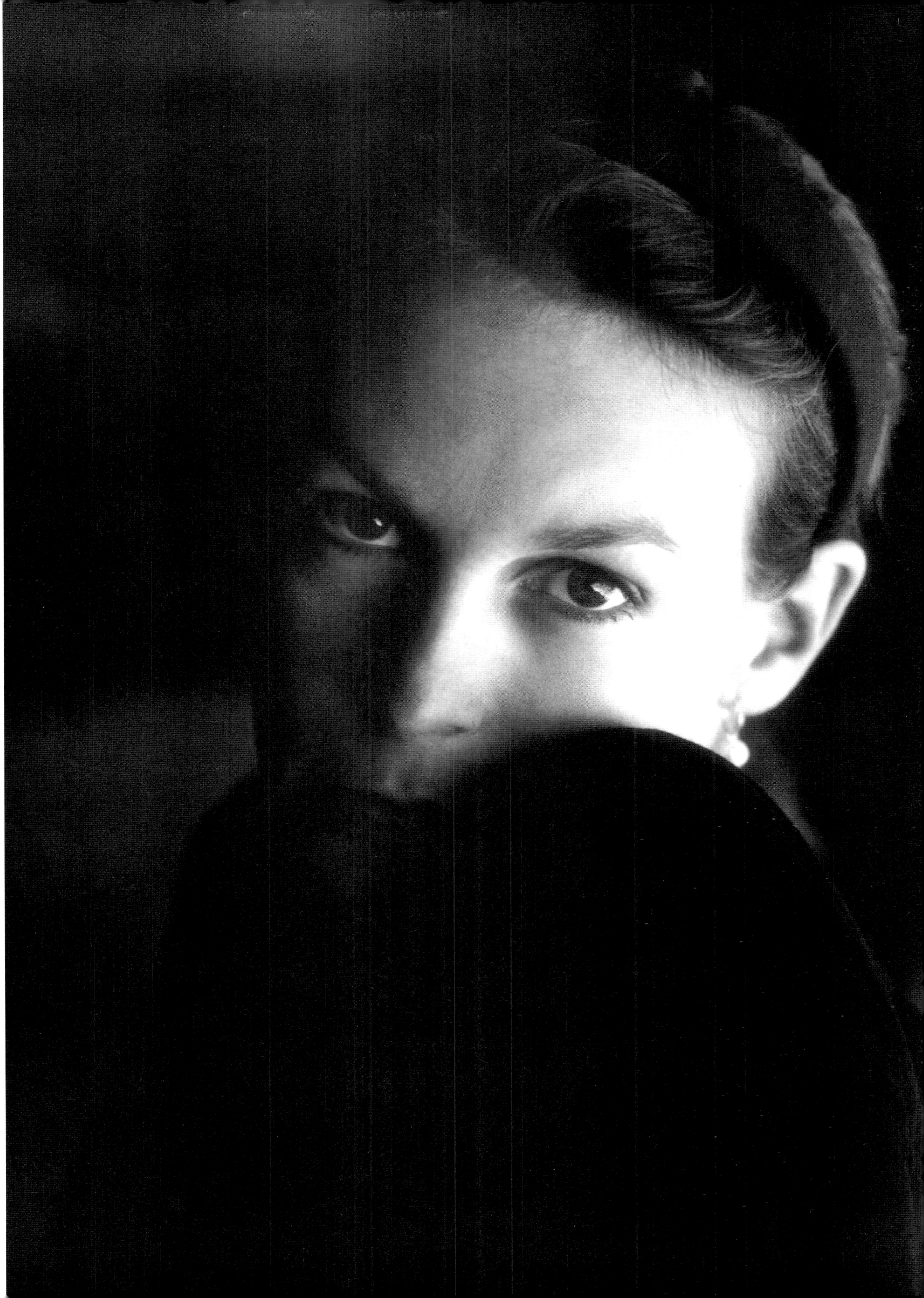

Federico Fellini
BY
Anthony Quinn

To work with Fellini you have to roll yourself into a small ball and crawl into his brain.

There you find yourself swimming in a light green sea. You are surrounded by strange, weird, colorful souls. It is all the fantasies and memories of his youth.

But be careful. It is hard to find an exit and get into the real world once you've been there.

But what a fantastic trip you've had!

New York City *1965*

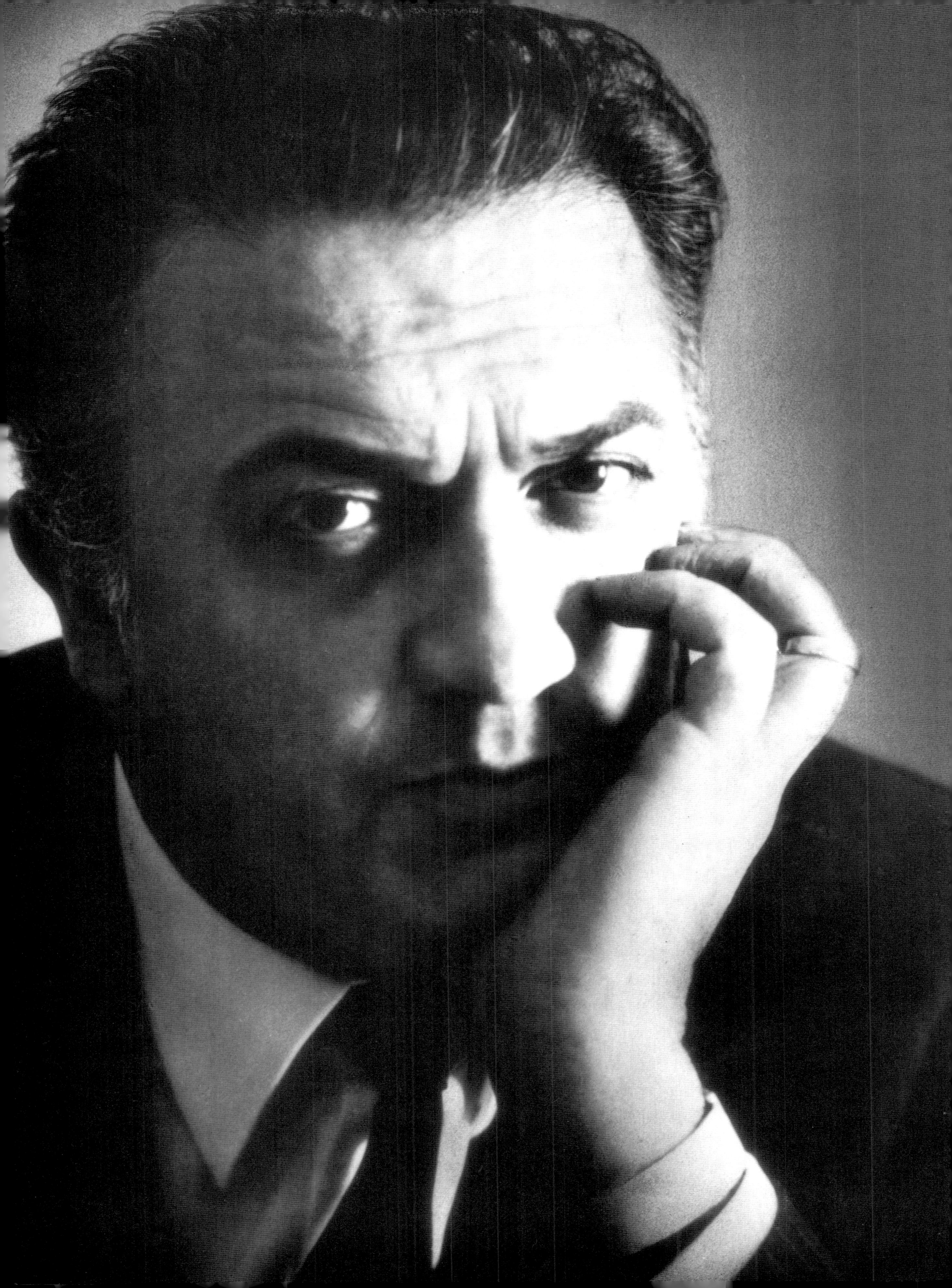

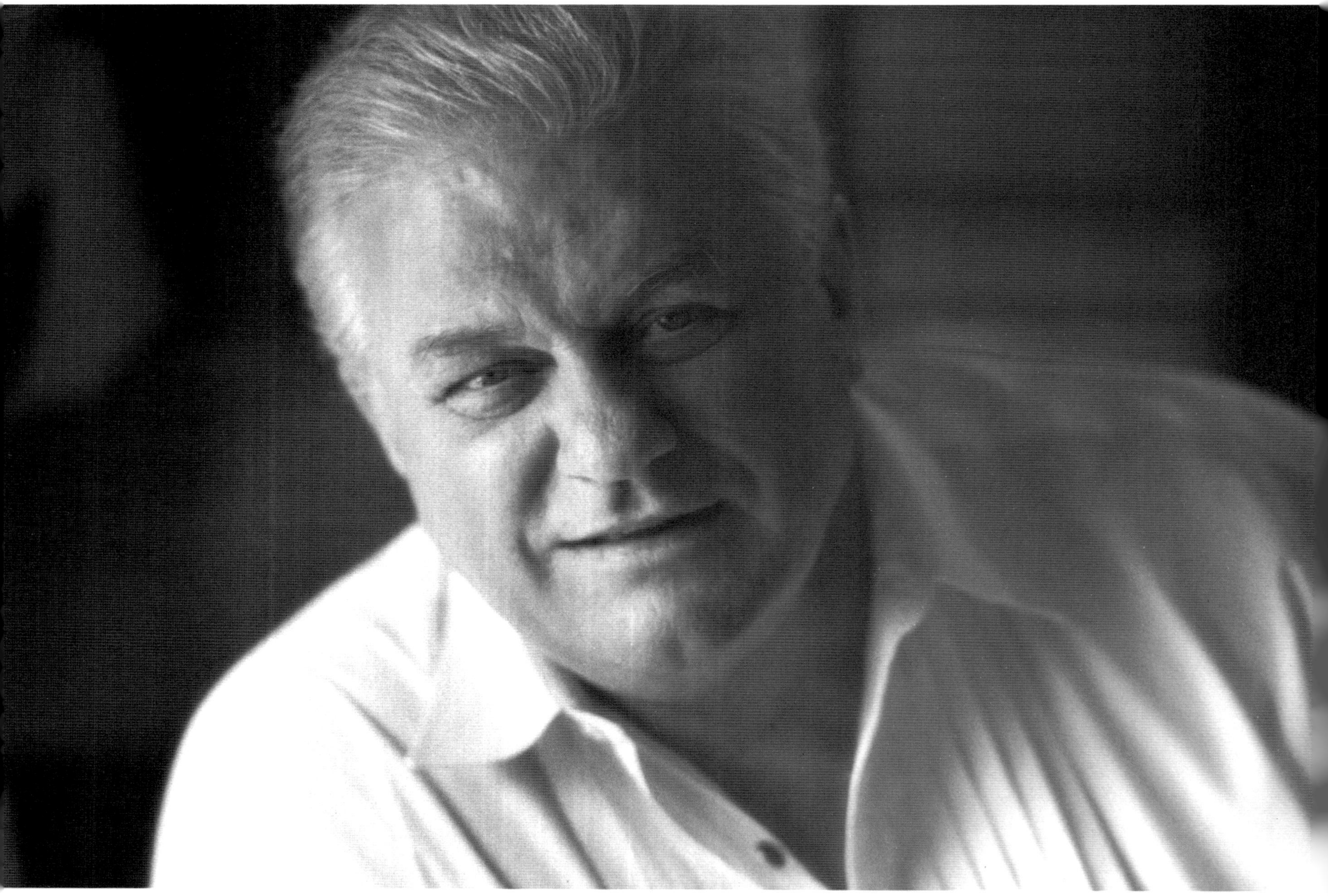

Charles Durning
BY
Burt Reynolds

It was in 1974 or 1975, and I was doing what was to become my favorite script over the years, *Starting Over.* Charles was to play my brother, and as if we were already brothers, that big Irish face just lit up when we met and he gave me a bear hug. I don't think I've ever worked with an actor who is so effortless in his approach to acting, and yet you can't take your eyes off him.

Charles also has that rare quality of trust. You just trust him immensely and he you. Steve McQueen and Charles Bronson, both wonderful actors, due to being shy or whatever had a hard time making friends. Charles became friends with both of these men from the first day they met.

Charles' dancing ability, of course, was one of the big surprises to the Hollywood community. For such a big man, he moves with grace and ease . . . like Jackie Gleason used to move. He taught dancing for years as a young man and also was a darn good professional fighter. He first fought at Madison Square Garden and was on the same card with another young man . . . who would go on to be one of our most respected actors, Jack Warden.

I don't think Charles would have me talk about his incredible war experiences, but just let me say this . . . here is a golden and brave man. He doesn't have to take a backseat to anyone in terms of what he gave of himself for his country in World War II. To call him complicated and brimming over with life would be a huge understatement. He carries no baggage from any pain that we can see, yet way down deep inside Charles Durning is a well of untapped emotion, that someday, hopefully, he will use in his performance that will blow us all out of the theatre. Not that he is doing badly now, with two nominations for an Academy Award and a Golden Globe award. But I truly believe in what Charles Durning has yet to do on the American stage and in films, and we are going to be blessed by this brilliant, talented, dear sweet man.

North Hollywood, California *1989*

Tom Hanks
BY
Sally Field

TOM IS ORDINARY LOOKING
    AND TRULY HANDSOME
SHY AND YET OUTGOING

HE IS SHARPLY FUNNY AND
    QUIETLY DARK

HAPPY AND EASY GOING AND
    SOMEHOW SAD AND INTENSE

HE CAN LIGHT UP A ROOM
    OR MASTERFULLY WORK THE ROOM
    OR SIT IN THE ROOM AND NEVER BE NOTICED

HE'S AN ENORMOUSLY TALENTED MYSTERY

JUST WHAT MOVIE STARS ARE MADE OF

I ADORE HIM.

Brentwood, California *1990*

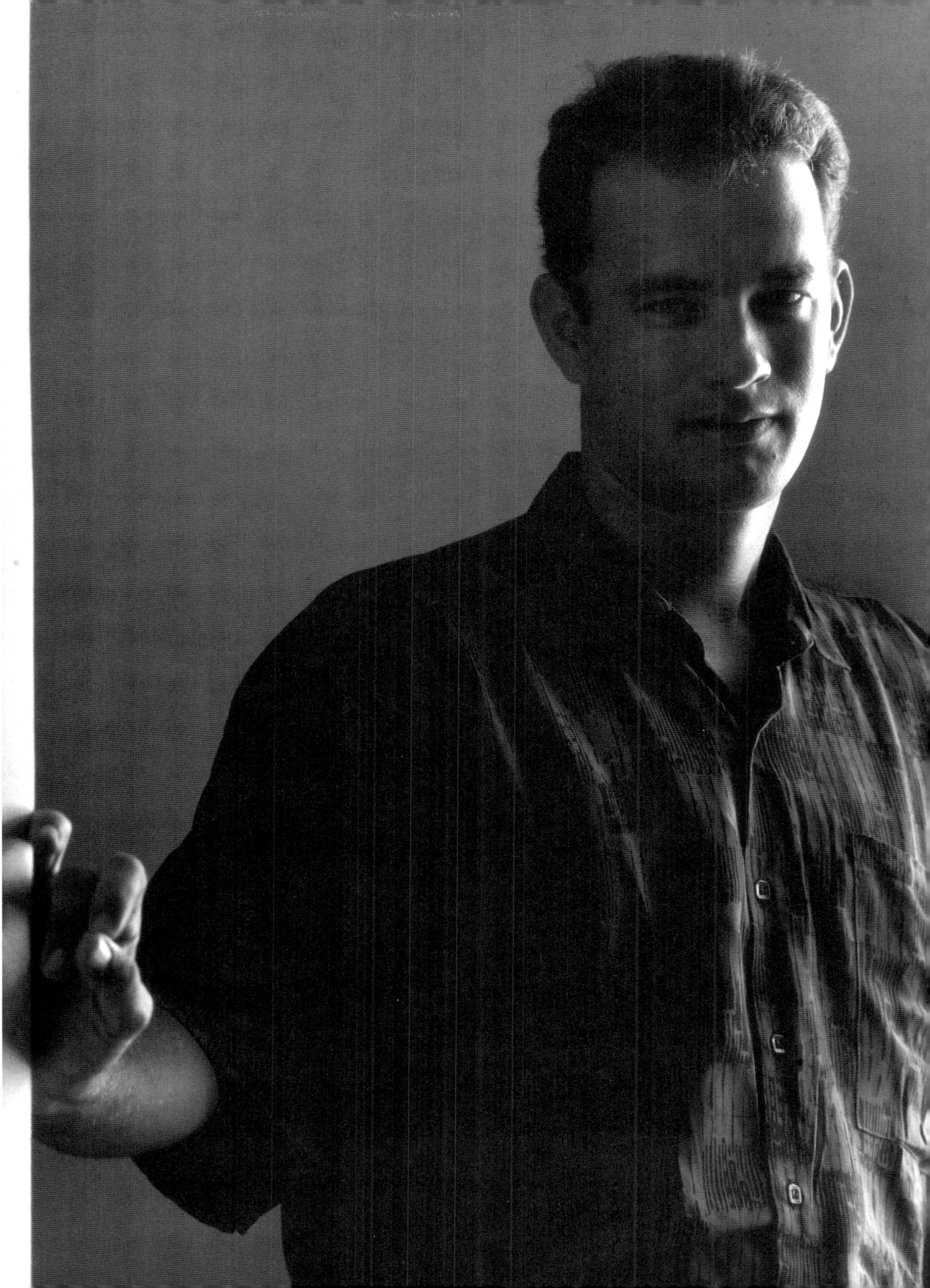

The Nicholas Brothers
BY
Gregory Hines

The Nicholas Brothers—tap dancers, daredevils, movie stars. Able to tap in syncopations never heard before. Able to leap off of tall staircases into splits. Able to fly and come down whenever they wanted to. My heroes.

Woodland Hills, California *1990*

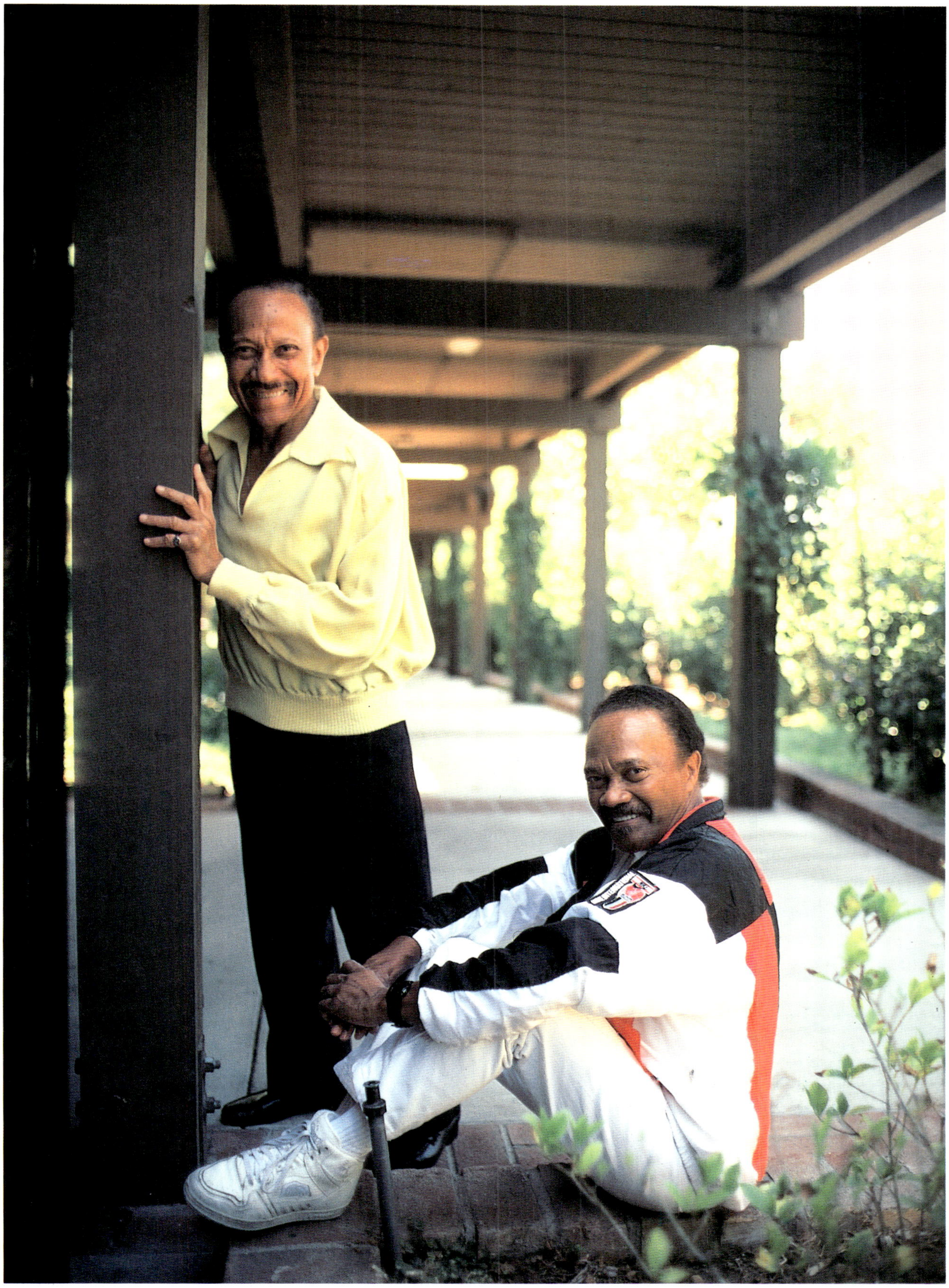

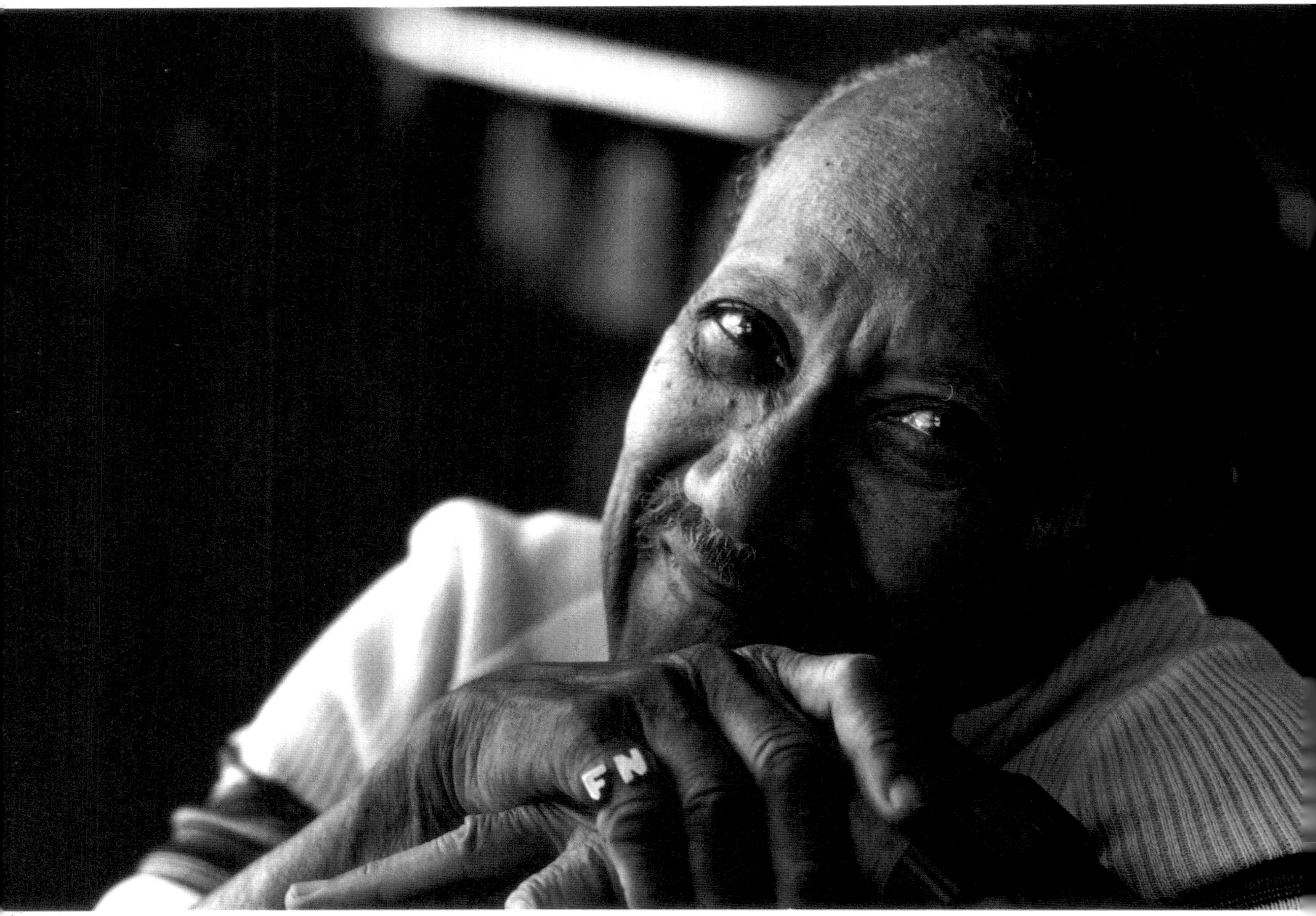

Woodland Hills, California *1991*

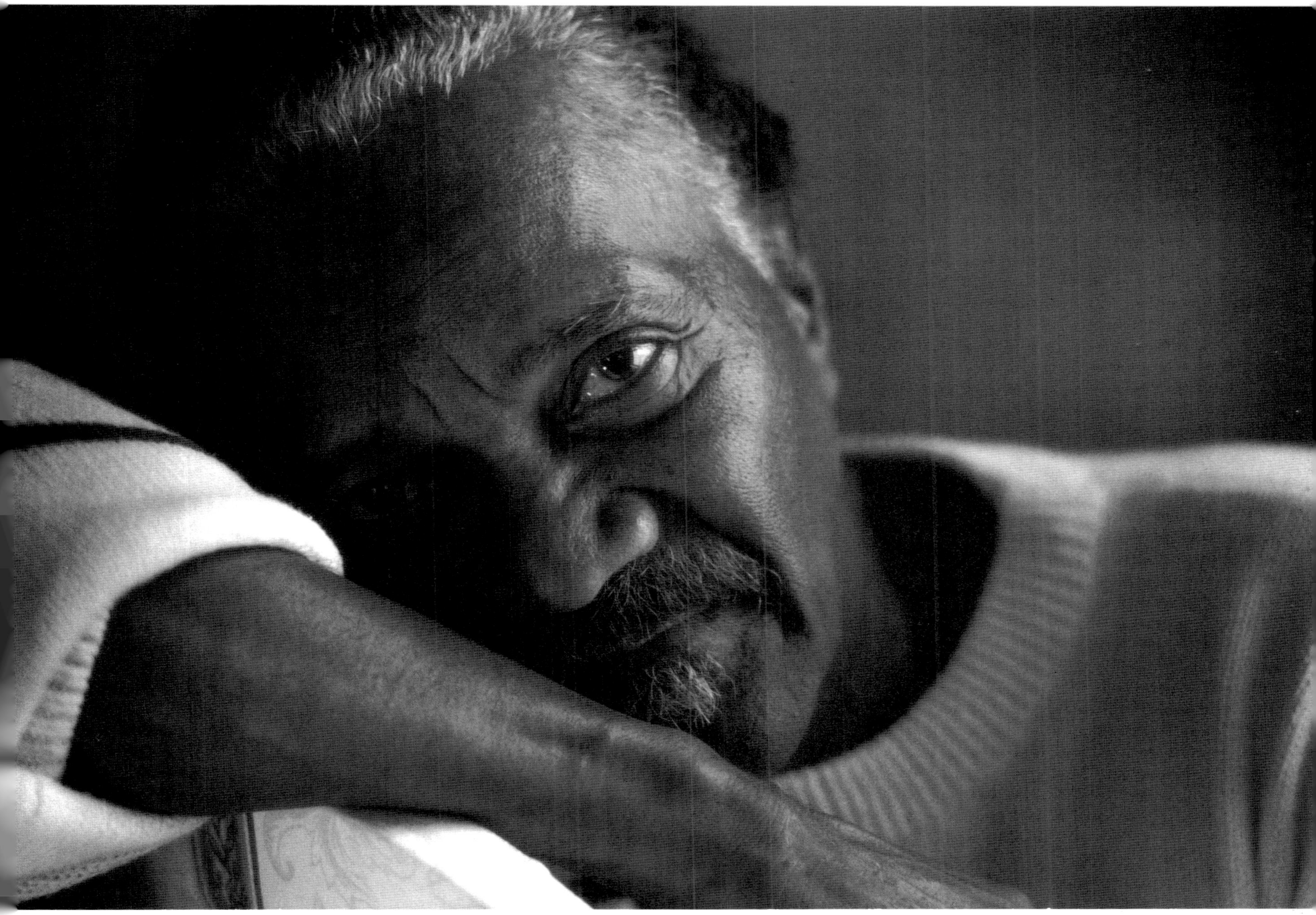

New York City 1990

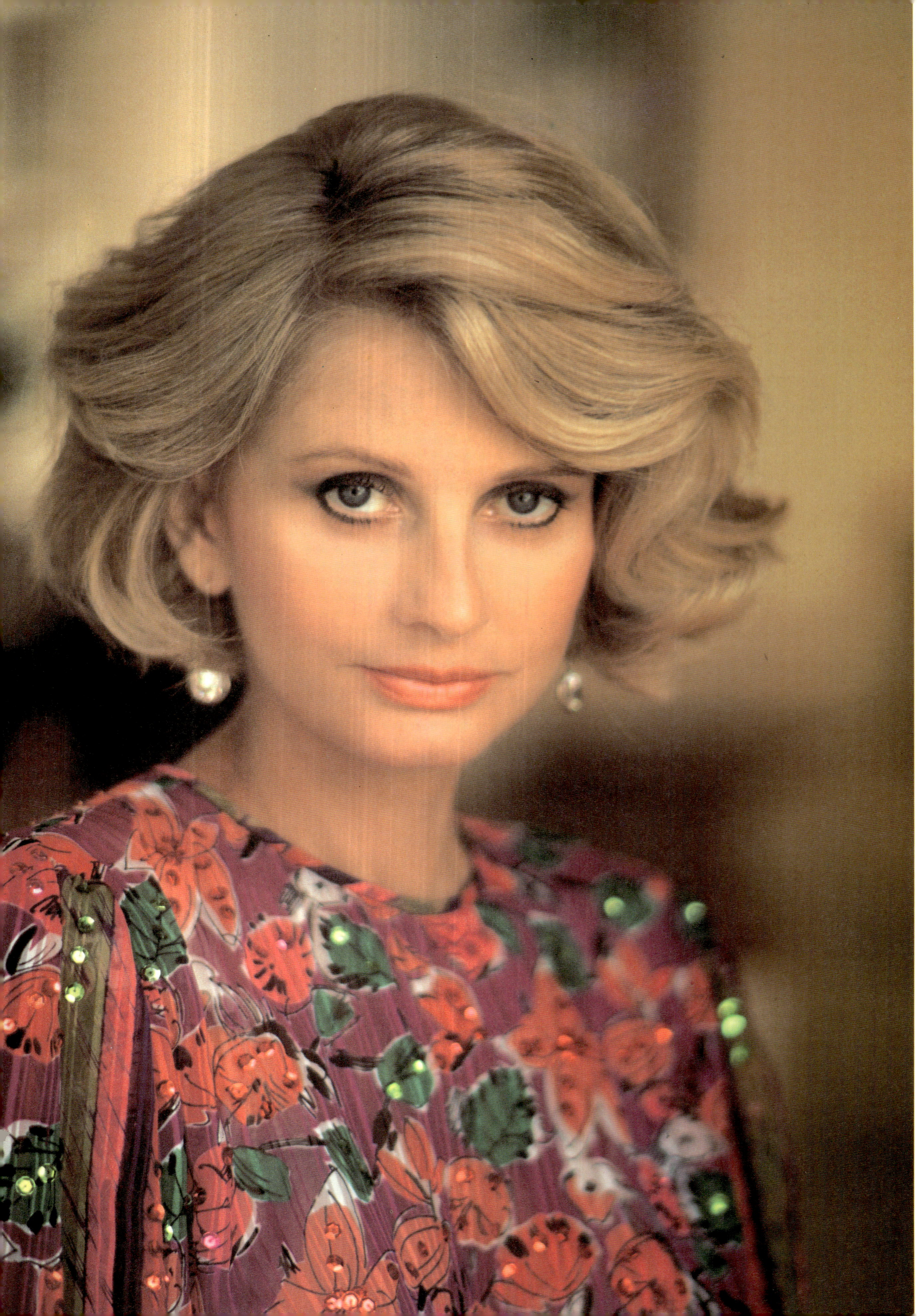

Jill Ireland
BY
Joan Rivers

For the longest time I knew two Jill Irelands. The first, sexy, charming, and enormously stylish, with a totally off-the-wall sense of humor, a man's woman in the classic sense, I used to run into her at horse shows. Looking great in riding pants and capable of making delicious small talk, she was the honey that turned every man into a buzzing bumblebee. Men's eyes followed whenever she walked by, and they found themslves flocking to her. There was no way to explain it except to say that she was the personification of things feminine and irresistible.

The second Jill was a devoted wife and mother. Jill passionately loved her husband and her family. And they responded in kind. To see Charlie and Jill together was always to see a couple who were courting, even though they had been married for quite some time.

A third Jill emerged when she became sick. This Jill was a woman of enormous courage. I knew she was in terrible pain most of the time, but neither I nor anybody else ever heard her complain. Instead, Jill continued to devote herself to being a wife, mother, and actress. And she looked to the future with astonishing optimism no matter what the doctors told her or how badly she felt. After her breast amputation I had her on my Fox show, and asked if she was considering a breast implant. "Never," she replied, "Don't you see, in my present state Charlie has the best of all possible worlds—If he wants a girl he looks to the right—if he fancies a boy he merely has to look to the left."

At that, Jill threw her back her head and roared with laughter. It was this wild humor, spunk, and courage in the face of such great adversity that knocked everybody out. And that's the Jill I remember.

Malibu, California *1988*

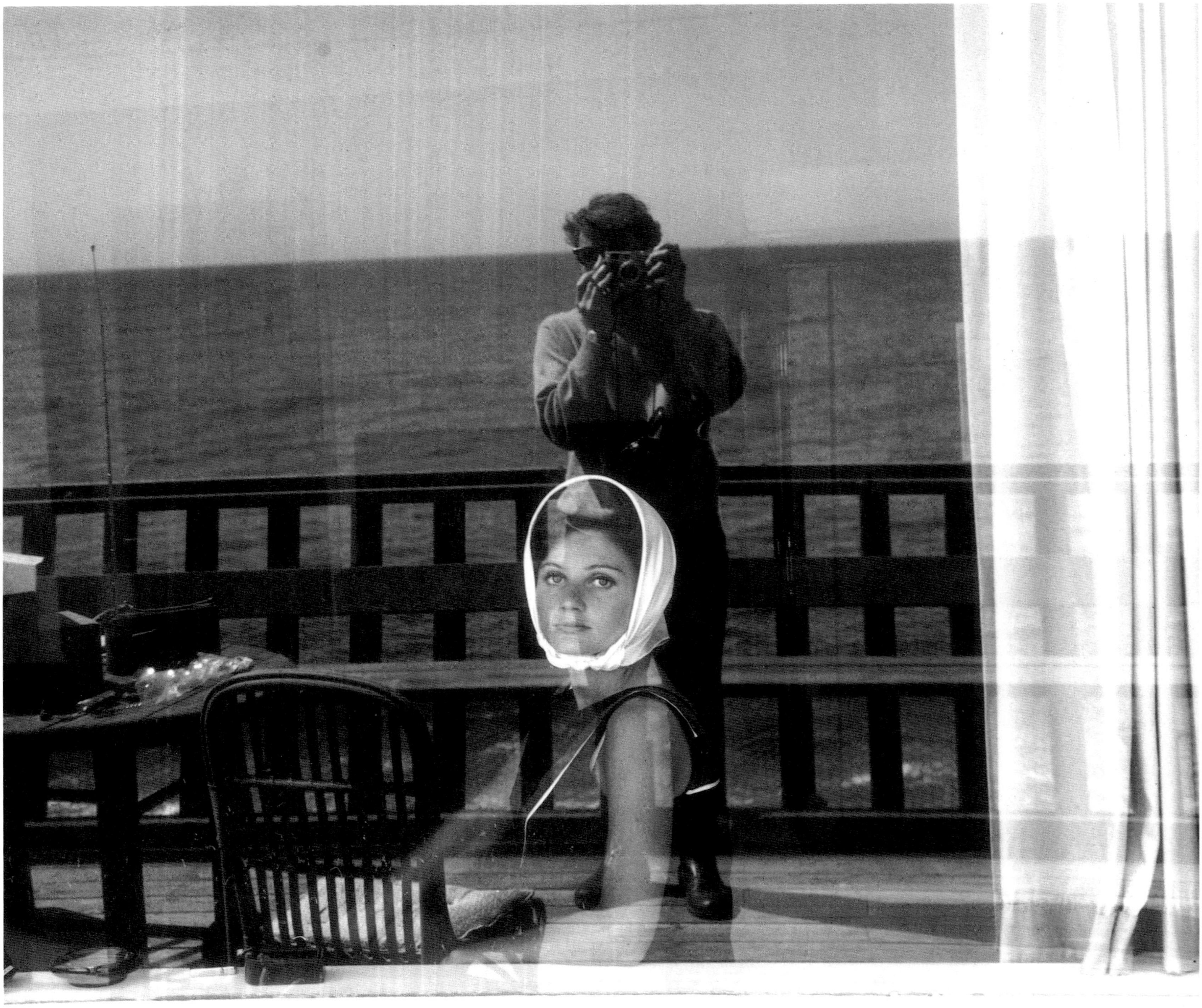

Malibu, California *1963*

Willie Shoemaker
BY
Burt Bacharach

Pound for pound, I always thought that Bill Shoemaker could be the greatest athlete of them all. He possesses a wonderful fluidity whether on a horse, golf course, or tennis court; he has the handle on being a fine human being on and off the racetrack. Whatever he lacked in power on a horse he more than made up for with great communicative hands and tremendous sensibility. To know him and have him as a friend has been a great privilege for me. To see him coming into the paddock wearing my jockey silks was always a highlight for me.

Shoe's the most direct and honest person I ever came in contact with in the horse-racing world. He's always tried to keep my expectations in check by telling me the real stuff about a horse that I owned but might have been getting too high on. He'd simply say, "Burt, he's a nice horse, he's going to win some races for you, but he's not going to be a great one, and I don't want you to get your heart broken." Another thing about Shoe, I never saw him abuse a horse. If the horse was beaten, he just tried to be as gentle as he could with the animal.

If looking for one word to describe Bill Shoemaker . . .

"Class"

Inglewood, California *1990*

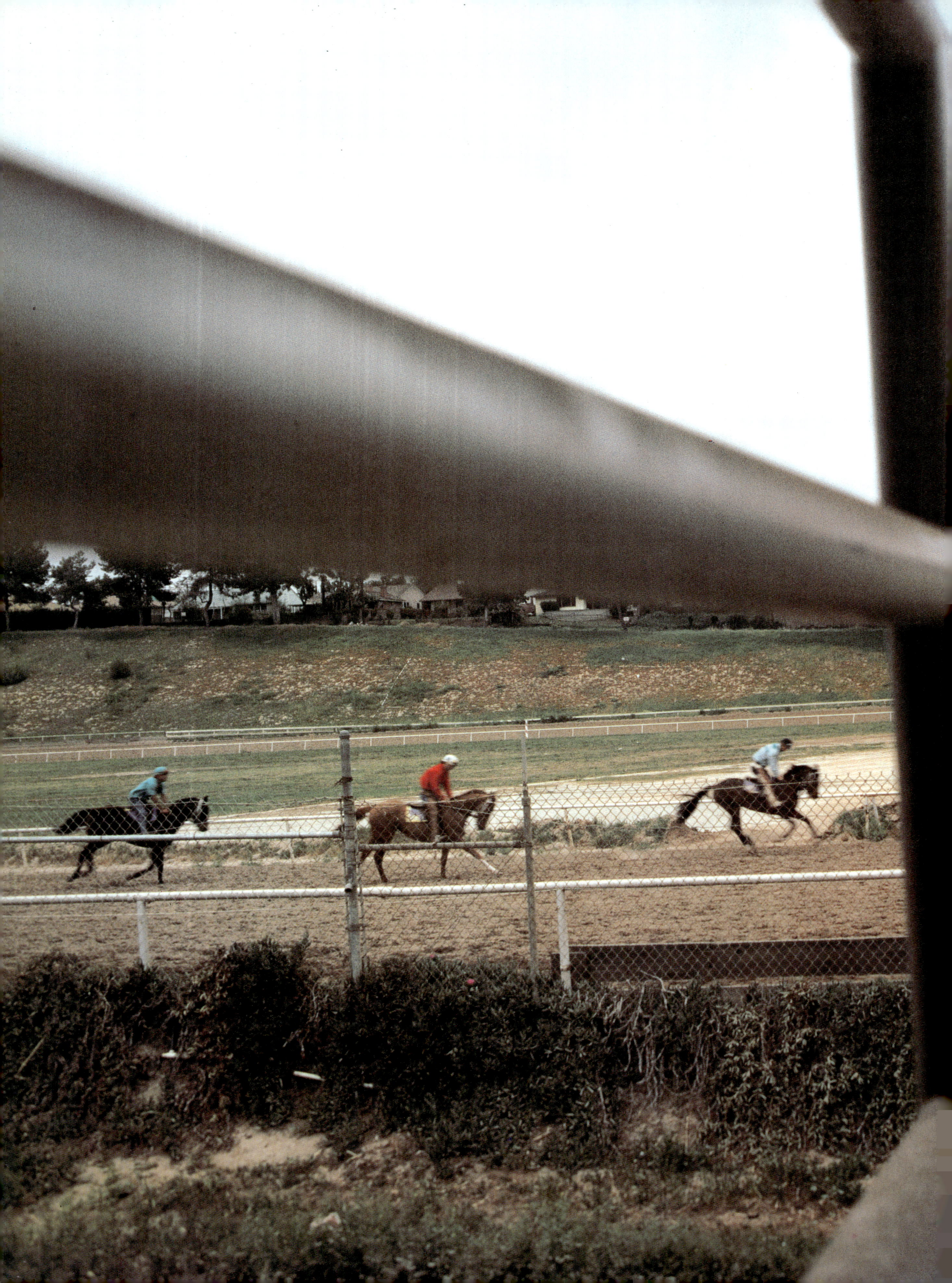

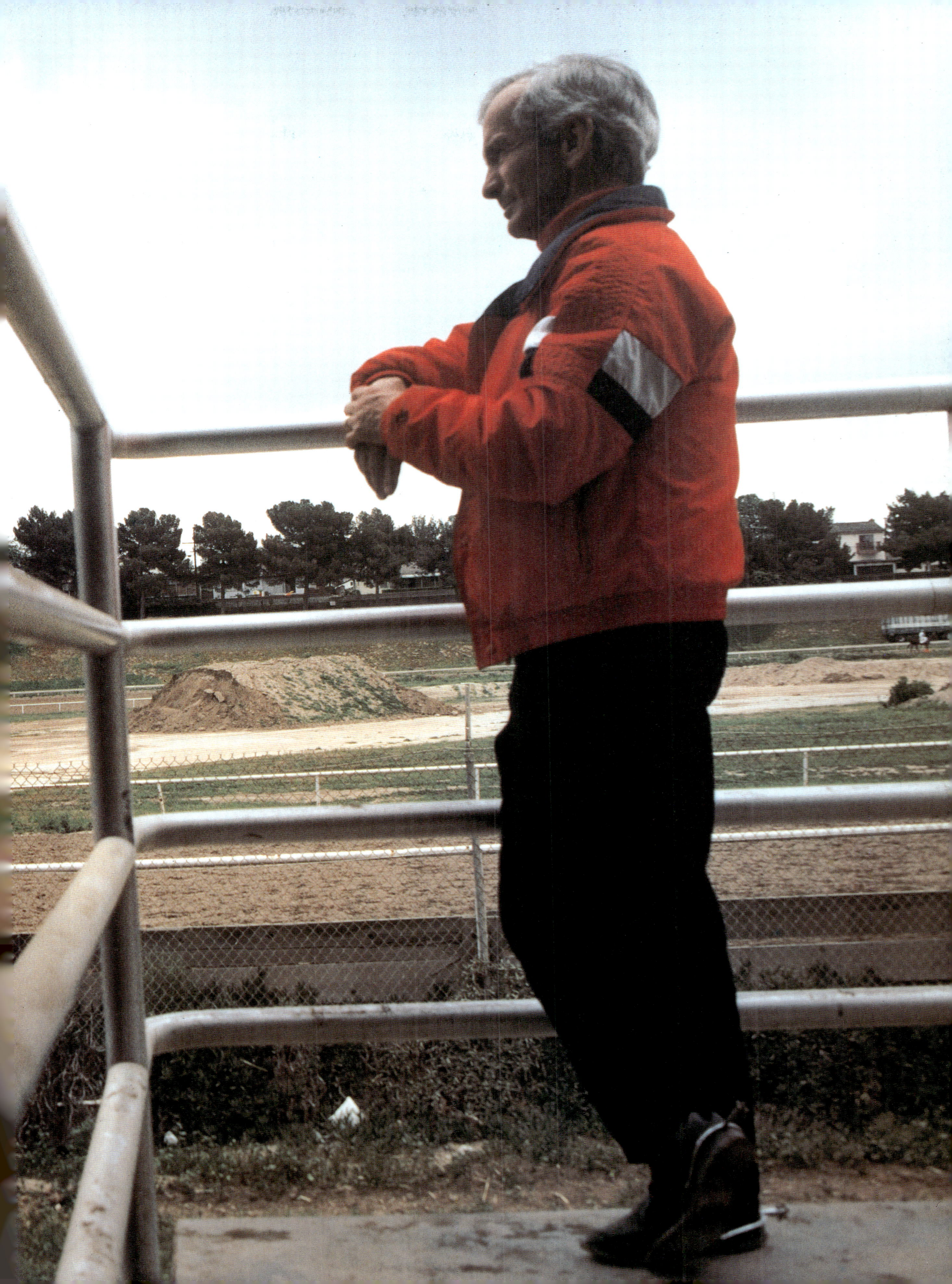

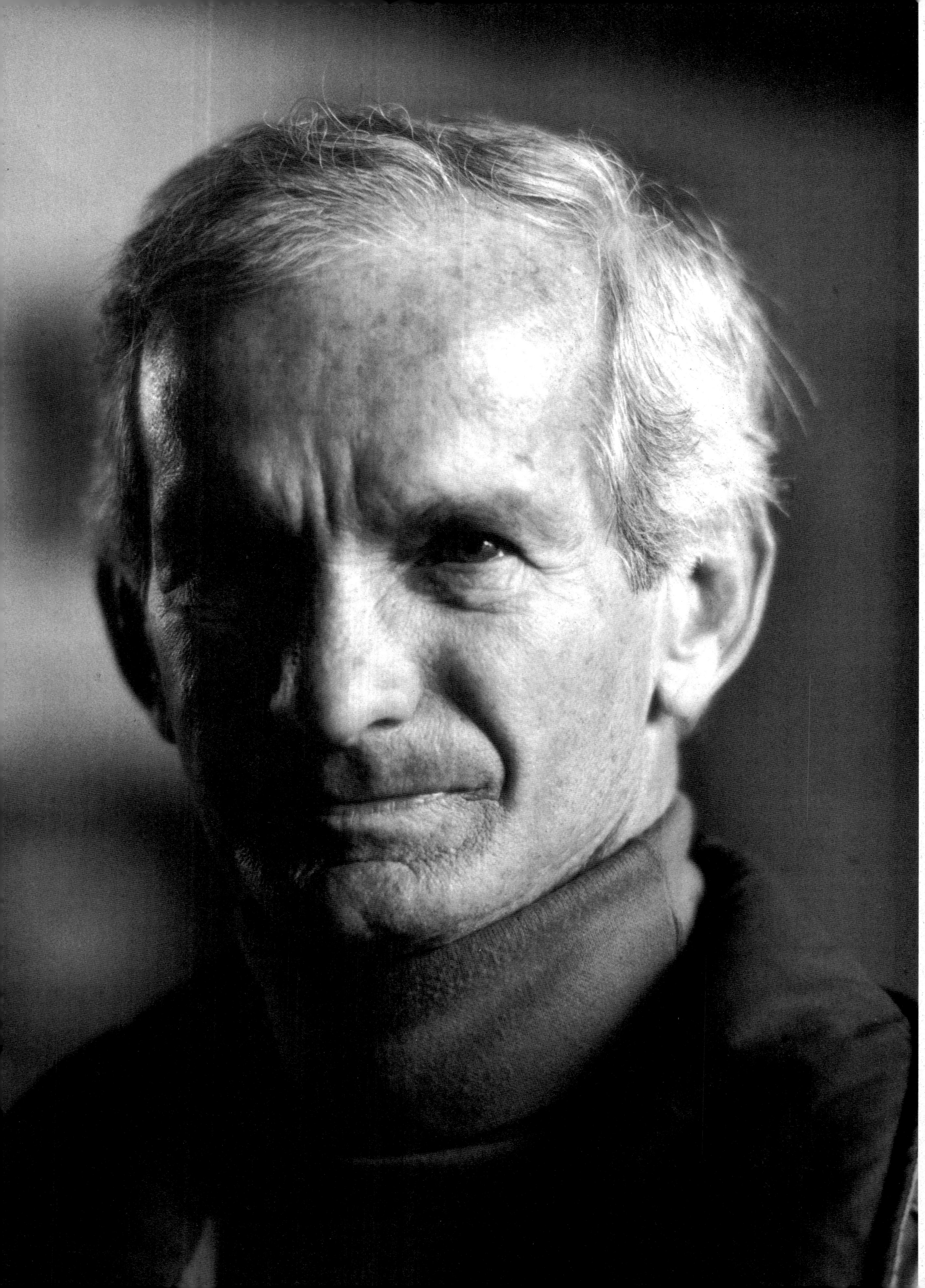

Viola Dana
BY
Kevin Brownlow

"You could shoot a cannon off on Hollywood Boulevard and never hit anybody after nine o'clock," Viola Dana once said, referring to the sleepy community she knew in the teens. That Hollywood was long gone, but where was Viola Dana? It was 1976 and David Gill and I were in Los Angeles, filming a documentary series about the silent era. We were particularly anxious to find Miss Dana, but no one knew where she lived, or even if she was still alive.

Hollywood Boulevard had changed a little since Miss Dana's day, and as I came out of Larry Edmunds Bookshop, I was conscious of being followed. Who was it—a mugger, a pick-pocket, a pickup? Since the streets were reassuringly crowded, I turned and confronted my pursuer. He was a young, mild-mannered Mexican who had seen me examining books on the silent era and thought I could help him. He was searching for actresses of that period to get their autographs. I was so relieved, I invited him for a coffee. He turned out to have an amazing list of addresses, among the names was that of Viola Dana.

I never saw him again, but I am profoundly grateful to that young man. For I had wanted to meet Viola Dana ever since James Card brought a print of *Blue Jeans* (1917, directed by John Collins) to the National Film Theatre in London. Until then, she had just been a name—an illustrious name, to be sure. One of the pioneers, she went back as far as the old Edison Company. She must be incredibly old!

David and I went round to see her a few days later. Viola Dana was small, as Pickford and Swanson were small. And she had the most remarkable eyes—"Dana eyes"—of an intense green. She looked younger than her age—it was just before her 79th birthday—and she was full of energy. She had such charm, and such a strong sense of humour, I was sure she must have Irish blood, like almost everyone else in early Hollywood. But no: her family was German and her real name was Flugrath. The Flugrath Sisters became famous—and they all married directors, each of whom had a tragic end. Edna, the eldest, married Harold Shaw, who was killed in a car crash in 1926. Leonie, who changed her name to Shirley Mason, and who was the youngest, married Bernard Durning, who died of typhoid fever in 1923. And Viola fell for John Collins. They met at the Edison studios in Bedford Park in the Bronx where she was a child actress.

"I fell in love with Johnny when I was eleven years old and I was so worried that he'd get married before I grew up."

Collins was an art director at the studio—that's what he'd be called now. Actually, besides putting up the scenery, he did every imaginable job. Ideal training for the director he soon became.

Viola was still in her teens when she persuaded Collins to marry her. He transformed her life.

"He did everything for me. If we went on location, he packed the grips. I didn't do a thing. He had his own ideas about the things I should do. He would see me do funny things about the house and he would remember them. He was almost like a Svengali. Right in the middle of a scene he would say, "Vi, come on, I'd like a few tears here." That's all he had to say, and the tears would start rolling.

"When Metro called, Johnny did the negotiating. He said, 'Well, of course, you can't have Dana without me. I direct her; we're a team.' They said, 'We don't know anything about you.' Reluctantly they took him on, and it wasn't long before they realized this man was a great talent. He wrote the script, he knew how to handle the actors, he cut the pictures, he even arranged the lights."

John Collins was one of the many victims of the 1918 flu epidemic. It was a devastating blow, the effects of which were clearly still felt by Viola all these years later.

"After he died, instead of being an actress, I think I became a bag of mannerisms. I don't think I was ever allowed, with a few exceptions, to do what I was capable of doing in the way of acting. Because I was little and supposed to be cute, I became a bag of tricks.

"There's nothing like your first love, believe me, nothing. You love again, but it's all different. The first love you well and truly remember."

Viola had known stardom in the theatre as well as in movies—she had played the lead in *Poor Little Rich Girl* at the Hudson Theatre, New York, in 1913. (Her sisters played the role, too.) Mary Pickford, who would play the role on the screen, was acting in *The Good Little Devil* at the Belasco at the same time, and the girls used to meet on the subway. Viola envied her

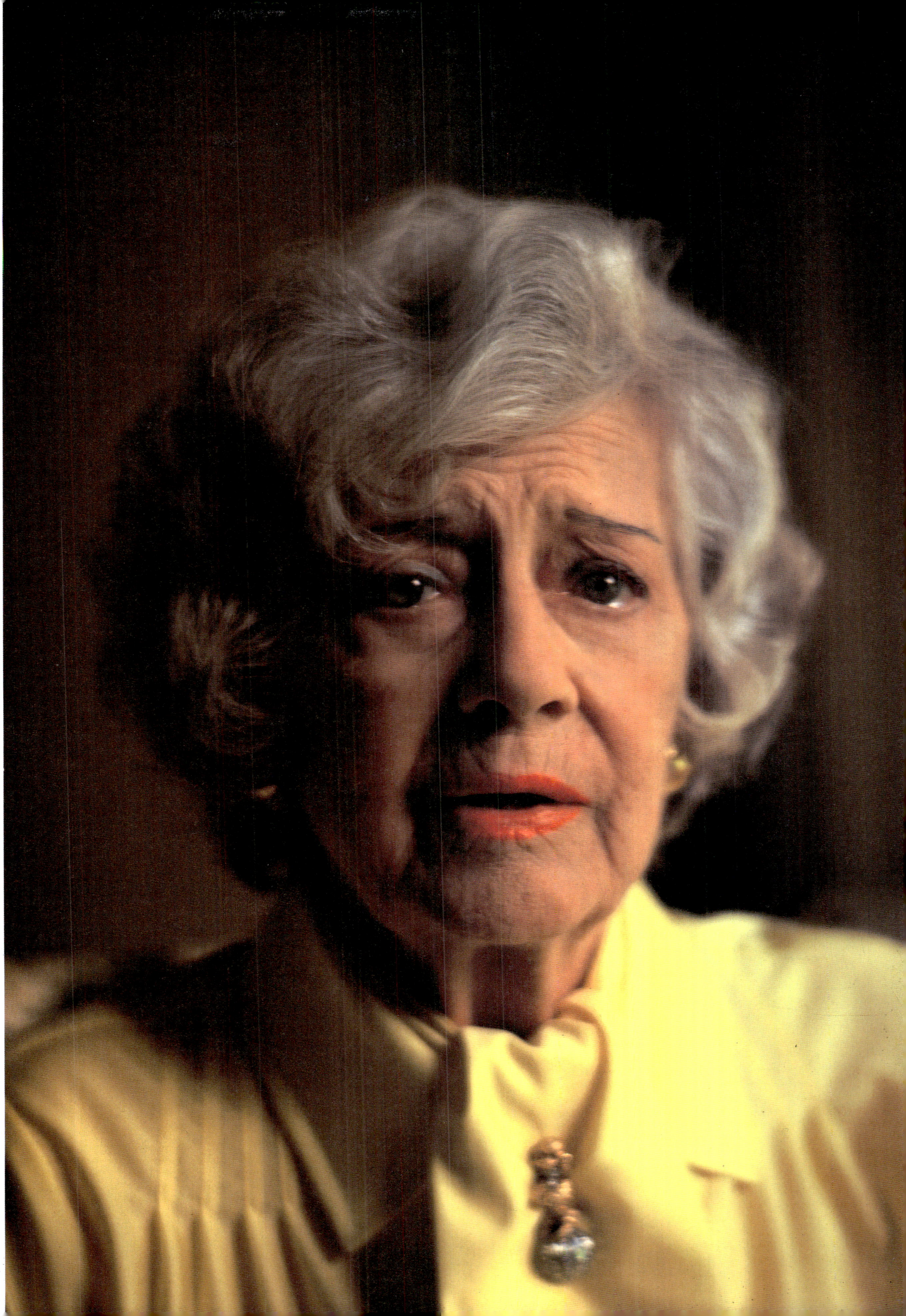

clothes. "My mother made my clothes, and I'm afraid I looked a bit like a Christmas tree." Like Pickford, she could play child roles for years.

"I used to go through terrible experiences, but I always came out pure. That was why mothers could let their children go to see Viola Dana. She was always a good girl, and believe me, it got kind of sickening, because I'm not like that. It wasn't me!" Viola laughed at the memory.

But she underestimated herself.

Those films of hers which survive show Dana to have been a fine actress, naturalistic, funny and touching. And she made a number of unusual stories. In *The Stoning* (1915), for instance, she played a girl who tries to live on in her village after the birth of an illegitimate baby. No one turns on her, no one hurls an insult, they simply ignore her. And one morning the girl's body is found floating in the river; the villagers' silence is worse than a stoning.

We had completed Viola Dana's interview when reports reached us of a camera fault. Apparently, Viola's interview was unsteady. It literally wobbled. We eventually learned it was a stock fault; Kodak had punched the sprocket holes incorrectly. It was a kind of fault one might have anticipated during the Patents War, but was hardly to be expected in the 1970s. We telephoned Viola.

She simply said, "Come on back. Let's do it again." "Luckily, Viola Dana is a peach," I wrote in my diary, "and gives us better than we got before."

Thus began a friendship that continued for the rest of her life. After the death of her sister, Shirley, Viola moved into the Motion Picture Home. She felt a little indignant that she should be in a home—she felt she was much too skittish. She did a funny impression of how old people walked. But she, too, was old, whether she admitted it or not, and soon she was grateful to be where she was.

"The place is very beautiful with all the spring flowers," she wrote in a letter, "and they really do everything in the world to make life a little happier for one. One has a feeling of security—we don't have to worry about our rent being raised. I feel very lucky not having to battle the world."

Ten years after we met her, David and I said our last farewell to Viola, in the Motion Picture Hospital. She looked as ill as she must have felt. "I don't have a bit of makeup on," she apologized. At this last meeting, she talked once again of Johnny Collins—and how much she loved him. But the old humour was still there.

"Johnny's mother was just a stinker. She had a face like a horse. She hated my guts, and when we got married, she went home and cried for a week.

"I've had a lot of experiences, haven't I? I'm worn out after an emotional life. I enjoyed it, though."

❑

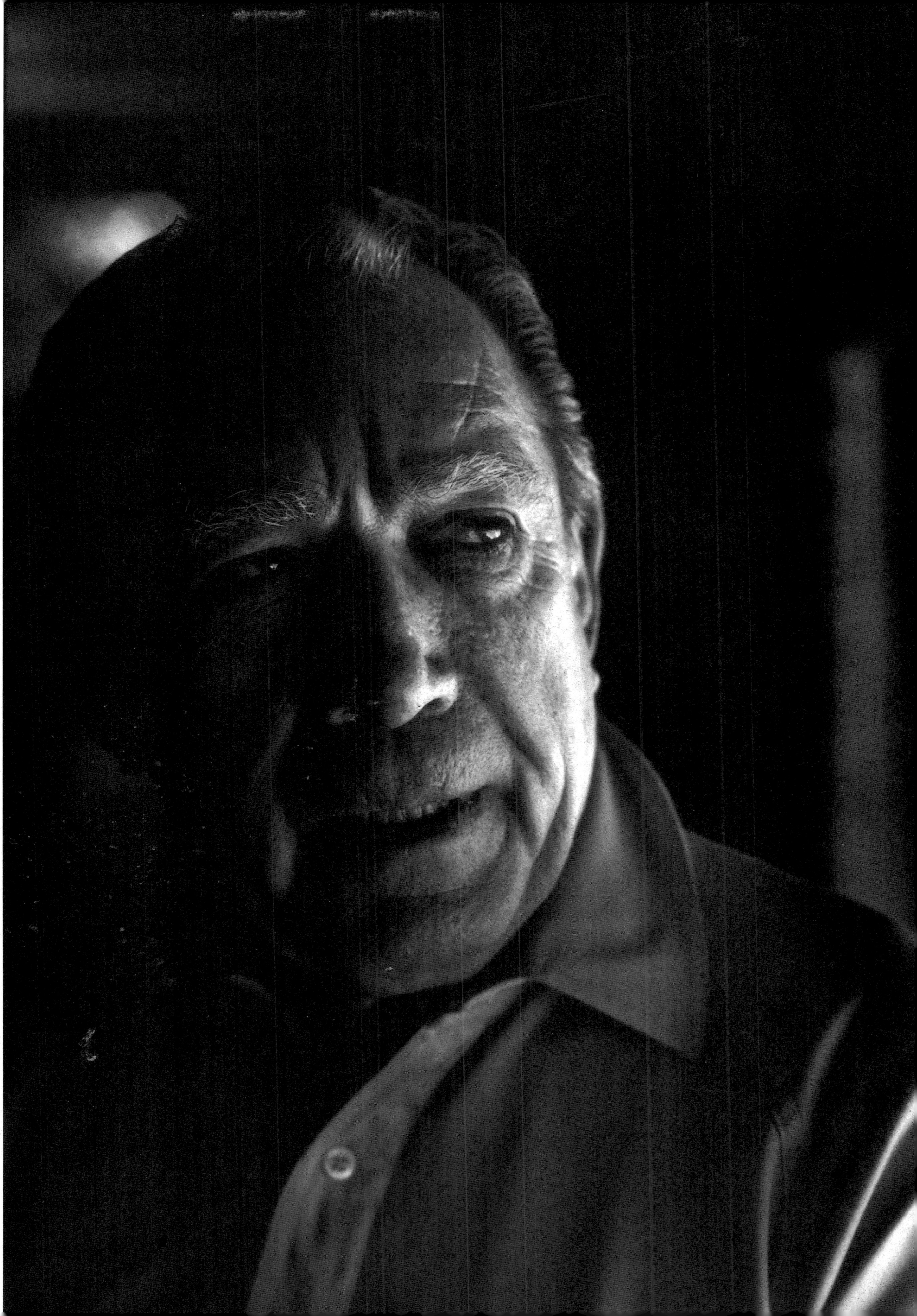

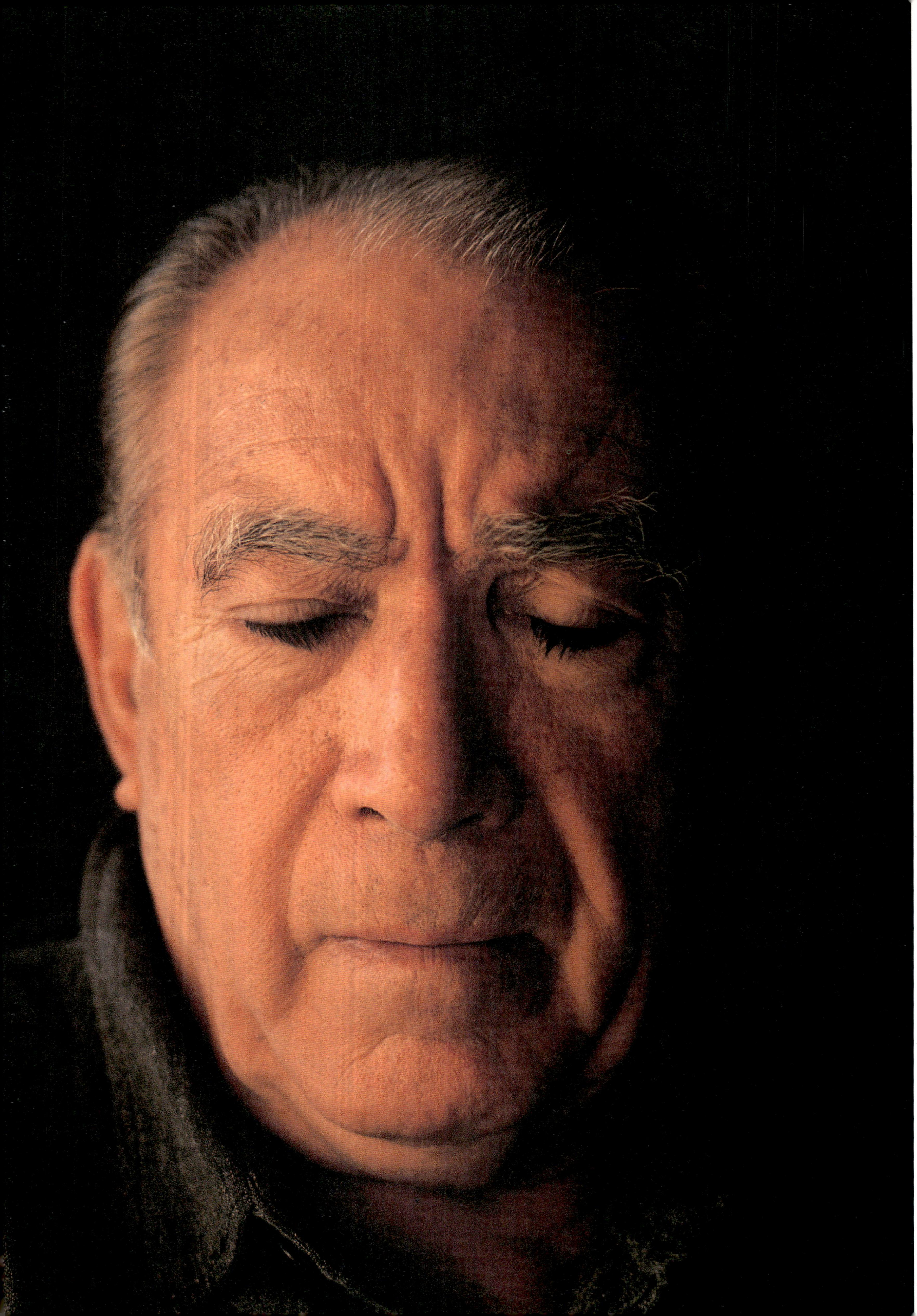

Anthony Quinn
BY
Don Rickles

Anthony Quinn is one of the most stimulating men I've ever met. His intensity is visible both on and off the screen. He's also recognized as an accomplished painter and sculptor.

On the other side of the coin, he really believes he's "Zorba" and at times can be seen eating with his hands. The world believes he's Greek, but his heritage is Mexican. However, he keeps it quiet ever since his taco restaurant failed. At one time he was a fairly good tennis player, but he quit when his friends, including me, got tired of saying, "Great shot, Tony."

I am proud to be considered one of his dear friends and to be able to enjoy our warm times together.

Sylvia Fine Kaye
BY
Peter Feibleman

Gentle, not genteel—clever, not obvious—understanding, not patronizing—critical, not judgmental—talented, not affected—the power behind any number of thrones, not her own: lyricist, composer, wife, mother, and all like that, she has almost died more often than most of us have almost lived. At the present time I am pleased to report that Sylvia Kaye is fine and vice versa.

After writing the above, I read it to Sylvia, who was, at the time, fighting emphysema. She laughed and said she liked it. Six months later—in October 1991, it was—she died.

I do not believe she would want me to rewrite it.

Beverly Hills *1979*

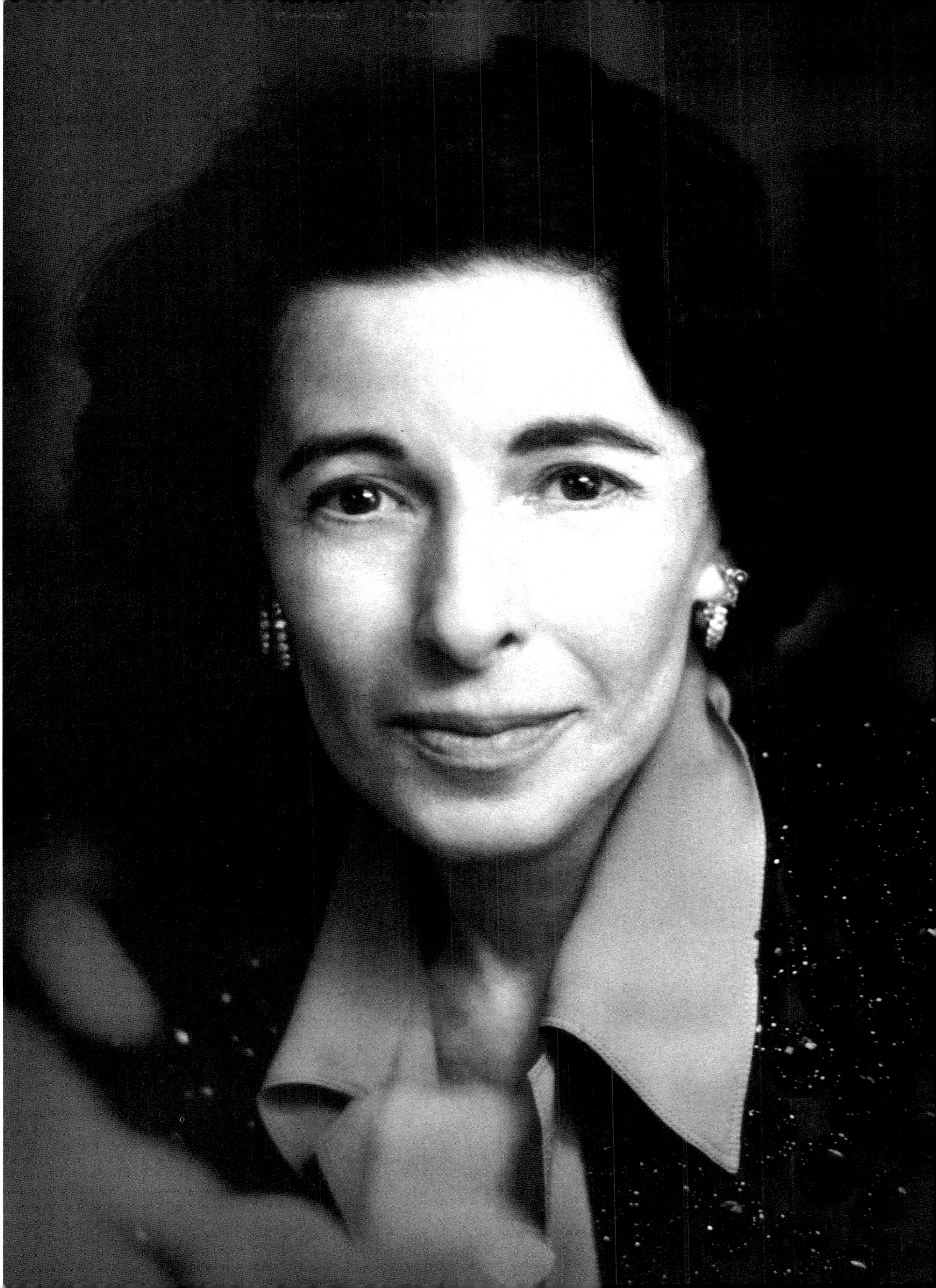

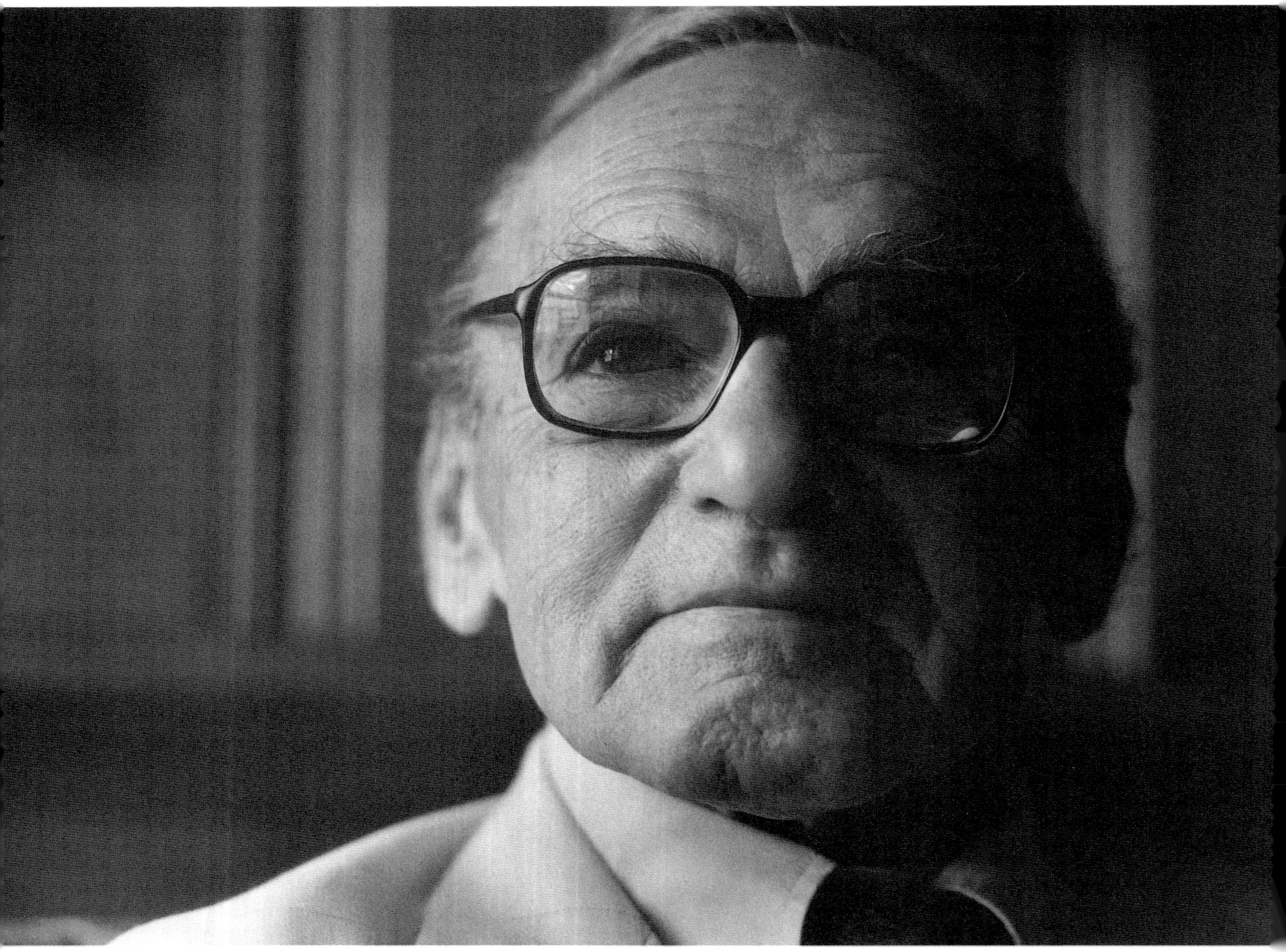

Sanford Meisner
BY
Mary Steenburgen

I only met Sanford Meisner in the first place because of my own prideful obstinancy. People said that the Neighborhood Playhouse School of the Theatre in New York City was impossible to get into, especially for a southerner like myself. People said that there was a teacher there who was wonderful and terrifying and who would demand more out of you than the Marines. People said, "Forget it." I applied.

That was 1972. The wonderful, terrifying teacher was Sanford Meisner and no one before or since has made so much sense to me.

Sanford Meisner is a master at teaching acting as a very personal craft. He takes a subject that's elusive and hands you the reins to it. He helps you to tell the truth under imaginary circumstances. His students would walk through fire for him—not because of his reputation or charms which are considerable, but because he gives them real and practical gifts.

Eighteen years later, Meisner is still teaching, he is still wonderful, and I know him to be anything but terrifying. He is, in fact, my antidote to terror. He has provided me with a truthful foundation that I always go back to.

Today Sandy speaks to his students with the aid of a voice box due to a laryngectomy in 1975. But I can close my eyes and still hear his voice in a hot classroom in New York City. "Tell me *why* you are doing that, Billy?" Or, "Rusty, put your attention on the other person, and he'll give you your moment." "Pamela, every little moment has a meaning all its own." Or, "You must have actor's faith, Mary, and trust that what you need is somewhere there inside you."

We do, Sandy. Many thanks to you.

Studio City, California *1990*

Robert Wagner
BY
Richard Widmark

In my experience it's very difficult for people in the film business to sustain friendships over a long period. I met R.J. when Darryl Zanuck had just signed him on at FOX. He was nineteen. Very outgoing—with a big smile. I liked him then. I still do. In the past forty years, I've watched him grow from a neophyte actor to an international film star of great skill. That's my friend.

Encino, California *1964*

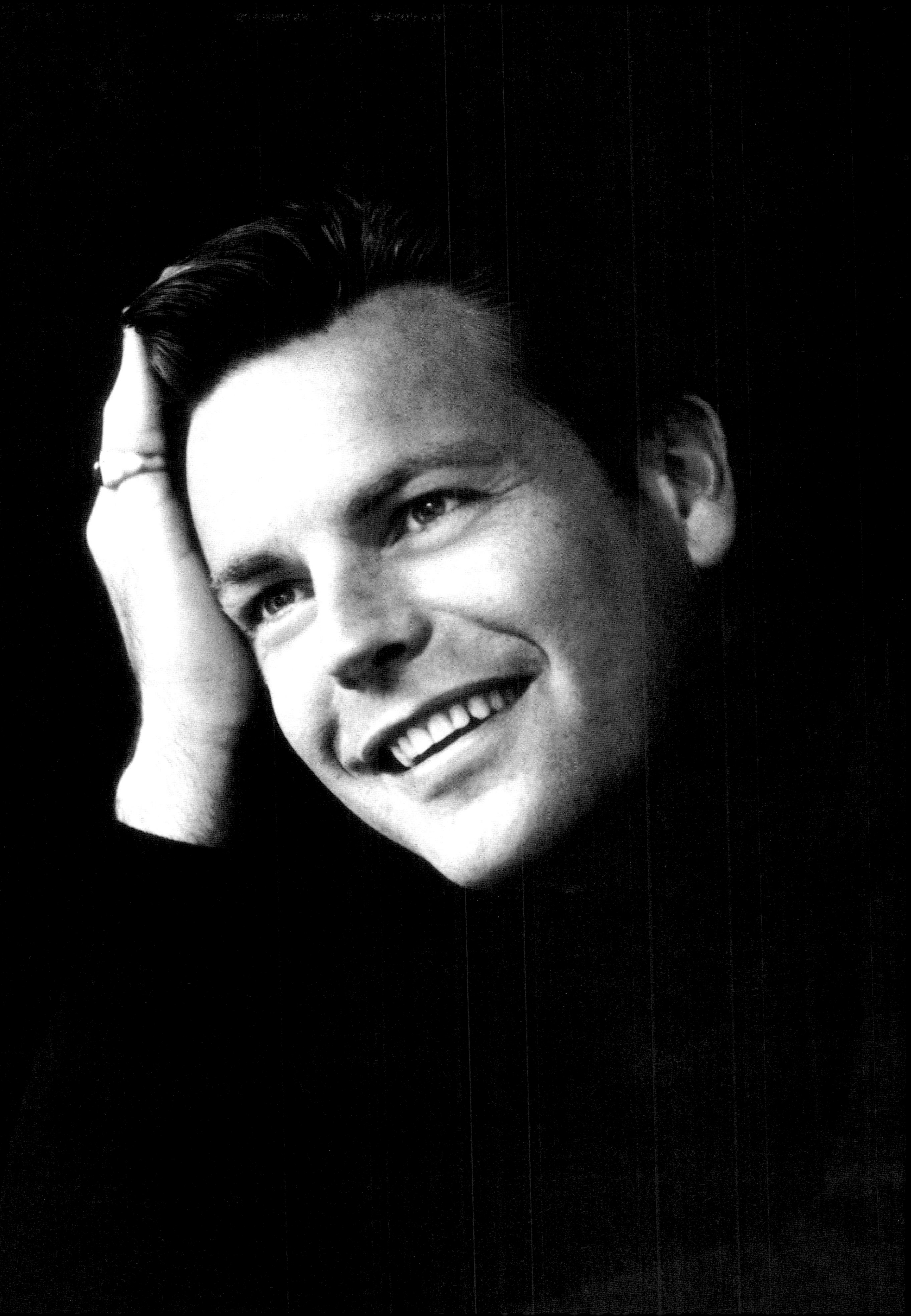

Deborah Kerr
BY
Robert Mitchum

In September of 1956, I arrived in Tobago, an island in the Southern Caribbean, to begin filming *Heaven Knows, Mr. Allison,* directed by John Huston. Upon meeting Miss Kerr, I was impressed by her chaste and genteel demeanor, an attitude eminently suited to the saintly character she portrayed, made touchingly mortal by a few freckles.

The ensuing period of our association revealed many more delightful aspects of this splendid lady, and began the rapid development of an admiration and friendship for her that I shall treasure always.

She is warmly human and sympathetic, and possessed of a humor that ranges from the subtle to the downright wicked.

When some Hollywood organization, charged with monitoring morality, became belatedly alarmed at the perils of pairing a nun and a marine on a desert island and sent a representative to check on our image of propriety, Mr. Huston planned a little surprise.

We contrived a scene wherein Sister Angela overcomes the suppression of her base animal urges and, panting and clutching, throws herself on Mr. Allison in a lustful frenzy. With no film in the camera, we "shot" the scene for our guest, who stood agape and immobilized in shock as John quietly said, "Cut."

Huston then turned to the stunned Mr. Grizzard and said, "You should have seen it before we cleaned it up."

There was a small Catholic church on the island and the Sisters attached to it were invited to see the rushes when they were shown. Deborah, always mindful of their presence, strived to maintain an on-camera deportment that would earn their approval. However, in one scene, in which she was paddling the rubber raft, her composure cracked.

Using a palm frond as a paddle, she was stroking away furiously, with Mr. Huston's voice from the camera boat urging her on to even greater effort. "Even harder, honey," he was saying, "Paddle even harder." With one desperate surge of energy, the paddle snapped in two. Holding up her bloodied hands, she looked straight into the camera and said, "That'll show you how effing hard I'm paddling, John!"

Beverly Hills *1985*

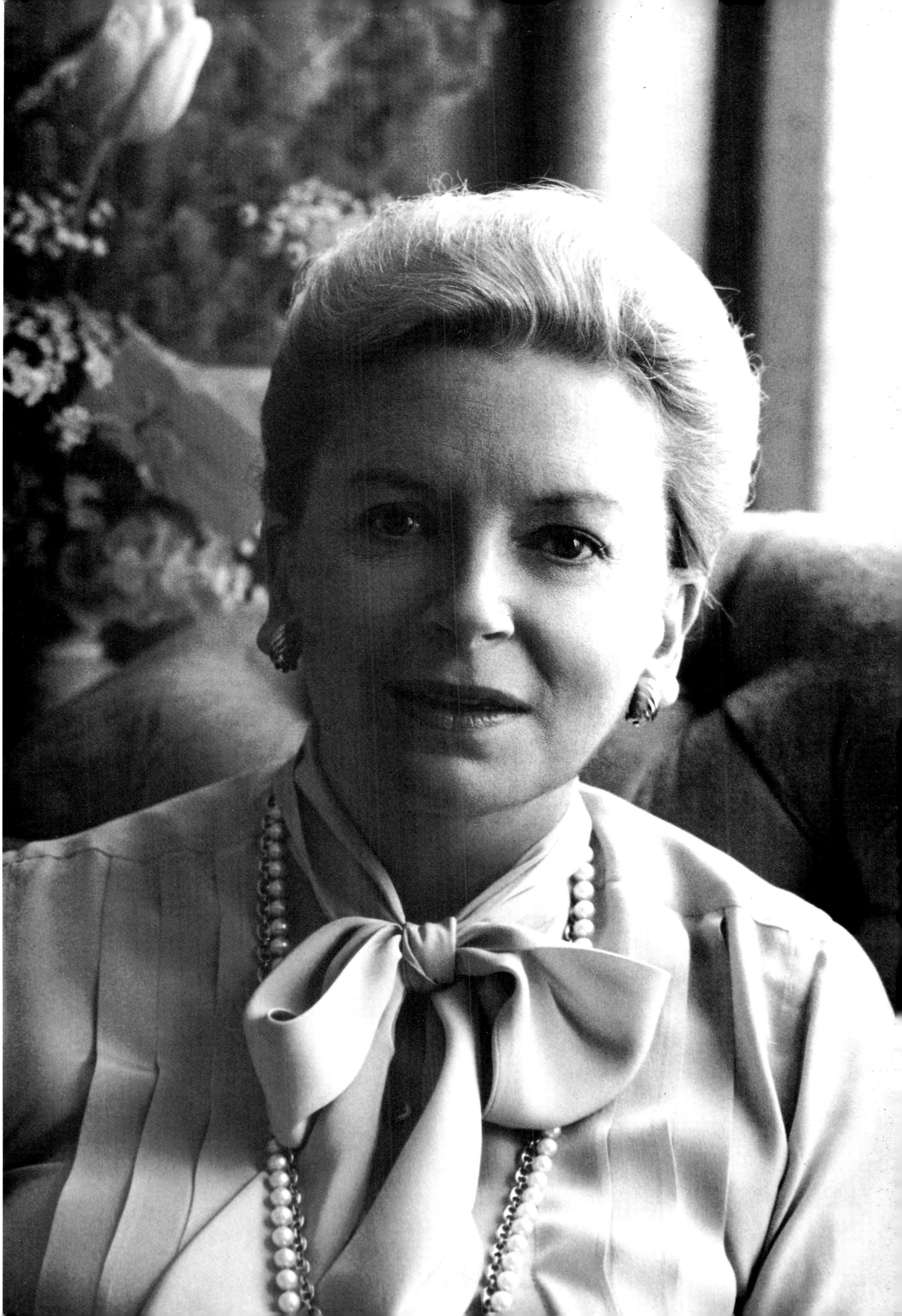

After working in a nasty swamp, the lady contracted a mild case of dengue fever which made her weak and feverish. Although she insisted on carrying on, I told Mr. Huston that I refused to work with sick people, and despite her protestations, she was banished to the Arnos Vale Hotel for a week until her fever subsided. She returned, somewhat fragile, but determined, wondering how we could have possibly got along without her.

Our next venture was *The Sundowners* in Australia, two or three years later. Here in the dust and heat of South Australia, she again demonstrated the courage and selfless good humor that made her a joy to work with.

As the work-worn wife of an itinerant sheep shearer, she demonstrated her remarkable ability to become the very character she portrayed.

Next we met in London in *The Grass Is Greener*, with Cary Grant and Jean Simmons. Mr. Grant forbade her to wear jewelry, contending that in their circumstances, she would have pawned her jewelry, while he himself was dazzling in emerald and diamond cuff links. Deborah just found the situation uproariously funny.

Most recently we got together in a made-for-TV movie called *Reunion in Fairborough*, and it was indeed for us a warm and welcome reunion.

She remains as truthful, caring, and sharing as ever. She delights in laughter, she is concerned and sympathetic, and as brave as she was during her bout with dengue and my own bout with "de Shrinkage," a local Tobagonian malady.

I honor her as an artist, and as a friend, and salute her as a great beauty—with a few freckles.

❑

Richard Brooks
BY
Robert Blake

The respect and love that I developed for Richard Brooks when we were doing *In Cold Blood* didn't come from his ability to communicate with actors in any normal or usual way, nor was there any of the usual jargon like "the spine of the character" or "your action," "inner conflict," "motivation," etc, etc.

No, indeed, I'll bet he never even went to an acting class in his life—not that he didn't know exactly what the scene was going to look like when he said, "Print." But in my heart, I don't think he ever knew how he was going to get it to go there. Yet I found myself compelled to trust his incredible ingenuity and resourcefulness to get the job done no matter what it took.

One cold and blowing winter day on those Kansas plains we were doing a scene stealing a car in a barn. In one split second in this scene I, Perry Smith, had to get my hands around Dick Hickock's throat and know in my soul that I was ready and able to kill him in a heartbeat.

Well, somehow the Robert Blake in me couldn't get to it.

Maybe it was late, maybe I was tired, maybe I didn't have the guts, but I had long since learned to fake it when nothing else worked. And after a few rehearsals I thought I had everybody fooled, including the Boss. Just before we went for the take, he put his arm around me and drew me off to the side. I don't remember what he said, but in a fleeting second he put a handful of that freezing snow down the back of my neck and when I turned on him he grabbed a handful of my shirt, punched me in the stomach, pointed to in front of the camera and said: "In there, you son of a bitch. In there is where it belongs." He threw me into the scene, yelled, "Action!" and poor Scott Wilson never came so close to getting killed in his life. In his inimitable way, the Boss knew just how to get me to do it, to get me where I had to go.

Another time we were working in a men's room—I'm standing there alone with most of my clothes off in front of a mirror with the hot water running to ease the pain in my injured leg, and when I look into the mirror I have this beautiful narcissistic fantasy about being a famous singer crooning a love tune to myself. What a piece of cake for an actor! I didn't even bother with rehearsing it because it was such a delightful idea I didn't want to run the risk of getting stale.

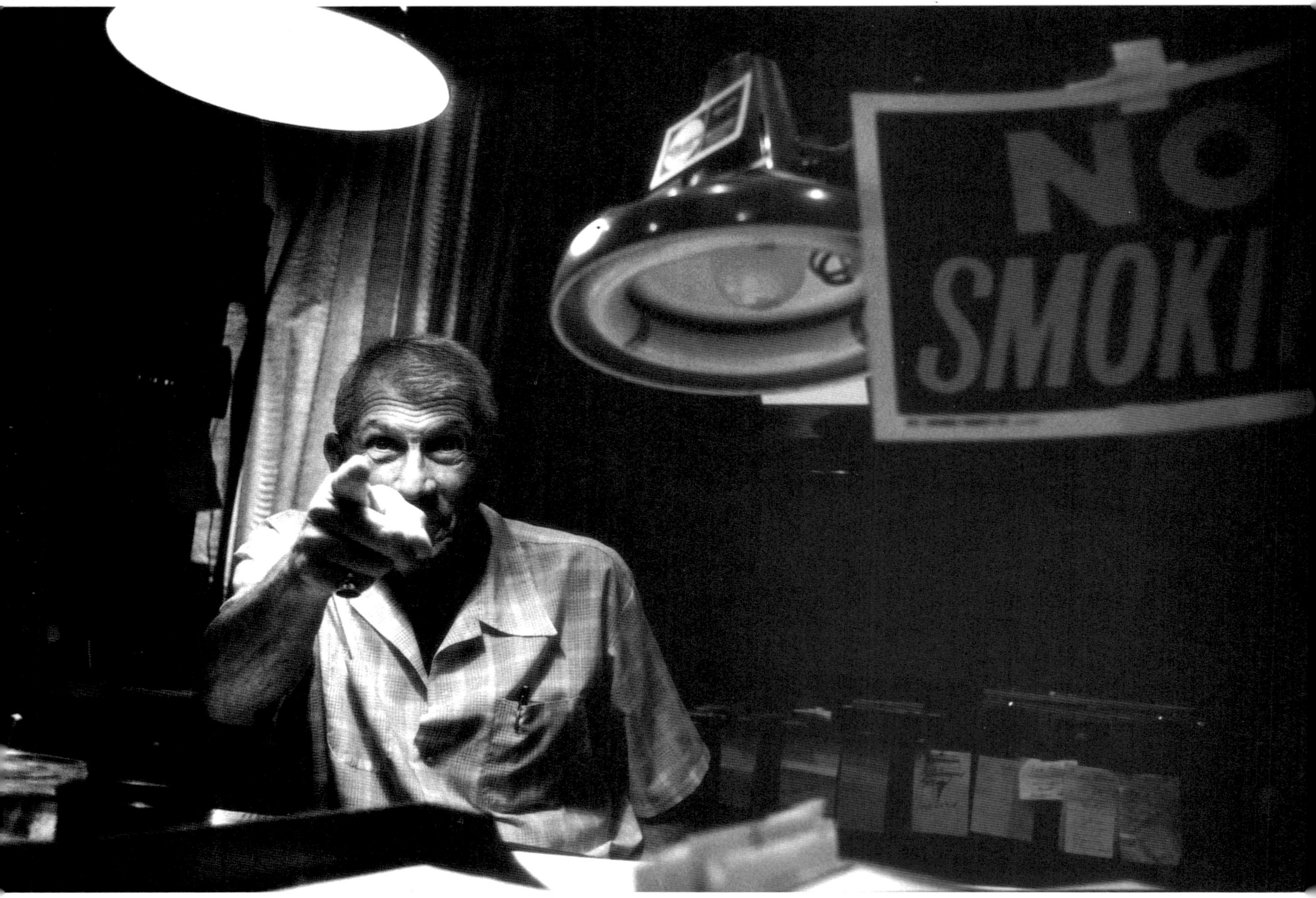
NO
SMOKI

So, there we were in the men's room, the lights are cooking, the camera revving up, the Boss says "Action!" and I look up at myself in the mirror and nothing, absolutely nothing happens. All I saw was myself, Robert Blake, the small, self-conscious dork in the mirror; the character was gone, concentration gone. I got so uptight you couldn't get a dime up my ass with a sledgehammer. But because I had been in front of the box since I was two years old I kicked into my faking gear and slid right through it. I heard "Cut" and "Print" and I knew I had outfoxed them for sure.

Then the Boss said: "I'd like another one just for insurance." After a few minutes of lighting there we were, ready to go. I dreaded having to fake my way through it again. Just before "Action" the Boss whispers to me: "When you look into the mirror, don't look straight at yourself—look a few inches off to the left of your face."

The scene began, but now I had enough faith in this strange genius to know that I hadn't fooled him and somehow or other he was going to bail me out again. When I looked into the mirror I let my eyes slide a few inches off to the left, and there in the mirror I saw the most beautiful creature I had ever seen in my life. She was so exquisite she mesmerized me. Slowly she smiled. I fell instantly in love, smiled back at her, and the whole scene was like a magnificent dream come true. I wasn't even aware when the Boss said, "Cut."

What he had done was taken his wife, Jean Simmons, who happened to be visiting him that day in Kansas, and put her next to the camera. He killed all the lights around her and put just one inky-dink on her face so that when I looked over, there was nothing but black and that beautiful surrealistic face like an angel peering out of Hell. I wonder what the Boss would have done if she hadn't been there.

One of the last scenes in the film was Perry sitting in solitary on a winter night, a few days before the hanging, alone. What the script called for was all the anger gone, the rage, the torment, the pain.

The Boss wanted a kind of spiritual Perry who maybe had crossed over to the other side. Well, I had spent three months working with all that other emotion; when it came time to do this scene I found I couldn't get rid of all that stuff. The Boss saw me muddling around and just before we rolled, he leaned over and whispered in my ear: "Robert, don't do this one. Let me do it for you." He walked off camera and said, "Action" and there was a long minute or two of nothing but that film rolling through the camera and me sitting there waiting.

Very quietly, from off camera, I heard the Boss's voice: "The Lord is my shepherd, I shall not want. He maketh me to lie down in green pastures, he leadeth me beside the still waters."

The Boss had such serenity it was coming clear from his soul. He knew what it was like to be in that place where you've already crossed over, and in that gentle instant he brought me with him and I just let myself go. It was like he brought me to a heaven that I understood.

"Surely goodness and mercy shall follow me all the days of my life and I shall dwell in the house of the Lord forever.". . . Thanks, Boss.

Culver City, California *1984*

Pola Negri
BY
Hayley Mills

A life that encompassed dramatic contrasts; she'd known poverty and enormous wealth. She had a beauty and fame that dazzled, and the greatest and most adored screen idol ever, Rudolph Valentino, had been hers.

I worked with Pola Negri when I was 17 years old. She was still a movie Queen.

Although she was rather short, she was very grand. Although then, she was far from young, she had great style.

Everything she needed for the film she insisted had to be real. The Cheetah was real—and dangerous. Her furs and jewels were real, and as security anxiously pursued her across the set—the twinkle in her eye was real.

And her smile was warm and her laugh genuine when she spoke to a child.

San Antonio, Texas *1980*

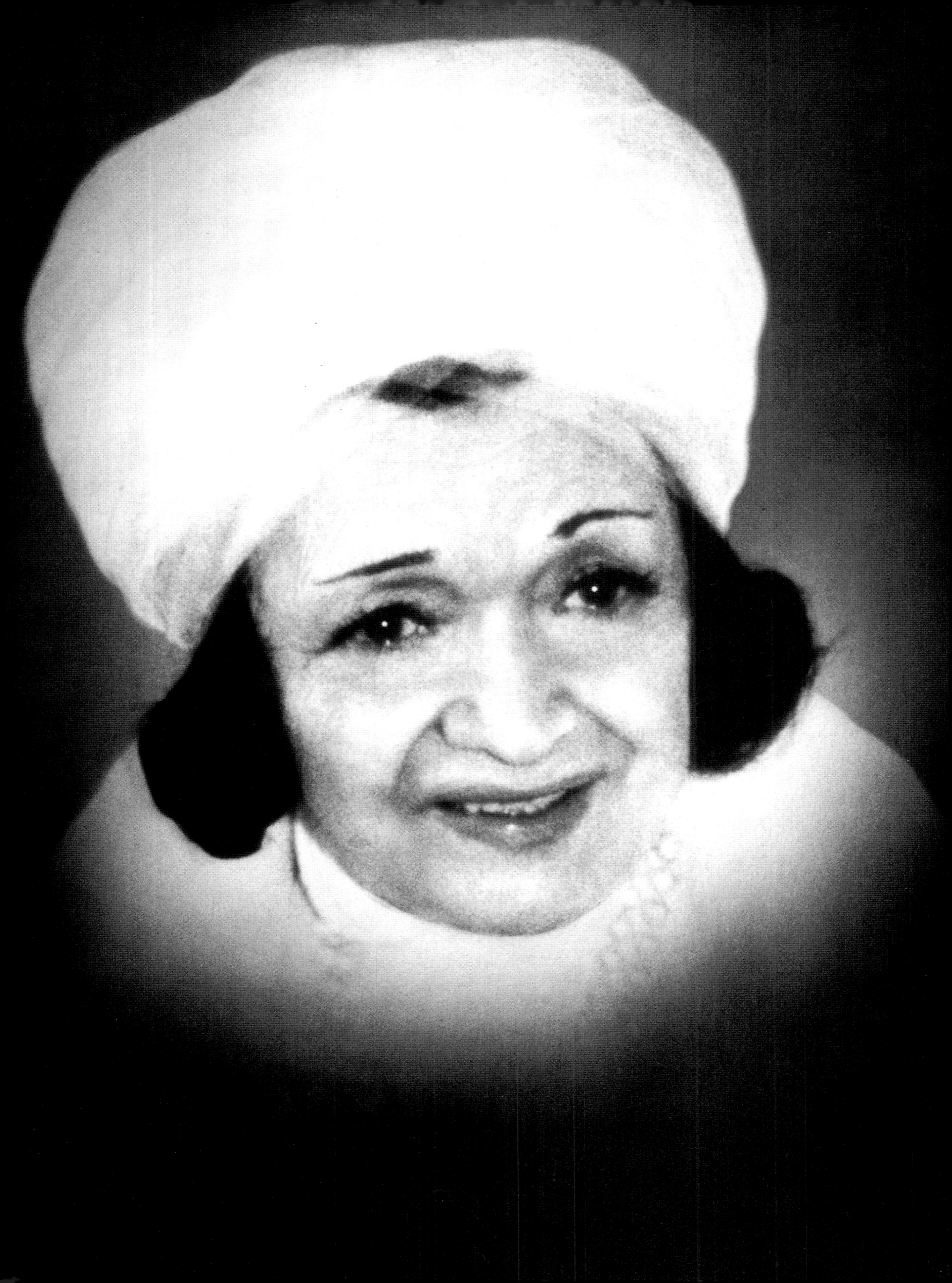

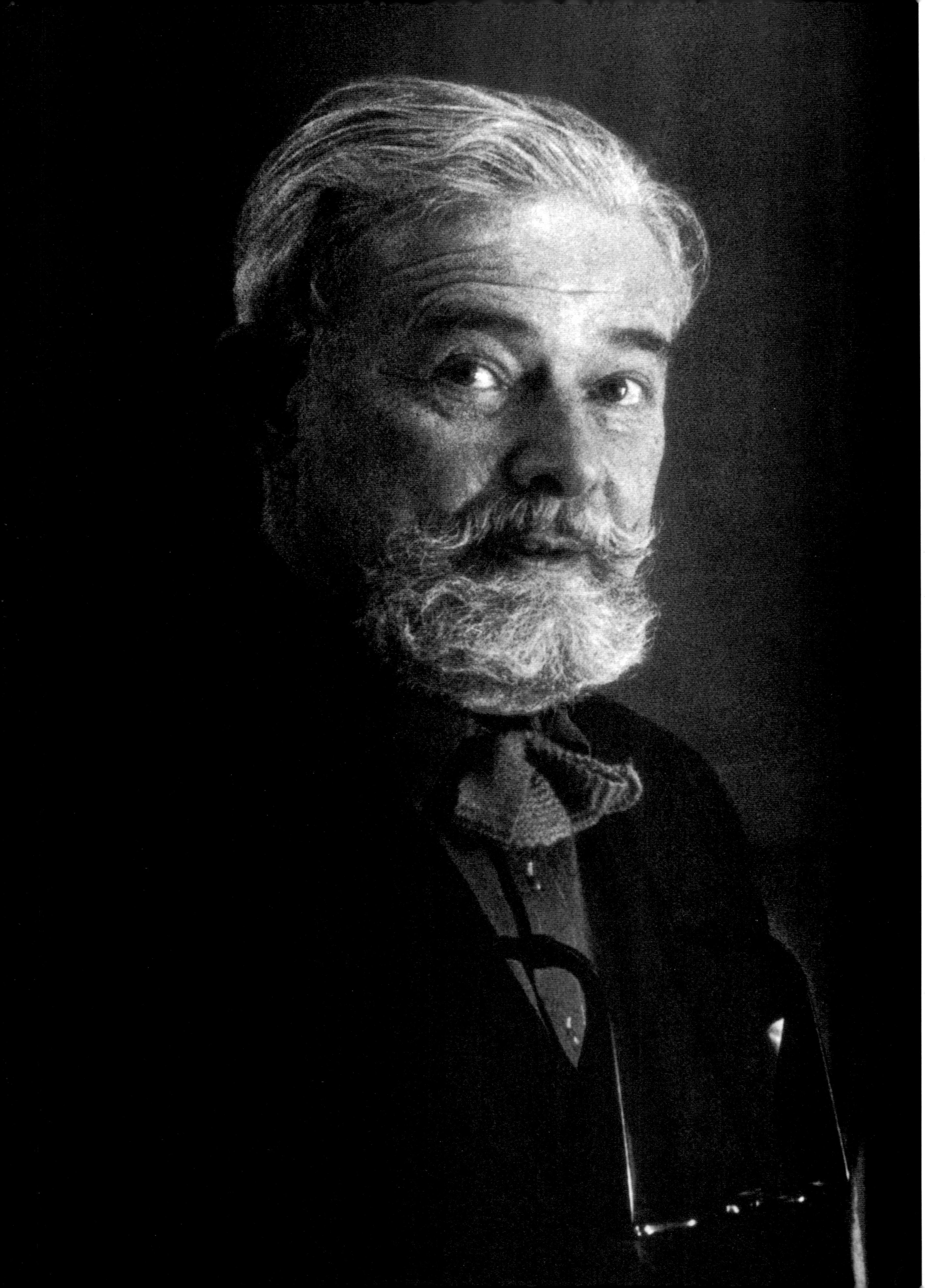

T. H. White
BY
Julie Andrews

He came to London to be interviewed on a television special that I was hosting. He said he had never done anything like that before and he wanted to learn—about lighting and cameras and being a "ham" and that sort of thing.

("The best thing for being sad," replied Merlin, beginning to puff and blow, "is to learn something." *The Sword in the Stone*, T. H. White)

This is a very good photograph of Tim. It shows the expression he assumed when he knew he was being cheeky. There are other photos of him looking remarkably like Hemingway—but Tim was taller and somehow less settled-looking and a bit more piratical.

He lived on the island of Alderney in the Channel Islands off the coast of Cherbourg, France. He encouraged the idea that he was a hermit ("keeps away the ruddy press!")—living alone with his beautiful red setter, Jenny, in two converted cottages on Connaught Square.

He invited me and my former husband, Tony, to come and visit: I was recuperating from the removal of my tonsils. ("The sea air will sort you out in a flash.") Prior to our arrival, he repainted and decorated his house, telling me, teasingly, that it would not be grand enough for a "big star." He painted the rooms bright colours, put down new linoleum and carpets, and hung up acrylic chandeliers and little glittering wall sconces. There was so much tinkling stuff, his Normandy-style home resembled a mini Versailles. He had painted the kitchen a fire engine red—including the refrigerator. However, he had not done any sort of cleanup on it. Almost upon arrival, I went at it from top to bottom, thinking I was doing him a favour. I discovered ledgers, filled with his notes and ideas for a novel based on *Tristan and Isolde* (never written), under the grill and in the gas stove—plus diaries, photos, leaflets, brochures, and warranties. He never let me forget my compulsion to tidy him up. He had a way of immediately spotting one's fatal flaws. "Let's pay Julie a compliment—before she gives herself one!" Then he'd add, genuinely, lovingly, "pretty Julie—sweet Julie" and I'd feel enfolded and happy.

When I knew him, it seemed he was drunk all winter, sober all summer. The dark days he was aggressive, maudlin, crying into his Pernod or brandy, his clothes unchanged, his beard yellow from tobacco. Summers he was joyous, genial, active, building his garden, stomping about the island full of ideas and projects.

New York City 1960

He came to stay with me in New York to see *Camelot* which was based upon his marvelous book *The Once and Future King.* If I remember correctly, he was asked to write a piece about the show for *Vogue* magazine. He stewed over it for days, pacing about the apartment, gathering his thoughts, not writing at all. When he finally sat down, the words flowed onto the page. I don't think he corrected more than about two. Trying to be a good hostess, I peeked into the study while he was writing and said, "Would you like a cup of tea or something, Tim?" Without looking up, he yelled, "GET OUT" in such a fierce voice that I hurriedly withdrew and never bothered him again, 'til it was done.

He wrote a poem for Richard Burton and one for me. He told me he intended to write something humorous about my nose, a parody of Herrick's "When, as in silks, my Julia goes" etc.—you can imagine how it might have turned out. But he had second thoughts about it, believing it would hurt my feelings. He wrote a kind and generous tribute instead. I treasure it.

Tim was Merlin. He knew so much that he could teach anything one cared to learn. He believed in all the things he espoused in his books! Chivalry, honour, decency, dignity, punctuality, wishing people well. He was a "white knight" in a time when, for most people, such things had become just a dim memory.

("He was the badge of everything that was good in the middle ages."
The Candle in the Wind, T. H. White)

He was shy, especially with women, though they intrigued him and he loved them. He was professorial, teasing, curious, a lonely little boy—and the wisest, gravest man I have ever met.

❑

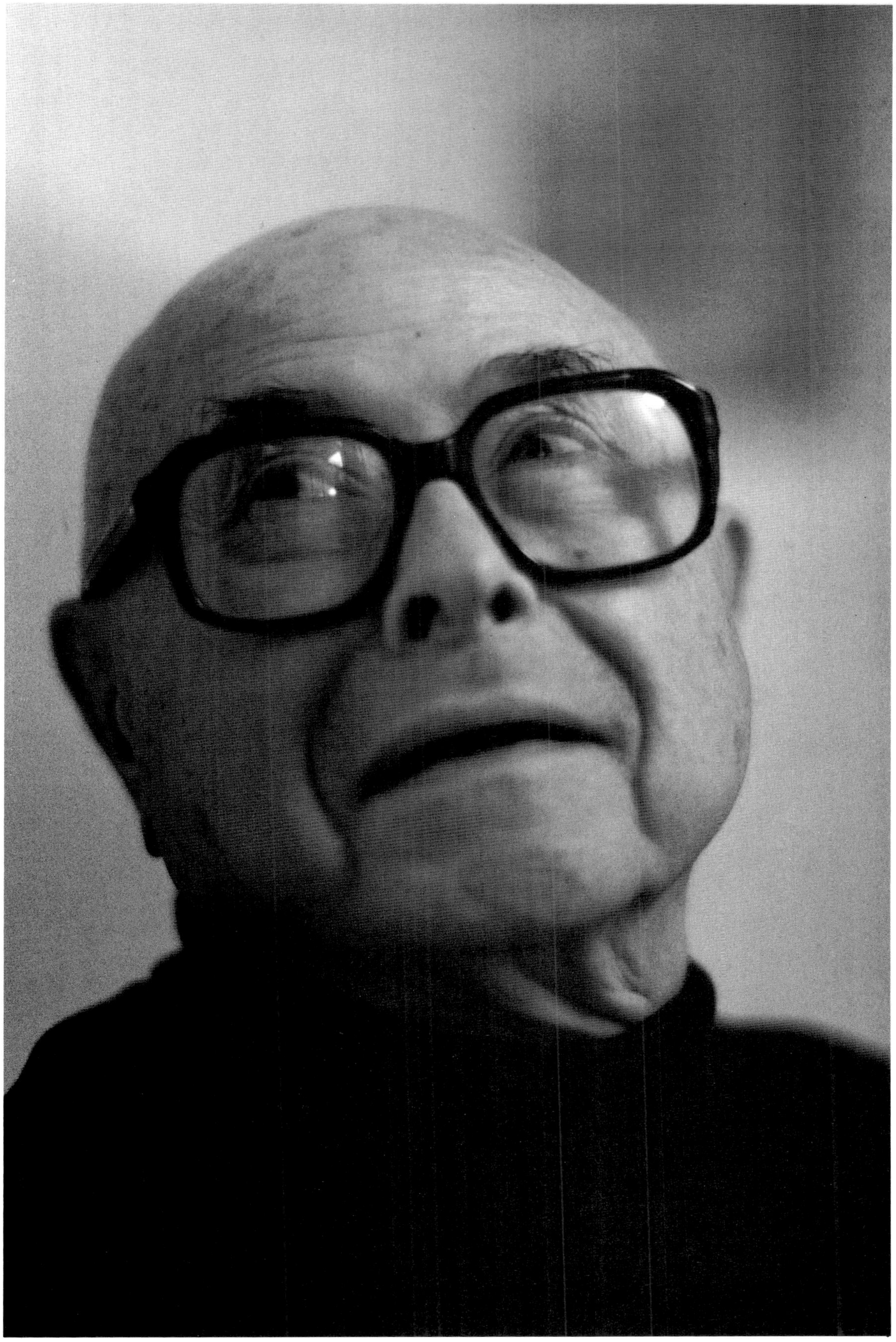

New York City *1990*

Robert Lewis
BY
Meryl Streep

Bobby was one of my acting teachers at Yale—I had three, but he was the only one who believed I had what it takes to be a successful working actor. In fact, the light of encouragement seemed to beam from his face like a beneficent Buddha. In the dark New Haven winter, the warmth of his reassurances and backstage reminiscences had the effect of making our often tense sixteen hour drama school days seem like the quaint early chapters of our own history, which, of course, they were. Bobby not only encouraged my instincts, he was *sure* they were valid. For an actor, whose creations are ephemeral, that confidence is often all you have to fall back on.

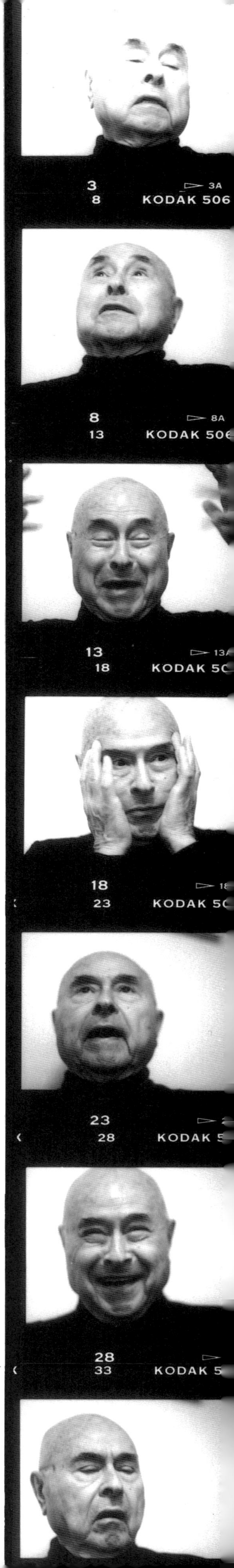

New York City *1990*

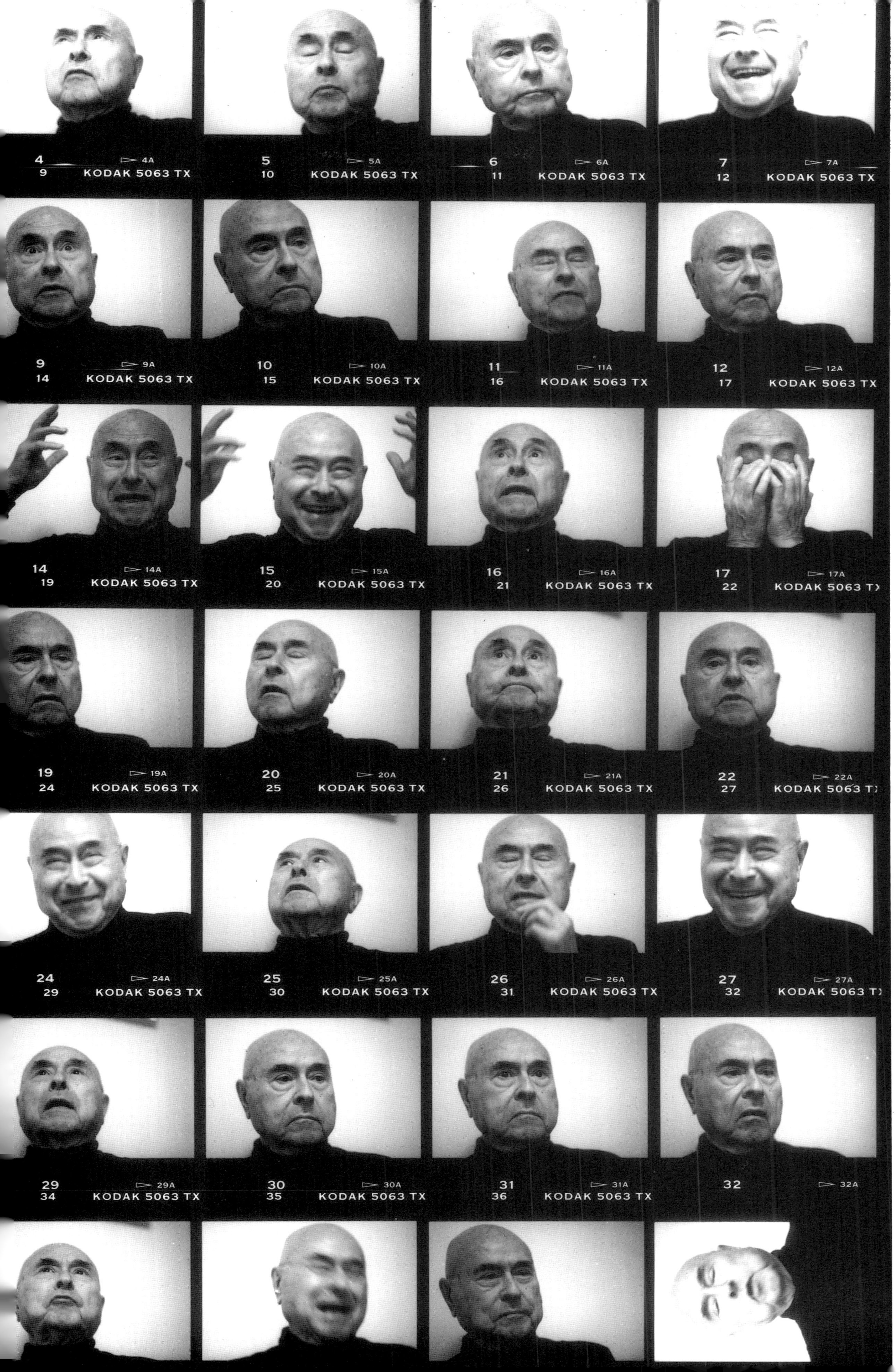
4 4A 9 KODAK 5063 TX
5 5A 10 KODAK 5063 TX
6 6A 11 KODAK 5063 TX
7 7A 12 KODAK 5063 TX
9 9A 14 KODAK 5063 TX
10 10A 15 KODAK 5063 TX
11 11A 16 KODAK 5063 TX
12 12A 17 KODAK 5063 TX
14 14A 19 KODAK 5063 TX
15 15A 20 KODAK 5063 TX
16 16A 21 KODAK 5063 TX
17 17A 22 KODAK 5063 TX
19 19A 24 KODAK 5063 TX
20 20A 25 KODAK 5063 TX
21 21A 26 KODAK 5063 TX
22 22A 27 KODAK 5063 TX
24 24A 29 KODAK 5063 TX
25 25A 30 KODAK 5063 TX
26 26A 31 KODAK 5063 TX
27 27A 32 KODAK 5063 TX
29 29A 34 KODAK 5063 TX
30 30A 35 KODAK 5063 TX
31 31A 36 KODAK 5063 TX
32 32A

Tracey Ullman
BY
Kevin Kline

I worked with Tracey on the film *I Love You to Death* and I've never had so much fun. She is no nonsense and all mirth; rigorously honest in her observation of character, and as compassionate in her acting of it.

She is utterly unique, deeply disciplined, boundlessly gifted, brilliant, generous, kind, and, I hope, a friend for life since I've said all these nice things about her.

Pacific Palisades, California *1990*

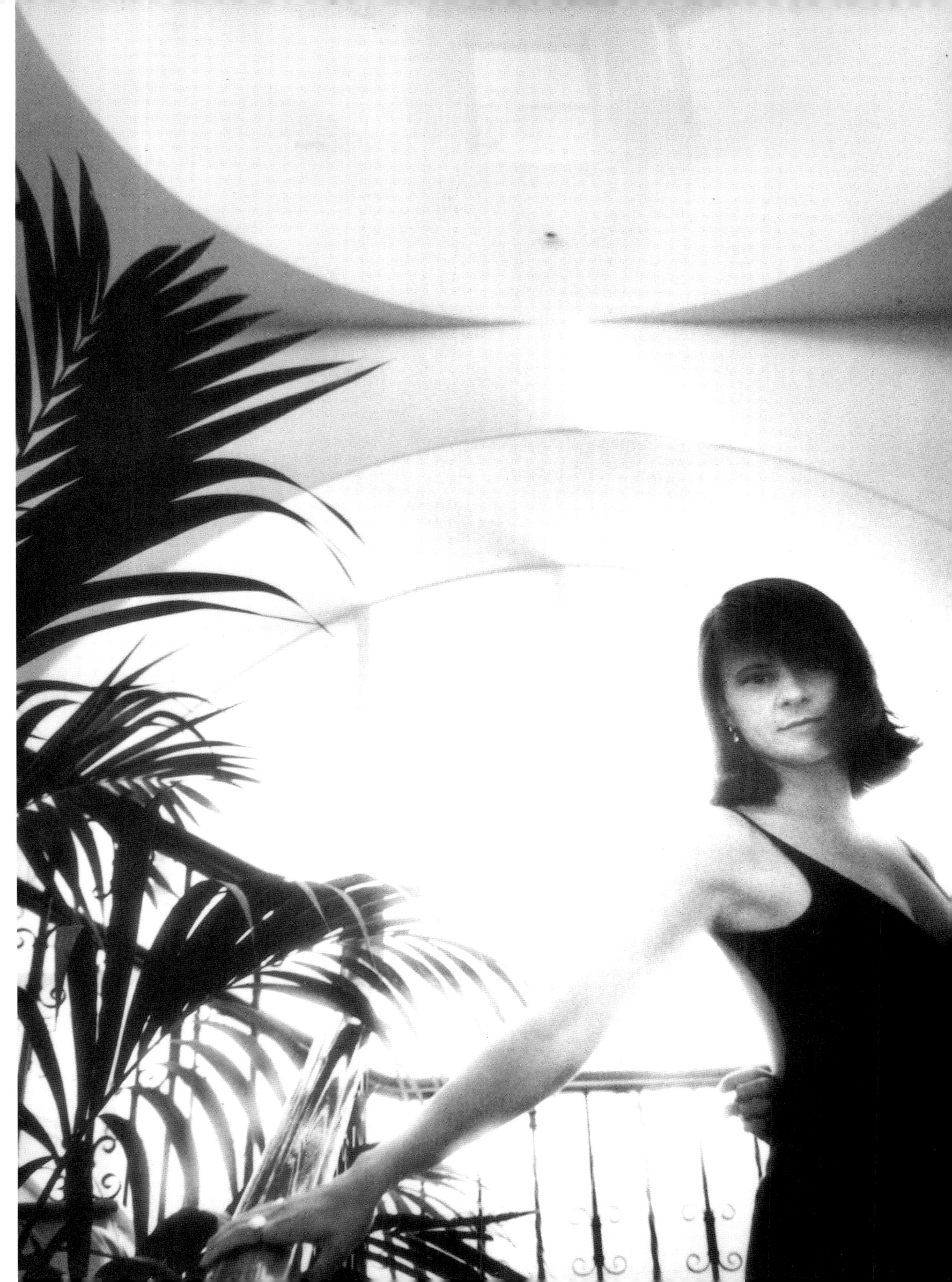

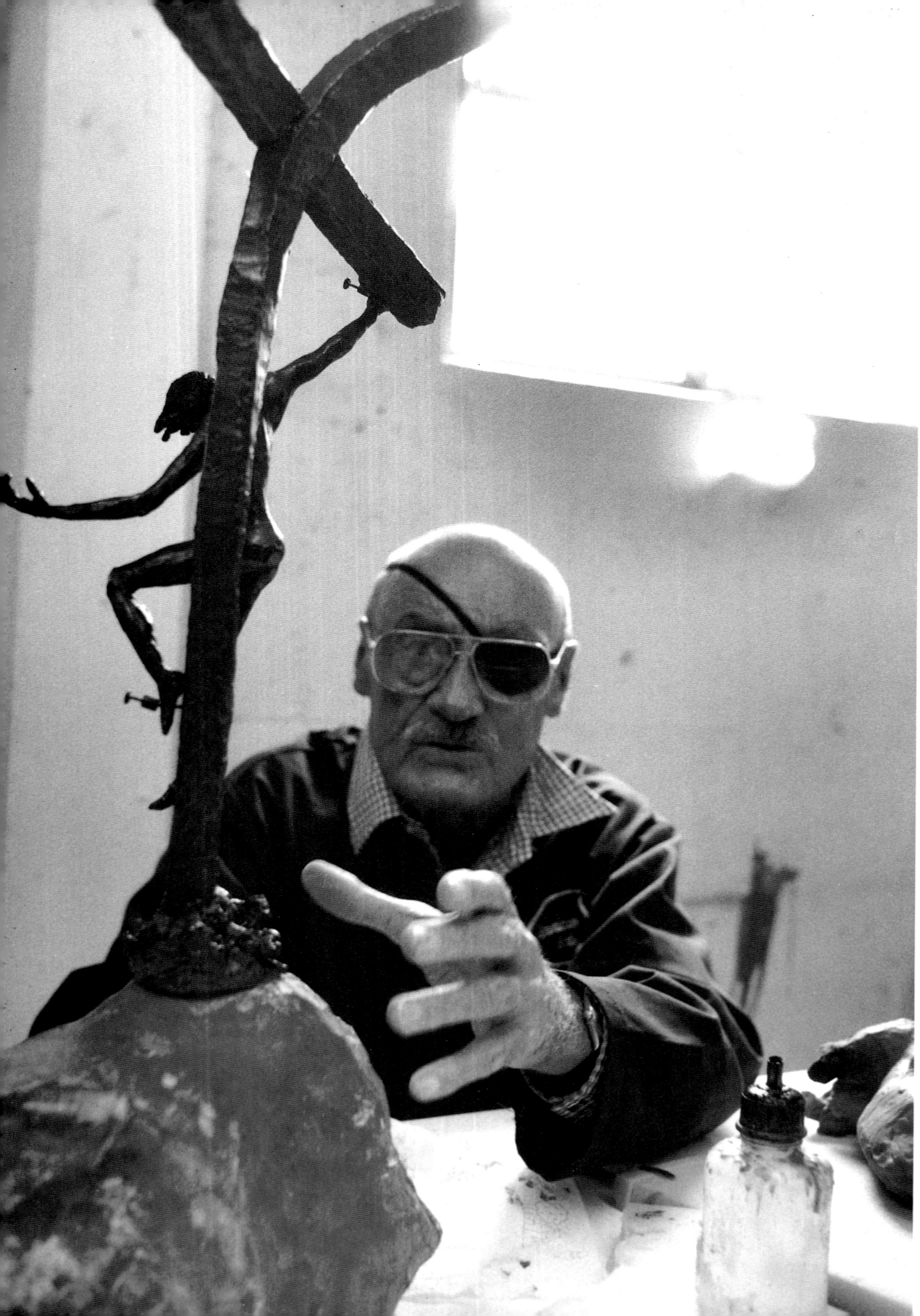

André de Toth
BY
Martin Scorsese

André de Toth is a "director's director," a special category that speaks for itself.

He is not a "popular" director—audiences may recognize the titles of his films rather than his name. Like other *genre* directors, de Toth is an unsung hero, mainly appreciated over the years by those who make movies.

I've always been fascinated by André de Toth's movies. Their underlying anger and determination often make them very disturbing. Take *Play Dirty* for instance. The characters have no redeeming social value, they don't think, they just act. They have a job to do, and they're going to do it. The nihilism, the pragmatism—it's at least unsettling. Disguise becomes a way to survive that brings doom at the end; soldiers killed by their own countrymen fooled by the uniforms. Take *House of Wax*: it's the best 3-D movie ever made—and de Toth has one eye! Throughout the first third of the film, the camera keeps tracking around Vincent Price, and around the wax figures—which look very much like real people. And every time somebody comes into a frame, you don't know whether it's a wax or a real person. When the wax museum burns, the eyes start to fall out of the dummies' eye sockets, and it's tremendously effective. (And I like that it takes place on Mulberry Street—my old neighborhood.)

My favorite de Toth picture is perhaps *Ramrod,* a grim, cynical Western which remains so surprisingly fresh. But I also like the gothic quality of *Dark Waters,* the way the psychology of the characters is reflected through the environment of the Louisiana bayous. Other de Toth titles that are favorites of mine include *Pitfall, Slattery's Hurricane, Springfield Rifle, Riding Shotgun, The Indian Fighter, Two-Headed Spy,* and *Day of the Outlaw.* There is a tension in de Toth's visual style that seems to reflect this continuous struggle between people and their surroundings. Be it in his "film noir," or in his "Westerns," de Toth's characters always move in a treacherous world where deception and cynicism are aimed at one goal: survival. In de Toth's movies there are no happy endings, only ambiguous ones.

Burbank, California *1990*

Anthony Hopkins
BY
Jonathan Demme

As an actor, absolutely scrumptious,
As a private citizen, utterly delectable
Hopkins is a walking, talking *chef d'oeuvre.*
A person to make your mouth water.

Studio City, California *1984*

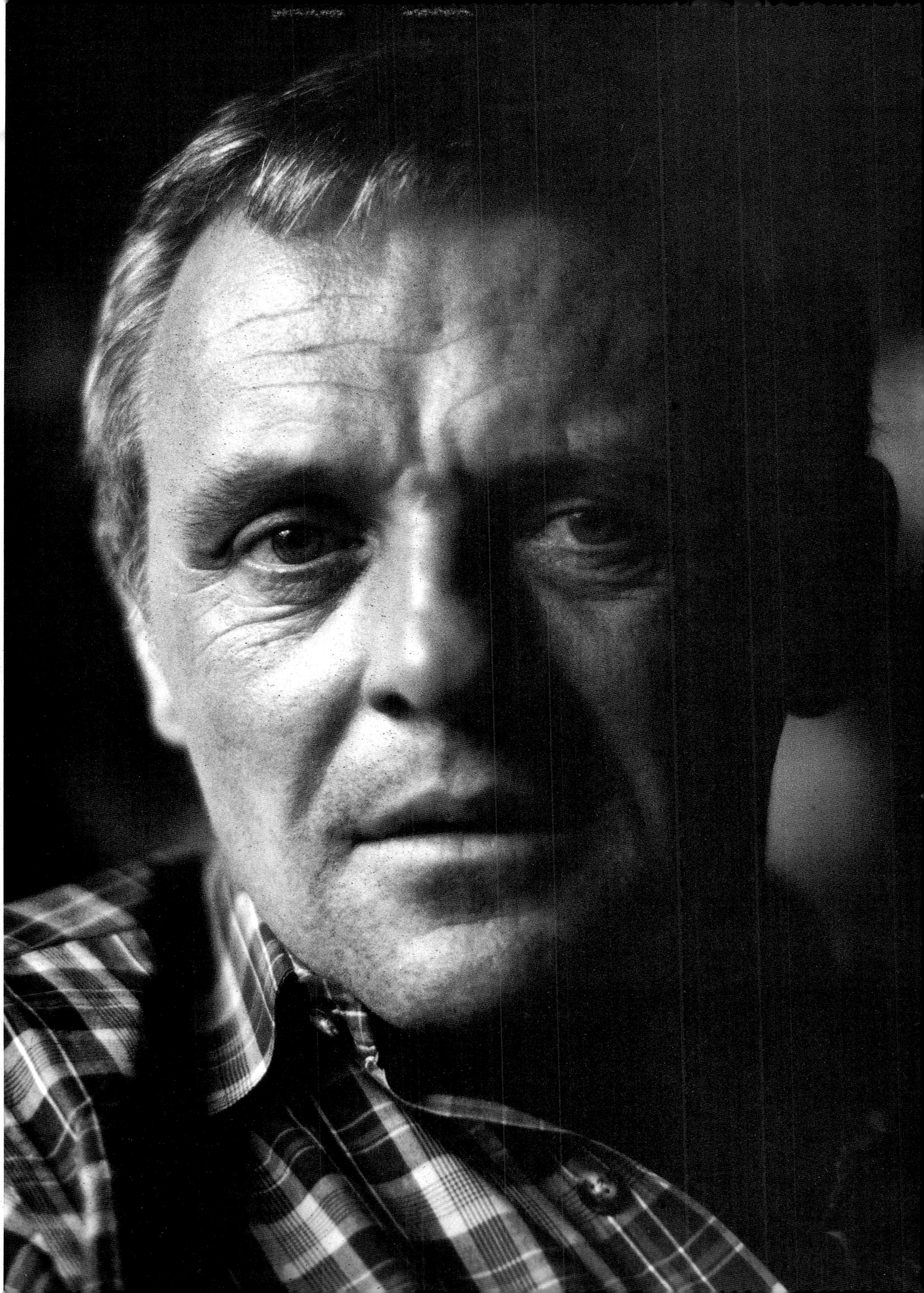

Jane Russell
BY
Bob Hope

I was very lucky to work with Jane Russell in *Pale Face* and *Son of Pale Face* because she was not only one of the most beautiful actresses, but also she had a sense of comedy, which helps a lot when you're trying to get a laugh.

From the time she made *The Outlaw* for Howard Hughes, she was a star.

Last year she acted as Mistress of Ceremonies for a big event for Hal Roach and she was delightful . . . and *still* beautiful.

Palm Springs, California *1951*

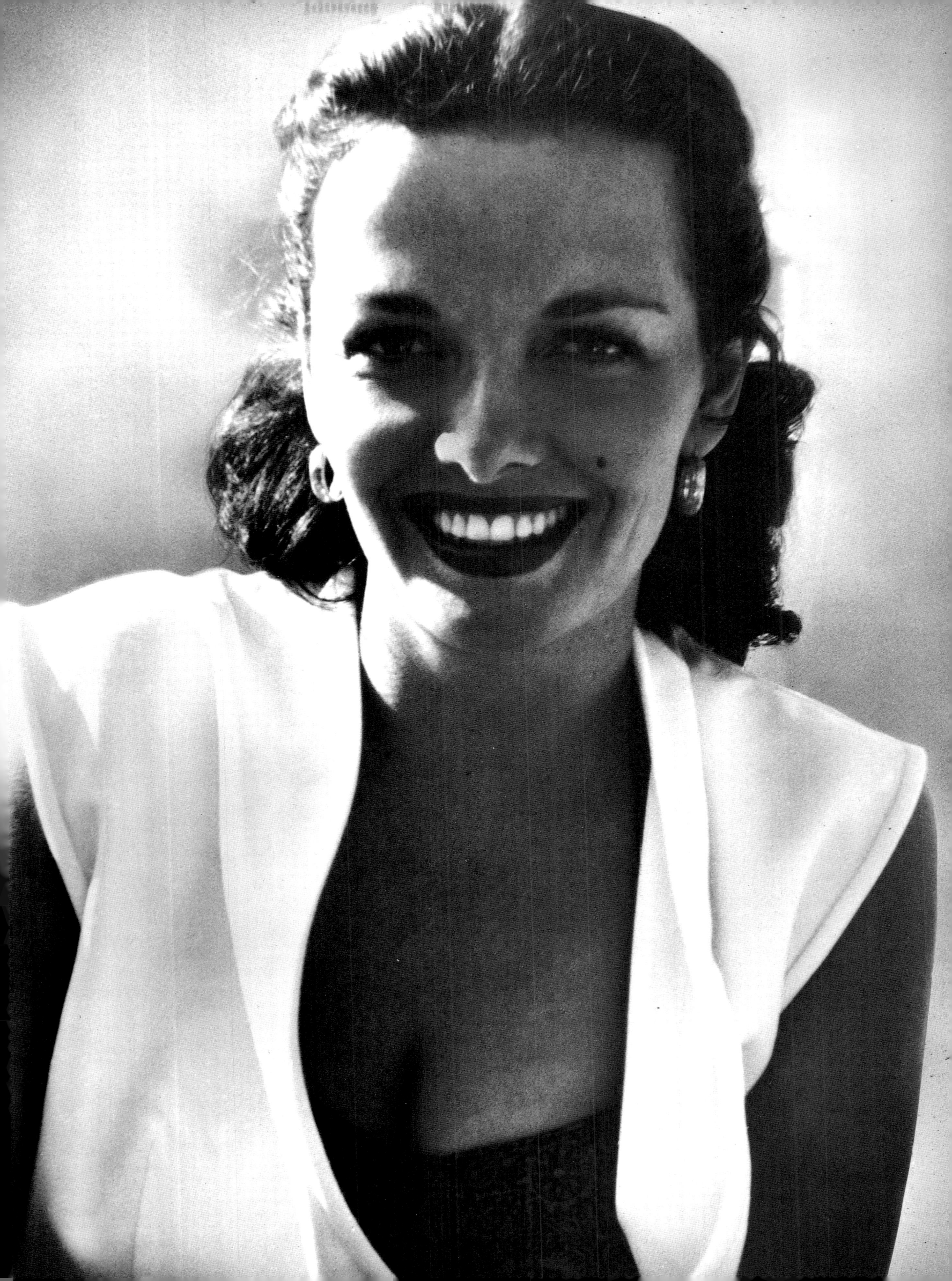

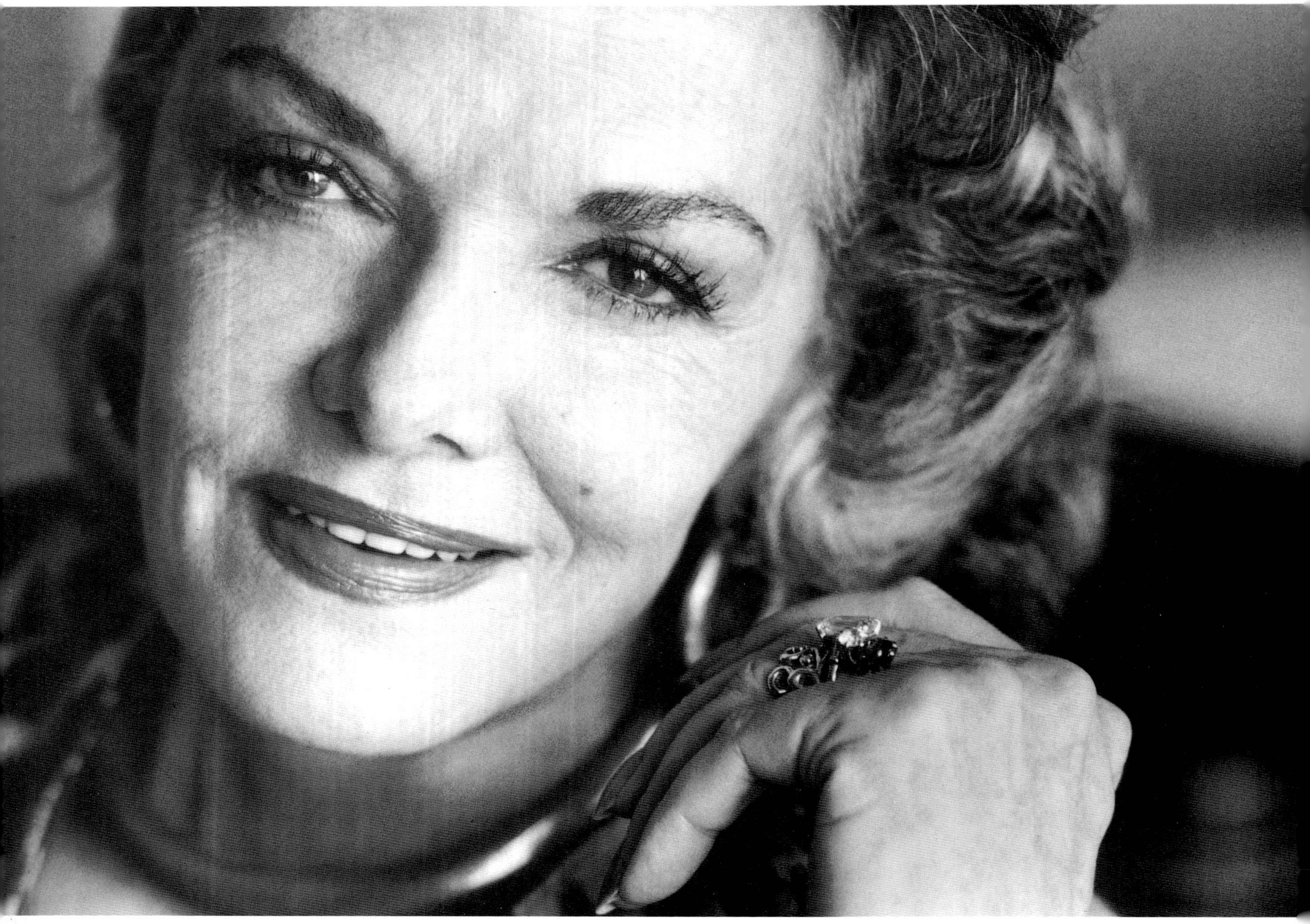

Beverly Hills *1991*

Index

Numbers in bold face indicate photographs.